Designs
and
Methods
for Youth-Led
Research

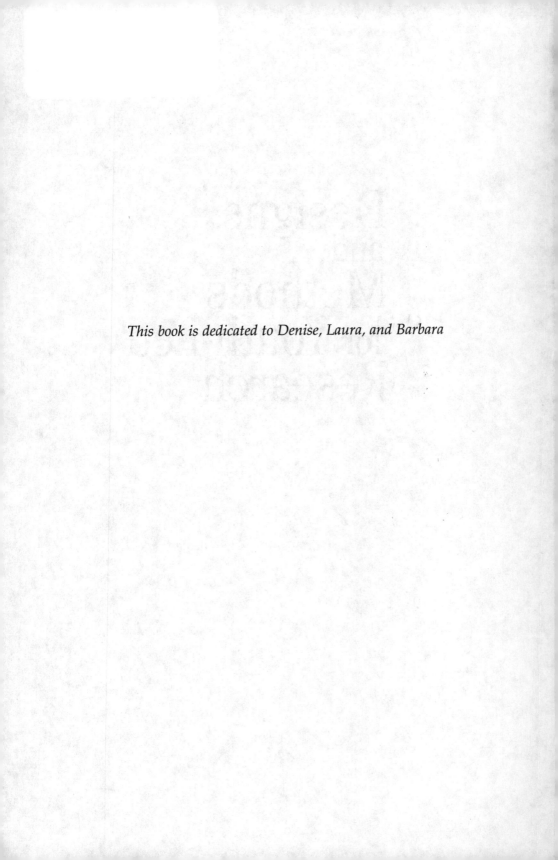

This book is dedicated to Denise, Laura, and Barbara

Designs and Methods for Youth-Led Research

Melvin Delgado

Boston University

SAGE Publications
Thousand Oaks ▪ London ▪ New Delhi

For information:

Sage Publications, Inc.
2455 Teller Road
Thousand Oaks, California 91320
E-mail: order@sagepub.com

Sage Publications Ltd.
1 Oliver's Yard
55 City Road
London EC1Y 1SP
United Kingdom

Sage Publications India Pvt. Ltd.
B-42, Panchsheel Enclave
Post Box 4109
New Delhi 110 017 India

Printed in the United States of America.

Library of Congress Cataloging-in-Publication Data

Delgado, Melvin.
Designs and methods for youth-led research / Melvin Delgado.
    p. cm.
Includes bibliographical references and index.
ISBN 1-4129-1528-7 (cloth)—ISBN 0-7619-3044-2 (pbk.)
    1. Youth—Research—United States. 2. Youth development—United States.
3. Social sciences—Research—Methodology. 4. Youth—Services for—United
States. 5. Social participation. I. Title.
HQ796.D392 2006
305.235'5'072073—dc22   2005009852

This book is printed on acid-free paper.

05   06   07   08   09   10   9   8   7   6   5   4   3   2   1

Acquisitions Editor:	Arthur T. Pomponio
Editorial Assistant:	Veronica Novak
Production Editor:	Laureen Shea
Copy Editor:	Colleen Brennan
Typesetter:	C&M Digitals (P) Ltd.
Proofreader:	Cheryl Rivard
Indexer:	Kay Dusheck
Cover Designer:	Candice Harman

Contents

List of Figures

Preface

The journey an author takes before deciding to write a book usually covers an extended period of time that is measured best in years or decades rather than weeks or months. My journey is no exception. Invariably, one scholarly publication, book, or article, for example, leads to another, which, in turn, builds on the previous one and explores some new dimension of the subject matter. Writing this book is best described as just that: a "journey." At first, the writing represented a daunting task. However, it slowly, but surely, emerged as a terrific and ever-wonderful ride that started in charted territory but quickly entered uncharted territory for me; it crossed temporal periods, national boundaries, continents, and oceans. It entailed reading reports, articles, and books, which quickly broadened my conception of youth-led research. Although I have always considered myself a willing passenger on this journey, I realized rather quickly that this trip would be unlike any previous trips I have ever taken in writing a book. This, I believe, speaks well for the nature of this field, how it interconnects with youth development and youth-led efforts, and how quickly it has evolved during the period of time that this book was conceptualized and written.

The writing of a book, unlike the writing of an article or book chapter, affords an author an unprecedented opportunity that is simply not possible in other forms of publishing: to explore a subject in depth. Thus, in my case, it meant starting out with a vision of what the "end product" would be, with the realization that this product would necessitate many twists and turns along the way.

This is exciting from an author's perspective but is not without its share of anxieties and challenges, since the journey of writing a book must ultimately not exceed a set, agreed-on number of words.

My decision to write a book on youth-led research is one that has a history spanning several decades. I have a long history of practice, research, and writing on the subject of youth development and youth-involved research, and I have published four books specifically focused on youth development: (1) *New Arenas for Community Social Work Practice With Urban Youth: Use of the Arts, Humanities, and Sports* (2001) focuses on the importance of activities for outreaching and engaging urban youth utilizing a youth development paradigm; (2) *New Frontiers for Youth Development in the Twenty-First Century: Revitalizing and Broadening Youth Development* (2002), in turn, seeks to broaden the use of this paradigm to settings not historically associated with youth services, such as museums, libraries, zoos, or outdoor adventure; (3) *Social Youth Entrepreneurship: The Potential for Youth and Community Transformation* (2004) examines the development of business enterprises by youth that have as a foundation social goals but utilize businesses as a vehicle for achieving them; and (4) *Social Work Practice With Refugee and Immigrant Youth in the United States* (2005) takes the paradigm of youth development and applies it to a population group that generally has not been addressed in the youth development literature, namely, newcomer youth in this country.

These books only touched on various aspects of youth-led research and did not do justice to the subject, which is complex, dynamic, and ever changing as innovative methods and approaches are incorporated into this field. The importance of the subject matter was too great to relegate to a passing reference or the publication of an article or book chapter on the subject. Nothing less than an entire book devoted specifically to youth-led research was in order.

Youth-led research and program evaluation is a subject that I have been involved in developing over the past twenty-five years. I first wrote about youth-involved research studies in the late 1970s and early 1980s: Latino youth based in a large New England city undertook three community surveys (Delgado, 1979, 1981). In 1998, I wrote about a group of Puerto Rican youth in Holyoke, Massachusetts, and their undertaking of a community asset assessment (Delgado, 1996, 1998). Youth-led research has also been predicated on the importance of communities of color in particular, being active members of research teams to minimize external bias by researchers (Marin & Marin, 1991). Thus, the writing of a book on the subject of youth-led research represents a logical extension of my previous writings on youth development and provides me with an opportunity to bring together youth development and youth-led research.

Writing about any form of youth-led initiative or movement brings with it a contagious excitement that originates in youth. Their energy, excitement, and hope for a better future cannot but rub off on anyone who has been privileged enough to work with them. Their willingness to question is an act that is very much endemic to their age group and is one that should be encouraged across the life cycle. This energy and questioning takes on greater meaning when combined with a social and economic justice perspective. This, unfortunately, may come as a great surprise to those practitioners who have not tried using research as the primary method for engaging youth. When it is predicated on principles of social and economic justice, research as a method, or vehicle, can be empowering for all who are fortunate enough to be a part of the process. It is important to emphasize that youth-led research is much more than just "research undertaken by youth" to increase the knowledge base of a particular subject. It represents a profound political and social statement about making research relevant, empowering, and capable of effecting significant changes to programs and youth services.

The fields of youth development and youth-led research are now well into their second decade, and this has provided ample opportunities for staff to be educated and trained in the philosophy, principles, methods, and activities of the field. This field takes a unique perspective on youth, and this requires staff that can embrace this view but also be creative in creating new opportunities for youth. The next decade promises to witness a continued explosion of youth-led initiatives in the United States as well as internationally. The continued convergence of the academic and practice worlds will provide numerous well-evaluated examples of programs incorporating the principles and methods outlined in this book. Further, it will create a corps of well-trained youth activists and researchers to staff, manage, and govern youth-led organizations. Eventually some of these youth will find their way into academic circles and will be in propitious positions to move this field forward with scholarly publications. Policy makers and funders will undoubtedly follow suit in helping to sustain this movement, and possibly expand it into other arenas.

Acknowledgments

A book of this nature is never accomplished without the support and input of countless individuals, and this book is no exception. First, I wish to thank Dean Wilma Peebles-Wilkins for her continued support of my scholarship over all these years, including this book. Ms. Suzanne Hogan must also be thanked because of her administrative support in getting this book to the publisher. A special note of thanks goes to Christina Weeter and Sarah Nacari, research assistants on this book. They played instrumental roles in helping to shape the contents of this book through their hard work, insights, and attention to details. I wish to also thank the anonymous external reviewers for their constructive feedback and encouragement. Finally, I must extend a special thank-you to Art Pomponio for his support and belief in the importance of this book.

PART I

Setting the Context

1

Overview

T he subject of youth and how best to meet their educational, physical, moral, spiritual, social, and health needs never seems to go out of vogue in this country (Wyn & White, 1997). This subject, as a result, has led to the development of a tremendous number of strategies and paradigms that are youth centered, such as youth-led initiatives (Delgado & Staples, 2005). The development of youth-led educational and social interventions necessitates the acquisition of an in-depth understanding of youth and their context, aspirations, assets, needs, concerns, and current and projected social profiles. It also entails adults assuming roles that are nonauthoritative in nature.

If social interventions are to be successful in both the long and the short run, then it is necessary for research to be undertaken that systematically and comprehensively answers critical questions about youth's well-being and perceptions of the world around them. This research, however, must address the perspective of youth themselves and actively seek to minimize adult bias throughout the entire process, if the results of the research are to be meaningful to youth (Schensul & Berg, 2004). This type of research, in addition, must not only answer key questions but also serve to create momentum toward achieving some form of social change. Youth-focused research, as a result, cannot be thought of as just "another" form of research. A shift in paradigms, controversial as it may be, is in order. This shift places youth in positions of power, as researchers instead of research subjects.

The subject of youth needs and well-being in the United States has rightly received increased attention in the past two decades. Unfortunately, much of this attention has focused on viewing youth as either problems or potential problems for the nation and on the social and economic costs resulting from their irresponsible behavior. Anyone undertaking a project to assess the economic costs of school dropouts, juvenile delinquency, drug abuse, and sexual acting out can readily find numerous studies, reports, and statistics on these and other subjects related to risk-taking behaviors of youth (Lakes, 1996; Males, 1996, 1998; Ungar, 2002, 2003; Watkins & Iverson, 1998). A deficit perspective, in essence, has characterized this approach and has helped shape much of the national attention and debate on youth and how best to direct interventions.

Rarely does a week go by without some major news announcement of how youth are "not measuring up" to what we, as adults, expect of them. The pervasiveness of this perspective has cast this nation's youth into a "problem" category, effectively casting a dark cloud over their potential to be productive adult citizens (Lerner, 1995). This deep hole, so to speak, has made it arduous for youth to view themselves in other than a deficit perspective.

Nevertheless, despite this gloomy perspective, there has been increased national and international attention to the search for social paradigms that can best capture youth talents and ensure their importance to the nation's future well-being (Hein, 2003; Lorion & Sokoloff, 2003). This search has resulted in a tremendous amount of excitement and energy for the field of youth services (Fraser & Galinsky, 1997). These paradigms share much in common, and one strong prevailing theme is that they all thrust youth into decision-making roles as either collaborators with adults or as leaders in their own right in the search for a more productive life and a recognition of their capabilities in the process of doing so.

Adults in general, but particularly those in schools and community-based organizations, have historically viewed youth from two primary perspectives as *objects* that need to be controlled because youth are incapable of knowing what is best for them, and as *recipients*, as they are really "adults in waiting" and in need of being socialized and educated accordingly. A third perspective, and one embraced by this book, sees youth as partners with adults. Youth are capable of making significant and lasting contributions now and only need opportunities and requisite support to do so. This partnership, as a result, is predicated on mutual respect (Klindera & Menderwald, 2001). Youth-led research, youth participation, and youth development, for example, best capture the goals of engaging youth in initiatives that effectively transform not only them but also their community in the process (Chan, Carlson, Trickett, & Earls, 2003; Innovation Center for Community and Youth Development, 2003; YouthAction, 1998).

A plethora of youth-led initiatives, as a result, has emerged over the past decade or so to provide a vehicle for youth to excise decision-making powers in crafting initiatives that target their well-being (O'Donoghue, Kirshner, & McLaughlin, 2002). Any form of community development or capacity enhancement without meaningful engagement of youth is nothing more than the use of smoke and mirrors to bring about significant social change and personal growth (Gamble & Hoff, 2004; Innovation Center for Community and Youth Development, 2004; Midgley & Livermore, 2004). A "business as usual" approach cannot be taken if significant changes are to occur in how we, as a nation, view youth and seek their involvement in crafting solutions to many of their concerns and needs, providing them with opportunities to develop competencies for life in the twenty-first century (Flanagan & Van Horn, 2003; Huber, Frommeyer, Weisenbach, & Sazama, 2003; Lerner, Brentano, Dowling, & Anderson, 2002).

Lakes's (1996) comments capture the hope and positive perspective of current-day youth and set the stage for a youth development paradigm:

> Our precious youth are the next generation to inherit the legacy of economic deindustrializations and community disinvestments begun in the latter decades of the twentieth century. We must start to encourage and facilitate partnerships of young people in sustainable, capacity-building approaches to revitalization of our inner cities. We desperately need their youthful energy and tireless strength, their boundless assets and valuable skills, their special qualifications and talented gifts for the important work ahead. (p. 18)

The emergence of a youth development paradigm is a case in point providing the youth-led movement with a powerful conceptual foundation for designing community- and institution-based programs.

This paradigm has certainly caught the attention and imagination of practitioners, social policy makers, and academics, across the country and internationally. More specifically, the past five years have witnessed an unprecedented amount of research and professional literature on this paradigm and the multitude of ways it can be used in youth-focused programs in a wide range of settings (Benson & Pittman, 2001; Delgado, 2002; Eccles & Gootman, 2002; Lerner, Taylor, & von Eye, 2002; Noam & Miller, 2003; Rauner, 2000; Rhodes, 2002; Villarruel, Perkins, & Keith, 2003).

The field of community practice, too, has witnessed a tremendous surge of attention, further lending itself to incorporate youth development and youth-led research and programmatic efforts (Gambone & Connell, 2004; KIDS Consortium, 2001; MacNair, 1996; Weil, 2004.) Community practice sets the stage for inclusion of numerous intervention paradigms stressing indigenous capacities, participation, and empowerment (Delgado, 1999; Fisher, 2004; P. W. Murphy & Cunningham, 2003).

Nevertheless, there has been at least one significant area that has generally been overlooked in using a youth development paradigm as the basis for including youth in critical community and organizational positions, namely, the field of social research (Kelly, 1993; Matysik, 2000). Well over twenty years ago, I lamented the absence of youth in research roles, and only recently has this movement for inclusion been taken seriously:

> The use of adolescents has too long been neglected in the human service field and must be seriously considered in the future. Participation in needs assessments research exposes youngsters to a broad view of community needs that extend past their immediate circle of contacts, and enables them to develop skills that may benefit them and their community in future years. (Delgado, 1981, p. 613)

The importance of this form of involvement cannot be easily dismissed as anecdotal. Rennekamp (2001), for example, raises the need for involvement of youth in research as a moral imperative for the field and the need for us to advise, strongly suggest, and ultimately insist that they play influential roles within the research process; the nature and importance of this role is determined by negotiation between the researcher, organization, and community. Checkoway and Richards-Schuster's (2002) observations on the state of youth-led research reinforce the need for a book specifically devoted to this subject and signify how the field has significantly progressed in the past several years: "At present, however, youth participation in community evaluation research remains relatively underdeveloped as a field of practice and subject of study. There are increasing initiatives, but they operate in isolation from one another" (p. 27).

The significance of the field is underscored by the increased number of scholarly publications on the topic and the number of presentations at professional conferences (Schensul & Berg, 2004). The importance was so great that an entire three-day conference on the subject was sponsored by the Kellogg Foundation (Wingspread Symposium on Youth Participation in Community Research, 2002), an entire special issue of a well-respected journal in the field of youth development was devoted to this content (Checkoway & Goodyear, 2003), and a book focused on youth participation and evaluation (Sabo, 2003a, 2003b).

A 1997 conference titled "First Annual Community YouthMapping Conference" typifies what is meant by this upsurge in attention (*Community Connections*, 1997). This conference involved youth and adults from sixteen mapping sites throughout the United States. Through the use of panel presentations, small breakout sessions, and informal opportunities for dialogue, participants were able to share success stories and identify common challenges and rewards. The following list of breakout sessions illustrates the potential subject topics for research conferences on youth-led research: Public/Private Governance, Maintenance and Updating Data, Access and Dissemination, Curriculum for Schools and Community-Based Organizations, Research Implications and Baseline Data, National and Local Funding Streams, and Youth Advisory Network. Youth-led research touches on a wide range of arenas and can serve as a mechanism for empowering youth.

The practice of social research has historically been reserved for the nation's formally educated elite social scientists; this exclusivity is coming under increasing criticism within and outside of academia (Cousins & Earl, 1992; Stoecker, 1997; Tandon, 1988). In quoting Gibbons et al. (1994), Oliver (1995) argues for the democratization of knowledge as a rationale for youth-led research initiatives:

The transformation of knowledge production is one of the central processes characterising the societies of the advanced, industrialized world. Knowledge production is less and less a self-contained activity. It is neither the science of the universities, or the technology of industry, to use an older classification for illustrative purposes. Knowledge production, not only in its theories and models but also in its methods and techniques, has spread from academia into all those institutions that seek social legitimization through recognisable competence and beyond. . . . The question of who owns knowledge and more specifically, who has the "right" to generate knowledge, has served to democratize information. This perspective has expanded the pool of those who are legitimized to be knowledge creators. (qtd. in Oliver, 1995, p. 2)

Information and knowledge are to postindustrial society what labor and capital were to industrial society (Bell, 1974). Consequently, it is not out of the question to consider monopoly of information to be closely related to monopoly of capital. Ultimately, who has the "right" to create knowledge? It has historically been the sole prerogative of professional elite (Comstock & Fox, 1993; Gaventa, 1993). There is tremendous power in being able to control the production of knowledge and information (Merrifield, 1993). Boyer (1990) criticizes the prevailing narrowness of the definition of scholarship as research with the primary goal of creating new knowledge. This form of scholarship effectively dismisses the value of other forms of scholarship such as teaching, application, and integration.

Sohng (1995), in turn, issues a call for the reconceptualization of knowledge production (research) from a detached discovery and empirical verification of generalizable patterns to one of uncovering resistance and struggle, thus creating a social-cultural context for research and the results emanating from this activity. Sohng notes:

Knowledge exists in our everyday lives. We live our knowledge and constantly transform it through what we do. Knowing is part of our life; it informs our actions. This knowledge does not derive from analysis of data about other human beings but from sharing a life-world together—speaking with one another and exchanging actions against the background of common experience, tradition, history, and culture. . . . It is this engagement and its impact on ways of looking and developing knowledge which is crucial rather than the articulation of a set of techniques that can be mimicked. (p. 6)

Contextualizing knowledge creation outside of customary institutions such as universities serves to empower communities, particularly those that have historically been the focus of research that is deficit oriented.

Universities and research institutes have traditionally been the staging grounds, or monopoly, in the preparation of this nation's and other nations' social researchers (Fai-Borda & Rahman, 1991; L. T. Smith, 1999). Learned societies and professional organizations, in turn, have been the places where researchers gather to exchange information and further develop their competencies. Brydon-Miller (1993) recommends that the term *researcher* refer to community and workplace persons as well as those with specialized training. Unlike conventional research approaches, youth-led research stresses the need for research of everyday life and the accounting of reality produced by the actors (subjects), with researchers participating in the everyday life of the subjects of the research (Puuronen, 1993).

Adults have historically and exclusively populated "learned" arenas. Although adults have and will, no doubt, continue to dominate the field of research, youth-focused or otherwise, youth must be incorporated as partners in these endeavors with the ultimate goal of having them assume leadership roles in all facets of this endeavor. Their contributions will bring a perspective that cannot continue to be overlooked by adults and the institutions they control. Having adults give up control over the research process may well represent the ultimate barrier youth will encounter in youth-led research projects or any other youth-led initiative.

Youth-led research, in essence, represents a commitment to identify not only how best to address a particular phenomenon but also how best to carry out action to address it (M. K. Smith, 1996). If knowledge is considered socially constructed, then youth participation becomes essential in development of a better understanding of youth's perspectives, opinions, needs, and assets (Dworkin, Larson, & Hansen, 2003). Discovering the underlying causes of a social problem firsthand represents a critical understanding of how best to address its manifestations within a local context and taking into account cultural norms. Youth can use their own terms to help frame the dissemination of the research findings to other youth (M. Weiss, 2003): "Conducting their own research and developing their own analysis not only equipped the young people to support their concerns, but gave them the credibility to come up with solutions" (p. 63).

Research on youth has and will, no doubt, continue to be a legitimate area for scientific inquiry. However, the idea of youth as researchers has only recently been advocated for, and not surprisingly, has raised a few eyebrows in the "scientific" community in the process. Inquiry, according to Rappoport (2002), is the engine that drives discovery, growth, and improvement to self and community. Thoughtful and systematic research, in turn, is the universal method that is used to direct purposeful action toward actualizing goals. Youth-led research, as a result, can increase knowledge and achieve positive social goals in the process. Youth have become a vehicle for developing a better understanding of the nature of the goal and the target of this change.

However, as one adult participant in youth-led research commented, organizations that sponsor these types of projects face a series of challenges, adult bias being one that may be deeply rooted and arduous to overcome (Horsch, Little, Smith, Goodyear, & Harris, 2002):

> At the organizational level, they've bought into it . . . just the fact that the young people are coming up with these little tangible suggestions gives it credibility. But the place we run into challenges is funders and more policy-level people who are coming in with [an] academic bias. . . . It's like being admitted to a club, in a way, and to believe that other people [like youth] can do that, when you've gone through ten years of various training might be hard, I think. (p. 6)

Social research in its various manifestations is within the reach of anyone seeking answers to important social questions, including youth. Thus, it is what I consider to be a new frontier in social research since we are only now willing to seriously explore its potential reach within the field. The consequences of these activities, however, go far beyond the confines of a classroom, human service organization, or an academic program.

Having youth play influential decision-making roles in designing and conducting research is democratic and empowering (Fetterman, 2003; Innovation Center for Community and Youth Development, 2001, 2004). An activity that historically has been denied to youth has suddenly and quite dramatically been opened up to them for the first time in a meaningful manner. Youth have a vital stake in the nature of the programs and services that have been established to serve them. Thus, what better way to ensure that these resources have tapped the voices of youth themselves than by having youth seek out, record, and analyze these voices and recommend changes as a result?

Although specifically referring to empowerment evaluation, Fetterman's (2002) comment nevertheless applies also to youth-led research: "Empowerment evaluation is fundamentally a democratic process. The entire group—not a single individual, not the external evaluator or an internal manager—is responsible for conducting the evaluation" (p. 2). Youth-led research represents an important conceptual leap in the broadening of a youth development paradigm among other social paradigms in the early part of the twenty-first century. Youth-led research can be expected to continue to increase in significance in the near future, and its evolution will no doubt influence other forms of youth development and youth-led projects.

❖ BOOK GOALS

The five goals for this book are simple in nature but have profound implications for youth, providers, policy makers, and academics:

1. Ground youth-led research within the broader youth development/youth-led movement within the United States and internationally.

2. Provide an in-depth and comprehensive understanding of the potential of this type of research for the field of youth development/youth-led research.

3. Assist the reader in developing a better understanding of how youth-led research can lead to important organizational and community changes.

4. Explore how service-learning as a construct can play a bridging role between schools, community-based organizations, and communities; and explore the role youth-led research can play in achieving this goal.

5. Inspire students at all educational levels to become better-informed consumers of research or even to become researchers themselves.

There is no denying that the subject of research, or "having" to take a research course at any level of education, is rarely embraced with enthusiasm by most students, regardless of their age. This lack of positive reaction is probably due to myths about the worth of research in this society and how "boring" or "difficult" research activities can be. They have not learned, unfortunately, that research in its various manifestations is very often the first step in achieving significant social change, or that the process of research can be empowering for both the researcher and the community participating in this venture.

All professions are in desperate need of a cadre of researchers who embrace the potential power this method has for informing and transforming society. Research must actively seek to inform change, and such change necessitates the use of many different types of research methods and approaches to answer the questions youth, in our case, believe to be significant in their lives and in the life of their communities. Exposing youth to the benefits and power of research may represent an initial significant step in providing the field of social research with a cadre of well-motivated and informed youth who wish to pursue careers in this field. These youth will be eager learners and will influence not only classroom discussions on the subject but also the scholarly outcomes that follow. Increasing the relevance of research brings with it a higher likelihood of positive social changes.

❖ BOOK OUTLINE

This book consists of four major parts and twelve chapters: Part I: Setting the Context consists of two chapters; Part II: Youth as Researchers: Approaches and Considerations comprises seven chapters; Part III: Field Examples consists of one major chapter highlighting four distinctive youth-led research undertakings; and Part IV: Future Challenges consists of two chapters, one of which is an epilogue.

Part I explains why youth-led research is part of a broader youth-led movement, and why youth are a population group worthy of such a movement. Part II exposes the reader to the theoretical underpinnings of youth-led movements in a variety of spheres and presents ways this subject content can be grounded within practice. Part III outlines for the reader a variety of perspectives, considerations, and steps that must be accomplished to conduct youth-led research. This part makes extensive use of case examples and illustrations. Finally, Part IV exposes the reader to the many rewards, challenges, and questions practitioners and academics will have to face in being part of a youth-led movement.

This book was written with a specific reader in mind: This reader embraces the principles and power of youth participation in decision making and recognizes that significant individual change is invariably tied to significant social change. In essence, youth can play important roles in changing their lives and the lives of others. Clearly, the reader who does not embrace this stance will find little value in the material covered in this book. The book should appeal to a wide audience, including those studying and working in fields such as youth development, community psychology, education, and social work. Although I am a social worker by education and experience, I have endeavored to broaden this book's appeal beyond social work. However, the reader will no doubt see social work's influence.

Unlike most conventional books on research methods and data analysis, which invariably find a home in research courses, youth-led research can also be viewed as a method of intervention. Thus, it can be used in research as well as direct intervention classes. Numerous national and international field-based examples have been selected to illustrate the potential of youth-led research across disciplines and geographical boundaries. The book has been conceptualized to supplement a basic graduate-level and upper-level undergraduate textbook specific to children and youth, social research methods, and planning/community development. In addition, I believe the book will be of interest to practitioners and organizations focused on youth services.

❖ OVERVIEW OF YOUTH DEMOGRAPHICS

The world's population of youth has steadily increased over the past decade and is projected to continue increasing into the near future, making it a subject of immense importance for all nations, including our own. More specifically, the percentage of youth living in urban areas surpassed 50 percent at the turn of the twenty-first century (Tienda & Wilson, 2000a). National and international demographic changes and trends, as a result, must influence how organizations, foundations, and government view the need for data to develop policies and make program recommendations, considering the potential role youth will play in generating these data. Youth, as a result of rapid social and institutional changes, must increasingly rely on their initiative, creativity, and ability to slowly navigate a "multidimensional labyrinth of choices and demands" (Mortimer & Larson, 2002, pp. 2–3).

Demographic profiles and trends historically have played important roles in helping policy makers, practitioners, and educators develop a more thoughtful agenda for research and interventions. The mere mention of demographics, however, generally gets an immediate and adverse reaction from most practitioners/educators, not to mention the general public. However, the mention of youth demographic profiles and trends gets an opposite reaction from this nation's corporations dependent on youth consumers. Why?

The subject of youth as a market for consumer goods is well understood in this country's business sector. The case of mobile telephones illustrates this point. It has been estimated that in the year 2004, there were over 36 million mobile phone users ages 5 to 24 years old in the United States; in 2001, only 32 percent of youths in this age range owned cell phones (W2 Forum, 2002). The subject of youth profiles and demographic trends warrants a brief overview because of its implications for any form of intervention focused on youth in this nation.

Hine's (2000) observations on this demographic trend stresses the profound implications that this society will feel as this age group works its way through all sectors of the country:

> During the first decade of the twenty-first century, the United States will have the largest number of teenagers in its history, more even than when the baby boomers bought their first blue jeans. The early years of this new century will, in large part, be shaped by this new generation, the largest infusion of youth in the U.S. population in more than four decades. (p. 296)

Fussell (2002), in raising questions about what happens to youth when situated within aging societies, in our case the United States, advocates for an intergenerational contract, one whereby adults invest in youth, and youth, in turn, support adults as they age.

A note specifically devoted to painting a sociodemographic profile of youth in the United States helps contextualize the numerical, social, and economic importance of youth in this country. Having an in-depth understanding of who youth are (e.g., knowing their ethnicity, race, age, residence, and economic power, and knowing about projected demographic trends) can help better prepare the reader for the importance of using youth as researchers currently and in the near future (Castex, 1997). Fortunately, recent U.S. Bureau Census data are readily available for use by communities across the United States.

In 1990, there were almost 27 million Americans ages 18 to 24 years old; after a dip in 1995, the young adult population rebounded to

28.3 million in 2000 and is expected to increase to 30.1 million in 2010 (Kerckhoff, 2002). A study focused on youth (18 years of age and younger) found that in 2000 approximately 70.4 million (26 percent) of the U.S. population was under the age of 18 (Forum on Child and Family Statistics, 2002). By 2005, there is expected to be nearly 73 million youth under the age of 18 in this country (Mullahey, Susskind, & Checkoway, 1999). In 2000, youth ages 17 and under numbered 72.4 million, making this cohort rival the size of the baby boomer generation (77.6 million adults) ages 36 to 54 years old (Lopez, 2002). By 2020, it is projected that youth under the age of 17 will account for almost one-quarter of the total population in this country.

The ethnic and racial composition of U.S. youth has also undergone dramatic change during this period. In 1990, 26.1 percent were African American and Latino. In 2000, that proportion increased to 29.7 percent and is projected to represent 33.7 percent in 2010. Thus, if projections are realized, the year 2010 will have the largest cohort of youth of color in the nation's history; this situation carries profound social, economic, and political implications for the nation as a whole, and some states in particular (Cullen & Wright, 2002; Kerckhoff, 2002; Ozer, Macdonald, & Irwin, 2002; Youniss & Ruth, 2002).

Special attention, however, has to be paid to how the racial and ethnic composition of youth, particularly those living in urban America, has changed over the past two decades and how it can be expected to change in the near future (D. E. Murphy, 2003). For example, in 2001 more than 50 percent of all new births in California were Latino. These Latino babies will constitute the majority of California children entering first grade in 2009 and the majority of those entering high school in 2017 (Jablon, 2003).

❖ YOUTH INVOLVEMENT IN COMMUNITY RESEARCH AND PROGRAM EVALUATION

A contextual grounding of any phenomenon is usually the first step toward a better understanding and appreciation of that phenomenon and its prominence in community, professional, and academic circles. An understanding of the context that led to the rise of a construct plays an influential role in practice. How can we understand the present and prepare for the future without a solid grasp of the history behind an idea? What is the history of youth-led research and evaluation in the

United States? Tracing the genesis of any construct or concept is always arduous to determine with any great degree of certainty. Generally, its appearance in the professional literature marks the time when it is officially recognized in professional/academic circles.

However, this "birthday" invariably overlooks the countless number of years when a construct has been in existence but no one bothered to write about it or publish anything about it in scholarly journals. Youth involvement in community research and program evaluation is no exception to this phenomenon. Few students in this country have not participated in some form of school-based research project that has entailed their going out into the community to learn about a specific issue, perspective, or problem (Egan-Robertson & Bloome, 1998; Egan-Robertson & Willett, 1998; Mercado, 1998). Consequently, research efforts of various kinds and in various institutional and community settings have been going on for quite a considerable period without a specific "field" being created to organize and capture these activities.

Sabo (2003a) traces the emergence of youth involvement in evaluation to the convergence of community development, action research, participatory evaluation, and positive youth development. As it has in most international movements, the United Nations has played an influential role in this surge in popularity, with the passage of the 1989 UN Convention on the Rights of the Child. This convention served to highlight the importance of children and youth throughout the world and led to an understanding of the common challenges nations face in better preparing this population for eventual roles as contributing adults.

The late twentieth and early twenty-first centuries have witnessed dramatic developments and advances involving youth in research capacities within this country. The emergence and wide acceptance of a youth development paradigm has played an influential part in this upsurge (Bumbarger & Greenberg, 2002; Roth, 2004). Thus, the popularity of this paradigm bodes well for the future of youth-specific programming. Advocates for youth involvement in research even go so far as to see this movement as an effective means of involving older youth in the youth development field, and developing powerful collaborative partnerships between youth and adults. Keeping older youth actively involved in programming activities has been a perennial challenge for the field, and there have been relatively few ways to accomplish this other than to hire them as staff (Schilling & Martinek, 2000).

It is not surprising that youth involvement in research and program evaluation has appeared in the field under a variety of labels, such as students-as-researchers, voiced research, peer research, youth-run research, participatory research, participatory action research, empowerment research, emancipatory research, participatory evaluation, collaborative evaluation, discovery research, voiced research, constituency-oriented research and dissemination, and action research (Bowes, 1996; Broad & Saunders, 1998; Hall, 1992; Krogh, 2001; Oliver, 1995; Pennell, Noponen, & Weil, 2004; Smyth, 1999; Stoecker, 1997). All of these labels stress the importance of participation, decision making, and action to one degree or another, regardless of setting (institution or community). Participatory evaluation, for example, is no longer considered out of the mainstream of the evaluation field, with youth participatory evaluation assuming a more central role within the field (Fetterman, 2003).

With notable exceptions, the move toward participatory forms of research has largely been led and influenced by non–university-affiliated sources. This, in large part, is the result of tensions between traditional researchers and the needs of the community (Strand, Marullo, Cutforth, Stoecker, & Donohue, 2003). Whereas those affiliated with the university environment use a more conventional definition of what constitutes "knowledge," those not affiliated with the university tend to emphasize practical outcomes and tie these outcomes directly to the priorities of the community.

These forms of research can be classified as "the specific collection of information that is designed to bring about social change" (Bogdan & Biklen, 1992, p. 223). Although Bogdan and Biklen's definition specifically addresses action research, it nonetheless captures well the primary social intent of any form of research that stresses participation, empowerment, and social change. This form of research does not exist exclusively within an age-specific providence. All of these efforts, however, can be conceptualized as "increasing participation."

However, I believe it is best to consider these efforts as representing a shift in paradigms, blurring the distinction between "researcher" and "research subjects" (Center for Popular Education and Participatory Research, 2003). Research that places participation as a central theme in the process of knowledge generation does not separate research from action and education (Altpeter, Schopler, Galinsky, & Pennell, 1999; Alvarez & Gutierrez, 2001). The social change or education that emanates from participatory research results in a "more equitable and democratic society" (Center for Popular Education and Participatory Research, 2003).

L. D. Brown and Tandon (1983) advance the stance that social research must focus on how best to serve the lower socioeconomic classes in their struggles against various forms of oppression. Horsch et al. (2002), in a meta-analysis of youth-involved or youth-led research projects, reinforce Brown and Tandon's conclusions:

> The most common motivator for involvement in research and evaluation is the ability to use research and evaluation as a vehicle for change. Some youth are not satisfied with a report to a funder that sits on a shelf; they need to see the results of their work in tangible, immediate, and important ways. This can be either through program changes or the fact that others were willing to listen and consider what youth have to say. (p. 4)

Stringer (1999) specifically addresses four dimensions pertaining to action research within a community context, with equal applicability to youth-led research projects:

1. Participation of all people in the research is one way of ensuring that it is a democratic process.

2. All participants are of equal worth.

3. The experience is liberating by providing freedom from oppressive and debilitating conditions.

4. It enhances the life of participants and enables the expression of an individual's full human potential. (pp. 9–10)

Thus, terms such as *democratic, liberating, equitable,* and *enhancement* capture Stringer's set of guiding principles for action research and effectively tie the act of research with the act of social change.

Torres's (1998) description of all of the elements addressed in sixth-grade "celebrations" and "letters home" projects also applies to any adult-led research undertaking:

> The students-as-researchers program was intended to give students authentic writing and learning experiences, a real question to explore, a topic important to their lives, and a real audience to address—an audience invested both in the students and in the students' research. (p. 67)

It is difficult to imagine any adult researcher who would not love to have a positive experience undertaking research, a burning question to answer that has importance to a wide range of people, and a vested audience that will anxiously await the results of the research.

Any community-based organization or school setting that articulates a vision of reaching youth will benefit from youth-led research and evaluation, regardless of its location and specific mission as an organization. Whether program evaluation and research involving youth-led teams are simple or complex in design depends on goals, funding, setting, and time considerations. This flexibility is one of the many appeals of this form of research. Regardless of study design, data will prove to be rich in results and experiences for both researchers and participants of the research (Alawy, 2001). The greatest compliment that one can give a research project is that the results were meaningful and the experience was meaningful for all of those who participated.

Regardless of the form used to capture this form of activity, having youth play influential and decision-making roles in a research enterprise is premised on the following five beliefs:

1. Youth have abilities that can be tapped in developing and implementing a research project.

2. Youth bring to a research project a unique perspective or voice that cannot but help the process of answering questions about youth.

3. Youth are vital stakeholders in the process and outcome of research.

4. The knowledge and skills youth acquire through active participation in research can transfer over to other aspects of their lives.

5. Youth-led research can help broaden and revitalize an activity that has a reputation as being boring, inconsequential, and of interest to only a small select group of adults.

Youth, however, are not the only constituency that has advocated for youth-involved research. The past few years have witnessed major national reports calling for a more comprehensive and participatory research, laying the conceptual and political foundation for youth-led research (Hatch, Moss, Saran, Presley-Cantrell, & Mallory, 1993; Schulz, Parker, Israel, Becker, & Maciak, 1998). The "Future of Public Health, Healthy People 2000" and "Health Professions Education for the Future:

Schools in Service to the Nation" are two examples of this national move toward involvement of disenfranchised groups in helping to set priorities for interventions through active and meaningful participation in research (Israel, 2000).

It may surprise the reader to know that a "formalized" role for youth-led research in the professional literature is well over 25 years old. Early references to youth-led community research in the professional literature are Bloom and Padilla (1979), Padilla, Padilla, Morales, Olmedo, and Ramirez (1979), and Perez et al. (1980), all of which describe an innovative peer-interviewer model for conducting inhalant, marijuana, and alcohol abuse surveys among Mexican American youth in California. This research was premised on the belief that youth are in a propitious position to get other youth to answer questions that would not be answered if adults were asking them. Youth-led research, in essence, serves to break down significant social, psychological, economic, and cultural barriers between research respondents and researchers and thrusts youth into a position of power and influence over the outcomes resulting from their research findings.

In the late 1970s and early 1980s, I developed a series of community needs assessment projects focused on the Latino community of Worcester, Massachusetts (Delgado, 1979, 1981). Unlike the project by Bloom and Padilla (1979) and Perez et al. (1980), this study had Puerto Rican youth conducting surveys of adults in three geographical areas of the city over a three-year period, asking questions from a wide variety of categories such as migration patterns, demographic characteristics, service utilization patterns, perceptions of community needs and resources, sources and amounts of income, future plans to return to Puerto Rico, and language competencies in English and Spanish. During the first year of the project, youth roles were limited to that of interviewers. During the second and third years, however, their roles expanded to trainers, field supervisors, coders, analysts, and writers of the final reports.

Since the 1970s and early 1980s, there have been a number of youth-led research projects reported in professional circles. These efforts occurred across all sectors of the country: in rural and urban locations; in settings such as schools, community-based organizations, and nontraditional places; and among various sociodemographic groups. The movement toward youth-led research has spanned a broad arena that prominently grounds this form of research within a community change and social planning context. The Redwood City,

California, initiative undertaken by community youth is such an example (Fernandez, 2002). As an after-school project, thirteen middle-school eighth graders conducted a series of need assessments for the purpose of achieving change in how city government provides programs and services for youth.

A number of prominent institutions such as universities and national professional organizations have readily embraced the concept of youth-led or youth-involved research, and this has spurred the movement forward during the early part of this millennium. Harvard University, through its Family Research Project, has undertaken an extensive analysis of fifteen youth programs throughout the country that have youth serving in research roles (Horsch et al., 2002). This analysis will no doubt play a significant role in shaping the field's better understanding of its emerging youth-led activity. Youth Action Research Group, based at the Center for Social Justice Research, Teaching and Service, Georgetown University, carries out research projects with youth designing, researching, and analyzing the challenges faced in their neighborhoods.

The San Francisco Department of Children, Youth and Families (2002), for example, on an annual basis recruits, trains, and employs twenty high school–age youth in research methods for the purposes of evaluating the forty community-based organizations funded to provide youth services. Youth researchers conduct program evaluations and present their findings to professional audiences, conduct community needs assessments, and facilitate community forums to disseminate the results and obtain feedback on programming suggestions. There is also an increasing number of examples in the field where youth and adults serve in collaborative roles in conducting research (Checkoway & Richards-Schuster, 2002; Krasny & Doyle, 2002).

Youth-led research initiatives have also found their way into need-specific and problem-specific arenas such as the disability field (Cook, Cook, Tran, & Tu, 1997; Hartman, DePoy, Francis, & Gilmer, 2000; Morris, 2000). Broad and Saunders (1998), for example, report on a study in Ireland involving youth leaving care (i.e., aging out of foster services) as peer researchers. Ward's (1997) report on a series of innovative strategies for involving children and youth with disabilities in research projects highlights the potential contribution of these youth in shaping strategies to address their needs and issues. Bryant et al. (2000) have used youth to undertake research on tobacco use among adolescents in Florida. Schensul, Wiley, Sydlo, and Brase (1999), in turn, have used youth researchers to study HIV/AIDS prevention. There appears to be no youth population subgroup that cannot benefit from youth-led research.

Adjustments will be required to take into account group characteristics and social circumstances. Nevertheless, the potential of youth-led research to better inform researchers, practitioners, and policy makers cannot be easily dismissed. Youth-led research may take on many different forms, goals, and budgets and is destined to continue to increase in prominence. The question is not whether or not youth-led research is applicable, but rather how this form of research can best be modified to take into account local circumstances and goals while including all types of youth.

By no means is youth-led research just a U.S. movement; its significance is too great to be bounded by one nation's geographical borders. Highly industrialized and developing countries alike have undertaken youth-led research within urban and rural settings (Munoz-Laboy, Almeida, Nascimento, & Parker, 2004). For example, the Triumph and Success Peer Research Project in Sheffield, England, uses youth ages 15 to 21 years old as a team, with support from professionals, to conduct surveys of youth for the purposes of developing youth programming (France, 2002). The Centre for Research and Evaluation model involves youth and adults on community research teams and steering committees. The research projects developed a model for involving youth and adults on community research teams and steering committees. The research projects were multifaceted and multimethod and specifically led to program development. Finally, in an El Salvador youth-led (15–21 years old) research project on studying the health risks posed by heavy use of pesticides in a rural community, the young researchers designed questionnaires, conducted pilot tests and interviews, entered and analyzed data, and presented the results to their community (Kato, Zwahlen, & Hubbard, 2002).

These national and international grassroots efforts at developing models for youth-led research have been accomplished with minimal exposure in scholarly journals and books. In many ways, the field of practice has led in this movement, and academics are playing catch-up. Practitioners have a desperate need for one source that will provide them with information on youth-involved research, for example, a book that can both meet the needs of practitioners and be used in the classroom to prepare future practitioners and researchers.

❖ DEFINITION AND CONCEPTUAL
    OVERVIEW OF YOUTH-LED RESEARCH

The importance of a solid conceptual base that can serve as a guide in
social interventions should be a welcomed addition to the field. A conceptualization that appeals to practitioners, academics, and—in the case
of youth-led research—youth can be quite powerful and unique in the
world of theory-driven initiatives. Youth-led research has a strong conceptual base, and practitioners as well as scholars can draw from a wide
range of conceptual perspectives. As a result, youth-led research can be
operationalized through a variety of avenues such as service-learning or
contextualized learning. This field also draws on many constructs such
as participatory evaluation, empowerment, peer research, and consumer-
driven research, to list but four. This propensity to draw on these and
other constructs serves to enrich the field but can also prove confusing
for academics and practitioners alike, not to mention youth.

London (2002) notes that youth-involved research effectively
draws from two broad streams of theory and practice, namely,
(1) youth development and (2) research and evaluation, and more
specifically participatory dimensions. There are a variety of paradigms
that can be used singularly or in combination to set a theoretical
foundation for these types of research projects. Thus, academics and
practitioners have many theoretical concepts and constructs on which
to base their interventions, including ones that are comprehensible to
consumers of interventions.

Participation as a central guiding value has achieved a broad base
of support across research-driven professional disciplines both within
the United States and internationally. Fetterman (2003), for example,
popularized the concept of "empowerment evaluation" as a vehicle for
using "concepts, techniques, and findings to foster improvement and
self-determination" (p. 88). Although this is a very simple definition,
its implications for participatory processes can be quite profound.
Cousins, Donohue, and Bloom (1996) advance the use of collaborative
evaluation that stresses meaningful participation on the part of those
who are recipients of services. This argument opens the door for youth
involvement in research. Harley, Stebnicki, and Rollins (2000) draw a
close association between participatory evaluation and community-
asset mapping. Evaluation results create a process of self-discovery
and competency enhancement in a community, such that both individuals and the entire community benefit.

Berg, Owens, and Schensul (2002) developed the "participatory action research" (PAR) model and defined it as

> an empowerment and inquiry model that teaches young people how to identify the components of a social problem that they and their peers experience, collect information about the problem using a variety of social and cognitive skills, and apply the results using both short- and long-term action plans. (p. 21)

PAR follows a long historical tradition of participatory initiatives and activities (e.g., participatory planning, management, and decision making), which appeal to a broader audience than just researchers (Brase, Pacheco, & Berg, 2004; Schensul, Berg, Schensul, & Sydio, 2004). (This model is discussed further in Chapter 9.)

Interestingly, youth-led initiatives, too, are not a recent phenomenon. The literature on youth-led initiatives can be traced to 1970, when they were a response to various national movements pertaining to social and economic justice. Community as a context, target, and vehicle for youth-led initiatives, in turn, opens up avenues for youth to undertake projects that have great relevance to them and their communities. In circumstances where these initiatives are developed out of a school-based curriculum, the potential for inclusion of academic subjects is increased. When initiatives are community based, there is a tremendous amount of variability and they can easily encompass arenas such as media, environment, violence, and health.

As I explain in greater detail in Chapter 2, youth-led initiatives can take many different shapes and, as a result, can fall into a variety of categories such as advocacy, planning, program development, policy development, community organizing, social enterprises, civic and political interests, and research (Davidoff, 1965; Hart, 1997; Hester, 1984).

Knopf (1970), for example, in one of the earliest known references to youth-led initiatives, describes and analyzes youth community crime patrol as a youth-led planning project. In the early 1990s, a number of youth-led patrols by Nation of Islam youth received national attention and recognition ("Farrakhan Praises Gang Members," 1993; "Nation of Islam Offers to Patrol Housing," 1991; "Prop-agandists or Saviors?" 1994). Fletcher (2002), in turn, focuses on school settings and describes students as planners, researchers, instructors, evaluators, and advocates. There really are no settings that cannot meaningfully involve youth.

However, regardless of youth-led initiative type, there are a number of significant similarities between projects:

1. Youth are in decision-making roles.

2. Adults are present but their role is dictated by youth.

3. Goals are multifaceted.

4. Planning techniques are always stressed.

5. Projects either explicitly or implicitly embrace positive social change outcomes.

6. Learning is never lost sight of throughout the duration of a project.

7. Although projects address serious issues and concerns, having fun is still an integral part of the experience.

It should also be noted that youth-led initiatives can be of varying duration, for example, fixed or open-ended and ongoing.

Youth-led research initiatives are often founded on a fundamental premise that connects and empowers youth to identify issues, challenges, and common goals for purposeful change. This central purpose is well captured by the Youth Research Institute of San Diego State University (National Latino Research Center, 2002):

> The main premise underlying this program is that affected youth can be utilized to assess the barriers that keep them and their peers from completing school and that research can be a mechanism that can be utilized by youth to better assess their needs and concerns. (p. 1)

Planning within youth-led initiatives has generally been viewed as a multistage process that can consist of three to five stages, depending on which framework the practitioner uses. At a minimum, the process must consist of development, implementation, and evaluation of a plan. Youth have played more active and meaningful roles in the first two stages and unfortunately have generally been totally absent from the evaluation stage (Rennekamp, 2001).

Historically, adults have taken the lead in deciding what programs are needed and how they should be conducted. Recently, however, there has been a widespread infusion of youth representation onto various planning boards, councils, and committees. This infusion of young people has begun to result in programs which more accurately respond to the needs of youth. But in many cases, the number of youth invited to be a part of these planning groups has been insufficient to affect the overall design of the resulting program. One or two young people serving on a council or board with a couple dozen adults often does more harm than good. (p. 1)

Phillips, Stacey, and Milner (2001) have defined the term *peer researcher* as a young person who has assumed the specific role of researcher in youth-related projects of significance to this age group. Practitioners and scholars may well argue that the evaluation stage of a plan has generally not been well regarded in the field of practice. One of the major reasons for this slight might have to do with the almost total absence of staff-consumer input into evaluation. Evaluation invariably represents a top-down effort with participation on the part of staff and consumers being relegated to answering questions rather than shaping the effort. Any effort to involve youth in evaluation will in all likelihood increase the relevance of this stage in the planning process. The lack of consumer-led evaluation in general, regardless of the age of the consumer, has effectively slowed progress of youth-led evaluation although efforts are prominently under way to rectify this situation.

Definitions of participation offered by Cousins et al. (1996), Fetterman (2001, 2002), and Berg et al. (2002) highlight the goals and processes of research as both a method of inquiry and a means for empowering and enhancing the competencies of youth. Berg et al. (2002) make specific reference to community-based research, while the other authors make reference to program evaluation.

Nevertheless, research has potential for transforming youth and communities far beyond the discovery of knowledge. It is an activity that can be effectively used for self-discovery and self-actualization, regardless of the sociodemographic characteristics of the persons undertaking the research. This presents a dramatic departure from the traditional view of research, which is that of a boring activity under-taken by individuals who typically are not the kind of people we nor-mally encounter in our daily lives, and with virtually no, or minimal, relevance to those being studied. Research, in effect, is closely tied to social change, thus increasing its relevance for day-to-day life.

Youth-led research, however, is not an activity that can easily exist without a supportive organizational infrastructure, culture, and knowledge of community, and therefore it is no different than any other youth-led activity (Youth in Focus, 2002). In essence, organizations and institutions require a necessary infrastructure to support young people and the adults collaborating with them, facilitating engagement in meaningful and long-term partnerships that benefit youth and also providing youth with clear roles, opportunities, and paths for engagement with other members of the community.

Organizations and communities, as a result, must not conceptualize youth-led research as an activity or project that is a one-time effort and can be resurrected as needed at some future date without serious consequences to the endeavor. Youth-led research is arduous to establish and maintain under the best of circumstances. Consequently, youth-led research must be thought of as an ongoing organization and community activity, just like other important activities such as fundraising and grant development. Once conceptualized in this manner, appropriate attention and resources can be allocated to it, and staff can be hired who have expertise in youth-led initiatives rather than just expertise in working with youth. Job descriptions, in turn, are developed and staff evaluated on items related to youth-led research.

❖ CONCLUSION

This introductory chapter provided the reader with an overview of the subject matter as well as a road map for the book. In addition to these goals, key concepts and terms were defined to ground the reader and facilitate the reading of this book. I hope that the reader is as excited about this book as I am. Youth have unlimited energy, imagination, and talents and are major stakeholders in programs addressing their needs. However, the fields of youth development and youth services are in desperate need for a more in-depth book on the subject of youth-led research. I hope that this book will play an influential role in helping to shape this emerging area of practice; I hope the book will appeal to youth, practitioners, policy makers, and academics alike. Innovations taking place in youth-led research have captured the attention of a wide audience and bode well for the future of social research.

Youth-led research represents an expansion of the youth-led movement both nationally and internationally. Like any movement involving youth in responsible decision-making positions, there is no telling how far they can go in helping to shape the future of research, whether the research is focused on youth or adults. Research as an area of practice is extremely important, and the systematic involvement of youth in this endeavor will aid to further energize this field. Youth, however, cannot simply decide to undertake research without active and meaningful support from adults within institutions and the community. Adults, too, play influential roles in the youth-led movement overall but particularly in the realm of research.

The following chapters systematically ground youth-led research within a broader conceptualization of youth-led initiatives. In so doing, the reader will develop an understanding and appreciation of the complexity of any youth-led initiative and, in particular, one focusing on research. I hope that the reader develops an appreciation for how the world of youth has expanded and will continue to expand, touching on a multitude of arenas in the field of education and youth-focused services. No nation can expect to progress without investing in its youth. Youth are capital, and as capital, they can wield prodigious influence in how communities, institutions, and nations navigate their way through the uncertainties that the twenty-first century has in store for the world.

It is fitting to end this introductory chapter with a quote. Yourniss and Ruth (2002) have eloquently stated the charge before adults in this century, and I cannot think of any youth-led field where this statement is more applicable than in youth-led research:

> Each generation of youth has an obligation to inspect society and move forward as best it can given the historical conditions that arise. In this regard, youth must remake history every generation. It is our complementary obligation as the older generation, then, to provide youth the resources that they will need in this task. While we cannot predict the future, we surely know how to help youth meet and confront it successfully. That is our choice and opportunity. (p. 268)

Youth-led research is the approach that can be used to study society and move it forward in a progressive manner. Youth-led research also can serve as a methodological approach for bridging disciplines in search of comprehensive strategies for improving the lives of youth, particularly those who are marginalized in this society and find themselves without a "legitimate" voice in helping to shape their destinies.

2

Conceptual Foundation
for Youth Involvement

The concept of participation within a democratic society is well accepted in the United States and countless other countries. There is no society in the world, however, that is governed by youth in all facets of daily life, even within institutions specifically devoted to the health, education, and well-being of youth. Adults, as a result, are in a universal position of power over youth. Youth, in turn, are vulnerable to exploitation in all spheres; the research arena is no exception (Save the Children, 2000).

Those who are fortunate enough to work with or teach youth, and strongly advocate for a particular initiative or movement, are invariably influenced by experiences, thoughts, and feelings about what they consider to be in the "best interests of youth." The best interests of youth cannot be considered within the narrow confines of national borders. These interests are best thought of in a global perspective (Estes, 2004; Reisch, 2004). Youth must be prepared to function and thrive within a global context. The United States and all other nations will benefit as a result of this perspective.

The United Nations Convention on the Rights of the Child (1989) mandates meaningful participation by children or youth in matters that affect them in accordance to their maturity. Particular attention has been paid by the United Nations Children's Fund (UNICEF; e.g., Lansdown, 2001) to include and encourage the participation of marginalized children on issues of significant bearing on their well-being. UNICEF (2002), although acknowledging a paucity of worldwide youth-led efforts, also specifically advocates for the active involvement of youth in projects directly affecting their well-being.

Worldwide recognition of the rights and potential of youth to play significant roles in society sets the foundation for youth-led initiatives (Golombek, 2002). Advocates of youth-led initiatives are no exception (KIDS Consortium, 2001), as they have experienced the power of youth-led initiatives and witnessed how they have positively altered the life course of youth, particularly those who are marginalized and undervalued in this society because of a sociodemographic set of factors, such as socioeconomic class, race, and ethnicity.

Nevertheless, a vision and desire to "market" youth-led initiatives cannot be expected to succeed without a strong theoretical foundation and, where available, research-generated data to support positions and recommendations. In the case of this book, it means that we must be prepared to document through research (quantitative- and qualitative-driven) our youth-led research efforts. This is an evolutionary process fraught with challenges, but one that must consistently move forward.

Youth-led research, as a result, should not be an exception to this point. The same standards that exist for assessing the importance and potential of other movements or paradigms must be used for youth-led research. Anything less means that this movement will not benefit as a result and will not carry the legitimacy (expertise, institutional, ethical, and consumer) to which other movements and paradigms have been subjected. Meeting these standards, as to be expected, will not be easy and will entail a considerable amount of time, thought, and energy. If movements are to be sustained and enhanced, however, collaboration between youth, practitioners, academics, and government must take place.

❖ YOUTH PARTICIPATION AS A CENTRAL THEME

The question of why youth aren't more represented in positions of decision making within the organizations established to reach them needs to be posed with an understanding that the answer to this question can prove quite troubling. This question is quite legitimate and it has been asked of women and people of color in this society. In fact, it is not unusual, although still controversial, to have special initiatives to increase youth's representation in decision-making positions. The success of these efforts can be debated, but the explicit goal cannot. However, the same cannot be said for youth.

As a group, youth are essentially invisible in this respect, but very visible and threatening in others. The following observation by Jason, a 17-year-old, typifies this prevailing perspective (Goggin, Powers, & Spano, 2002):

> If you had a problem in the Black community, and you brought in a group of White people to discuss how to solve it, almost nobody would take this panel seriously. In fact, there'd probably be a public outcry. It would be the same thing for women's issues or gay issues. But every day, in local arenas all the way to the White House, adults sit around and decide what problems youth have and what youth need, without ever consulting us. (p. 3)

I would also add not involving them in finding relevant solutions.

In another example, Sabo (2003b) quotes Beth, a 17-year-old researcher, highlighting the feelings of alienation many youth feel in their lives:

> For me, it seems that kids really need to own something. Kids don't own anything. They don't have any say over what kind of schooling they're thrown into; they don't have any say as to what their families do; they basically don't have very much control over their lives. The way that I look at it, it would really make me happy if I knew that at least one kid felt as though he or she had some sort of say in this place and had some sort of ownership over what happens in this place because kids, I think, are very alienated from what is happening in their lives, you know. (p. 21)

Youth alienation can be successfully addressed only through provision of meaningful activities to shape their environments and circumstances.

Jason and Beth are by no means exceptions, but the general rule, concerning their feelings of being undervalued and disenfranchised from decision-making roles within their lives. Their experiences very often represent a formidable barrier in engaging youth in any youth-led initiative. To ignore the disempowering experiences youth have faced in their dealings with adults would be a serious miscalculation on the part of program staff. Youth, after all, will eventually get their turn when they achieve adulthood.

A number of authors have proposed reasons why there is a general absence of youth in key decision-making roles in U.S. society. These reasons interact with each other to make a powerful case against youth empowerment and in favor of excluding youth from decision-making roles (Delgado, 2002; S. Howard et al., 2002; P. Kirby, 1999; Males, 1996, 1998; Morrow & Richards, 1996; Mullahey et al., 1999; Smilowitz, 2000):

1. Adults' general lack of interest in or disdain for the input given by children and youth

2. Adults' lack of confidence in youth's experience and expertise

3. A difference in the operative reality between youth and adults in how they live their lives

4. Adults' casting onto youth a wide range of fears and stereotypes

5. Adults' lack of awareness and understanding of how youth process information, making it difficult for adults to tap into how different stages of development influence perceptions and behaviors

6. The fact that this work is labor intensive and therefore expensive to actively involve youth or seek their opinions in decision making

7. Fear that empowerment of children and youth will translate into disempowerment of adults

8. The need for a process and procedures to systematically address differences of opinions and potential conflicts among youth

9. The presence of inertia, which undermines any form of innovative changes within organizations, including placing youth in decision-making roles

10. The difficulty and time it takes for a shift in paradigms to occur in order to place youth in decision-making positions

An even cursory review of this list of barriers highlights the significance of the challenges facing advocates of youth-led initiatives in their quest to broaden the decision-making roles within society. None of the barriers listed are insurmountable; however, in combination they produce a synergistic effect that requires the adoption of a paradigm that might be considered "radical" or "revolutionary." I say this not to dissuade the reader from moving progressively forward with a social change agenda based on social and economic justice themes, but to alert the reader to be fully cognizant of the rocky road ahead. The use of a competitive race metaphor is appropriate to illustrate this point. If runners enter a race thinking it is only 100 meters long and find out near the finish line that the race is really a marathon, they will quickly become disheartened and drop out of the race.

A shift in paradigms, such as the one being proposed in this book, might well require a lifetime of devotion to achieve. It is not a mad dash to the finish. I am under no illusion that the youth-led movement, and in this case that related to research, will not have a challenging journey throughout the early part of this century and millennium. The youth development/youth-led movement, including youth-led research, has encountered and surmounted numerous challenges and barriers since its wide-scale introduction in this country and other countries throughout all hemispheres of the world (Larson, Eccles, & Gootman, 2004). Several social perspectives have been particularly relevant to this movement. However, service-learning (or contextual learning) has had a disproportionate influence. This orientation, in turn, has been fueled largely by paradigms such as empowerment, youth development, and, more recently, community capacity enhancement, and the need to draw on these types of paradigms to help inform and set a foundation for analyzing youth-led research.

The subject of consumer participation in research has slowly, but dramatically, expanded in scope over the past several years with all facets of the research process being addressed, allowing youth-led research to be grounded within a more expansive movement. There is worldwide acknowledgement that scientific and technological advancement in Western society has played an influential role in creating benefits for residents. Much of this advancement is investigator driven (American Association for the Advancement of Science, 2003). Nevertheless, there is also awareness that these advances have not come without disempowering consumers, by limiting their involvement to being subjects rather than active members of the research process.

Royle and Oliver (2001) report on the development of job descriptions, person qualifications, and procedures for identifying and supporting consumer involvement in all aspects of the research process, including writing research reports. This review process can entail raising issues not previously addressed, reprioritizing the importance of recommendations, and making suggestions for future research. Although Royle and Oliver's observations are in response to adult consumer involvement, they are also applicable to youth-led research because of the principles that they embrace and the flexibility inherent in how decisions are made.

Consumer involvement in designing research is not restricted to small-scale projects. The United Kingdom, for example, has actively pursued a policy of consumer participation in the design and conduct of controlled clinical trials as an integral part of the research process (Hanley, Truesdale, King, Elbourne, & Chalmers, 2001). A content analysis of researcher reactions to consumer involvement in these trials was overwhelmingly positive. Consumer involvement, however, has not occurred without barriers and challenges along the way. Oliver et al. (2001) comment that involvement of consumers is fraught with challenges such as cultural divides, language barriers, and need for skill development. Being progressive on race, ethnicity, gender, sexual orientation, and physical and cognitive challenges, for example, does not necessarily translate into being progressive on matters related to youth participation (Burgess, 2000). It is remarkable how adults may be very progressive in their thinking about inclusion and participation on a variety of factors, except age (youth).

The youth-led and youth development literature often relies heavily on the concept of participation in putting forth a social change agenda with youth as a central feature of these paradigms (M. Anderson, Bernaldo, & David, 2003; Innovation Center for Community and Youth Development, 2003). The concept of engagement, too, can also be found in this literature, and at times used interchangeably, with participation. The terms *participation* and *engagement* will be used interchangeably throughout this book, seeking to capture the following three dimensions (Forum for Youth Investment, 2001):

1. Active Participation: Youth are committed emotionally, physically, and cognitively.

2. Action and Contribution: Youth are able to initiate and sustain activities that make meaningful contributions to their community.

3. Decision-Making Power: Youth have choices in how they spend their time and are supported (e.g., experientially, instrumentally, and informationally).

The interplay of these three dimensions seeks to empower youth to make contributions to themselves, family, and community.

Kirshner, O'Donoghue, and McLaughlin (2002) define youth participation as consisting of a wide constellation of activities that seek to empower youth. Thus, the three dimensions outlined previously provide both the depth and breadth needed to do justice to a construct as important as participation/engagement. Ginsburg (1996) uses the phrase "teen-centered methodology" to capture the central purpose behind youth-led research through the provision of a "naturalistic forum" for youth to voice their opinions and feelings. Further, youth involvement in research helps to ensure that (a) research questions are not only pertinent but are asked in a "youth-friendly" manner; (b) research findings lead to interventions that are relevant; and (c) outcome measures are framed in such a way that they take into account a youth-specific change agenda.

Participation on the part of youth in designing interventions has the potential of addressing a wide range of current and future aspects of youth's lives (Community Unity Matters, 2000):

> Current research shows that if young people are to become competent, caring and responsible contributors to their communities, they need meaningful opportunities to participate, to lead, to contribute, both side-by-side with adults and on their own. Why? Because such "stakeholder" opportunities satisfy their very deep-seated developmental needs for belonging, recognition and power, and help them develop the skills and values they need to succeed in school, work, and life. (p. 3)

Thus, the benefits of youth-led movements are both immediate and future driven, and can reach as far as the imagination can take them. Youth participating as partners with adults in research is considered a viable path for addressing the consequences of the unequal power differential within conventional research, which views those being researched as objects (Atweh & Burton, 1995).

With proper training, support, and opportunities, youth can be quite natural at community organizing (M. Anderson et al., 2003;

Delgado & Staples, 2005). Assessments using research instruments (such as surveys) for systematically gathering data on specific issues can easily be the basis for undertaking a community organizing initiative within schools or communities (Sherman, 2002). Youth participation in the life of organizations and communities translates into youth taking ownership, by playing a role in defining needs and problems and finding appropriate solutions (Mullahey et al., 1999).

Chan et al. (2003) stress the need for children and youth to play an active part as full participants in creating and applying benchmarks on developmental assets. They add:

> Unless children's own interpretations and perspectives are garnered, social scientists will necessarily obtain only an adult-centered interpretation of their lives. To create a more complete picture, children themselves should be involved in the research process so that their subjective interpretations can be put to a critical test and incorporated into research design. (p. 65)

Involving youth as researchers requires that at least four key questions be answered in the affirmative, as noted by K. M. Brown et al. (2000, 2003) in their report of evaluation results from the Sarasota Youth Initiative:

- Can youth conduct research effectively?
- Can youth understand the complexities of the topics that are involved?
- Can youth comprehend the intricacies of specific issues?
- Do youth have the maturity to address challenging situations? (p. 1)

All of these questions must be answered in the affirmative; otherwise, youth-led research has no future. Each of these questions highlights a different dynamic aspect of research by focusing on youth as researchers and the emotional, cognitive, and sociopolitical aspects of research.

Answering yes, however, does not mean that youth do not require training and support. Provision of this support must take place within a climate that recognizes and embraces the following assumptions (K. M. Brown et al., 2000, 2003):

1. Training youth cannot be approached without regard for their age and must actively involve them in all aspects.

2. Cognition levels are different for youth when compared to adults, and this must be accounted for in the development of a training curriculum.

3. Different levels of conceptualization between youth and adults exist, but this does not make one better or worse than the other.

4. Patience level is lower for youth, and training format is affected.

5. Attention span differences will necessitate training formats to be structured accordingly.

6. Youth have a higher likelihood of experiencing wider emotional swings during a research project, and this must be recognized and addressed with proper support within and outside of the training curriculum. (pp. 3–4)

These assumptions stress the importance of proper screening, training, and support for youth researchers.

❖ SERVICE-LEARNING

The popularity of service-learning (also called "contextual learning") has increased dramatically in the past decade, particularly within schools and even universities (Strand et al., 2003). Human service organizations, too, have found service-learning to be an attractive mechanism for engaging community residents. Youth are provided with an opportunity to learn while serving their community. Teachers, in turn, are provided with a pedagogical tool for integrating social and academic content into their curriculum, and doing so in a manner that is engaging for youth to learn. Strand et al. (2003) note that community-based research is an effective mechanism for service-learning to transpire within a wide range of settings and embracing a variety of educational and social goals.

The importance of service-/contextual learning goes beyond any one age group, although it is more frequently applied to youth. This perspective toward learning is multifaceted and has increased meaning when applied to youth. How it is conceptualized, as the reader will soon find out, is greatly influenced by the setting conceptualizing this form of learning/teaching, making for a wide range of possible projects. In essence, service-learning lends itself quite well to blurring the boundaries between school and community (Pittman, Yohalem, & Tolman, 2003).

Definition and History of Service-Learning

Service-learning falls within a number of perspectives and, as a result, can be conceptualized and operationalized in a variety of ways, thus widening its appeal across professional groups and settings. However, it is widely considered to be a part of experiential learning. Experiential learning (community service, internships, volunteering, service-learning) is considered to be any activity that actively engages the learner in study, with the student being the ultimate beneficiary of the process. Experiential learning promotes desirable outcomes when the activities are purposeful and relevant, and have youth playing decision-making roles (Zeldin, 1995b; Zeldin, Kimball, & Price, 1995). The beneficiaries of service-learning, however, are not just students but also the institutions sponsoring these initiatives and, ultimately, the community (Andersen, 1998; Fletcher, 2002; McAleavey, 1997).

Kendall (1990) notes that "service-learning programs emphasize the accomplishment of tasks which meet human needs, in combination with conscious educational growth" (p. 40). Honnet and Poulsen's (1989) observations on the synergistic effects of service on learning highlights the positive relationship each has on the other: "Service, combined with learning, adds value to each and transforms both" (p. 1). In commenting on students as researchers within the classroom setting, particularly when they use ethnographic and sociolinguistic inquiry, Bloome & Egan-Robertson (1998) note that they do much more than learn and increase their competencies; the work that they produce has value for their peers, members of the community, and the broader community, including teachers: "In brief, students are not just doing to learn or learning to do, they are learning and doing" (p. xiii).

Service-learning has been referred to as a philosophy of education and a method for instruction (Andersen, 1998). It is relatively easy to see how its philosophical roots can be traced back to the field of education, although some readers, myself included, may well argue that other fields, too, can just as easily make a claim for this form of service and learning in their historical roots. Nevertheless, probably more than any other field, the field of education has made the greatest contributions to this movement.

The educational historical roots of service-learning can be traced to the 1930s with the publications of seminal books such as *Youth Serves the Community* (Hanna, 1937) and *Dare the School Build a New Social Order?* (Counts, 1932). However, as I note later in this chapter, the influence of John Dewey is unmistakable.

The 1960s and 1970s witnessed the explosion of service-learning in U.S. schools and signaled its maturity as an approach (National Service-Learning Cooperative, 1999). In the later twentieth century and early twenty-first century, service-learning expanded its scope into community-based settings. These advances resulted in the field of service-learning coming into contact with a noneducation audience and also caused a great deal of excitement about multidisciplinary collaboration and multisetting initiatives, with this book being a prime example of this interest.

There are many different definitions of service-learning in the education and human service fields. In fact, to say that there are numerous definitions would be a severe understatement. Well over ten years ago, Kendall (1990) uncovered 147 definitions in the literature. The proliferation of definitions of a popular concept is to be expected. Youth development, too, has benefited or—as some critics would argue—has been limited because of a profusion of definitions. A multitude of definitions pertaining to a concept must ultimately be considered a developmental phase that can last several years or considerably longer. As it is in any developmental perspective, a consolidation of knowledge will result in a clearer understanding of a phase or stage, lending clarity to a paradigm. I believe this process is quite natural.

The National Youth Leadership Council (1994) does a fine job of summarizing the key elements generally found in most definitions:

Service-learning is a method of teaching that enriches learning by engaging students in meaningful service to their schools and their communities. Through careful integration with established curriculum, lessons gained from hands-on service heighten interest and enhance academic achievement, citizenship, and character development. Service-learning is a proven key to educational reform that masks significant contributions to community development. (p. 1)

Service-learning is an educational activity that can transpire within any setting and benefit all those who are involved. Further, it is an activity that is not passive or focused on any particular age group. Service-learning, in other words, is not exclusively for youth and can occur in any setting and take on a variety of forms. Nevertheless, its appeal for use with youth is undeniable.

The emergence of a "new" way of teaching and engaging youth in pursuit of their education has been around in various forms in the education field for a considerable amount of time, and reflects on the importance of learning activities that are collaborative and "real-world" oriented (Sagawa, 1998). Nevertheless, this movement, so to speak, received considerable national attention with the passage of two national acts: the National and Community Service Trust Act of 1993 and the School-to-Opportunities Act of 1994. The passage of the School-to-Opportunities Act of 1994 emphasized the importance of school-to-career transition for youth and placed a prodigious amount of emphasis on youth learning through the use of hands-on activities. Service-learning, as a result, took on greater importance by providing students with an opportunity to both learn and provide a service to their schools and community, thus promoting a sense of civic responsibility (McAleavey, 1997; Root, 1997). The passage of national legislation, however, was more of a reflection on what was already going on in the field rather than a "jump-starting" of this movement.

Eyler and Giles's (1999) comments on how learning gets manifested in service-learning underlines the potential of this approach for what can be considered a transformative experience in youth:

> We have been impressed by the ability of students to bring the information and skills learning in the classroom to bear on a project and help a community group achieve an important goal. We have been impressed by the power of service to motivate students to want to know more. We have been impressed by the ways in which service-learning creates connections—between feelings and thought, between studies and life, between self and others, and between college and community. It is clear to us that these programs lead to better learning and that the learning leads to more effective service. (p. xiv)

The experiences associated with service-learning can be considered transformative in quality. Eyler and Giles (1999) have coined the term *perspective transformation* to capture the experiences of youth in carrying out service-learning projects. These transformative experiences will challenge stereotypes and personal values, create empathy, and result in the uncovering of surprising information pertaining to how individuals with trauma in their lives have survived and even thrived under adverse conditions.

Goals of Service-Learning

An activity such as service-learning lends itself to incorporation of a multitude of social and educational goals, depending on the organization sponsoring it. Cervone and Cushman (2002), in developing a schema for improved teacher-student partnerships, drew on curiosity, humility, and mutuality as guideposts in the process of discovery, or knowledge building. Service-learning as an activity or strategy lends itself to incorporating these guideposts. Bjorhovde (2002), in turn, focuses on teaching philanthropy to children and classifies service-learning alongside activities (role plays and games) and actual giving as part of experiential learning.

Kielsmier (2000) views service-learning from three interconnecting viewpoints: (1) as a philosophy, by seeking to identify youth assets and expecting youth to contribute to the well-being of their community and society, regardless of their age; (2) as a community development model, by bringing about social change within the community by actively addressing significant issues and needs; and (3) as a teaching and learning model, through the use of active learning that places value on critical thinking and problem solving, thus resulting in student achievement in the realms of academics, citizenship, and character development.

Sagawa (1998), in turn, identified seven critical goals associated with service-learning, representing a holistic view of youth and their potential for significant contributions to community and society:

1. Increase academic performance, either directly, by reaching students who learn more effectively through experiential, hands-on education than through traditional methods, or indirectly, by motivating students to achieve as they connect classroom learning to the real world.

2. Teach life skills, develop problem-solving abilities, and increase understanding of the community.

3. Prepare young people for the world of work, expose them to careers, and help them to develop specific skills that will lead to employment.

4. Get things done that would not otherwise be addressed by existing public programs or the private sector.

5. Bridge gaps in understanding among people of different backgrounds.

6. Develop active citizens who are engaged in the community through their volunteer service and other forms of civic involvement, such as voting and awareness of current affairs.

7. Help young people learn that with rights come responsibilities. (p. 2)

The reader should be as impressed as I am by the ambitious and comprehensive set of goals usually associated with service-learning and its potential to achieve change at multiple levels, starting with the individual and working its way into the family, neighborhood, and the broader community. The goals identified by Sagawa (1998) are quite explicit in their ambition to create positive social change for youth participants and their social environments in a manner that connects youth-serving institutions and communities, while empowering youth in the process. Each of these goals taken alone would be significant in scope, but in combination, they take on almost mythical proportions pertaining to their influence.

Nevertheless, there are still a considerable number of challenges in the field. Fletcher (2002), for example, notes, "However, the powerful role of students as applied researchers often is downplayed in the classroom. When considering meaningful student involvement in service-learning, teachers are challenged to see the potential of student research, including its effects on students and the community" (p. 4). The connection of service-learning to youth development, and more specifically to participatory action research models, is no stretch by many accounts, either theoretically or practically (Richmond, 2000). These perspectives share a set of underlying theories that emphasize youth learning, decision making, empowerment, and social and economic justice (Berg et al., 2002).

Research Findings on Service-Learning

The importance of research for establishing the legitimacy of a field of practice is widely accepted within professional circles. No field can be embraced with fervor without an empirical basis for its claims. Service-learning is no exception. Initially, the theoretical foundation can be laid without heavy emphasis on empirical validation, although this is never advised. The emerging field will soon require that evaluation efforts be undertaken as an initial step in substantiating and testing its claims for positive social change.

The field of service-learning has benefited over the years from research, although in comparison to other types of experiential learning, it is still considered to be in its infancy (McAleavey, 1997). The research on cognitive outcomes has generally relied on the use of self-reports, a method that has questionable reliability and validity (Steinke & Buresh, 2002). However, problem-solving protocols, although in need of further refinement, show much promise in helping the field to move forward (Bringle & Hatcher, 2000; Steinke & Buresh, 2002).

The relative paucity of outcome research has resulted in a demand for research on service-learning due to the need for data to substantiate these types of programs (Eyler & Giles, 1999). Relatively few studies, however, have focused specifically on academic achievement. Student grades, for example, do not necessarily suffer or benefit from service-learning (Elyer & Giles, 1999; Kendrick, 1996; Markus, Howard, & King, 1993; T. I. Miller, 1994; Sugar & Livosky, 1988). The research, however, is still generally overwhelmingly positive about the influence of service-learning on youth, adults working with youth in partnership, schools and other community-based institutions, and the community as a whole (Eyler & Giles, 1999; Melchior, 1997; Perkins & Borden, 2003; Scales & Leffert, 1999).

An exhaustive review of the literature on service-learning outcomes is beyond the scope and goals of this book (see, e.g., Billig & Furco, 2002; Claus & Ogden, 1999; J. Howard & Scott, 1998). I present the following research studies, however, to help the reader better appreciate the variety of perspectives on "benefits" and how they have been measured. These studies serve not only to inform the field but also to broaden the social arenas that can ultimately benefit from service-learning initiatives, with research being but one of those arenas.

Billig (2000a, 2000b), like many other researchers, found that service-learning activities benefit students academically and socially.

W. Morgan and Streb (2001) found service-learning to be positively correlated with improved self-concept, political engagement, and increased tolerance of others. Service-learning outcomes, however, are greatly increased when students have decision-making power in the planning and implementation of service-related projects. Westheimer and Kahne (2000) found that students involved in service-learning experienced a greater sense of efficacy and developed new understandings and insights into their environment. Further, they also experienced a renewed sense of motivation for civic involvement.

The Council of Chief State School Officers (1995) concluded that service-learning increases student self-esteem, promotes personal development, and enhances a sense of social responsibility and personal competence. In a study of service-learning among middle school students, Scales, Blyth, Berkas, and Kielsmeier (2000) found that participants in this form of activity showed greater concern for others' welfare than did the control group immediately after the conclusion of the project and over an extended period of time. In their review of three major national evaluations of service-learning initiatives, Melchior and Bailis (2002) found numerous benefits for participants, such as reduced absenteeism from school, increased homework hours for middle school participants, increased school engagement, higher math and science grades, and core GPA.

In a meta-analysis of findings on service-learning, Andersen (1998) used a youth development paradigm as the conceptual base to examine personal and social development among participants. Andersen concluded that service-learning facilitates character education as well as civic education, and participants experience a greater sense of social connection, acceptance of diversity, higher academic achievement, and a greater sense of competence and self-esteem. D. Kirby (2001), in a review of research findings to reduce teen pregnancy, found that programs with a service-learning component were more likely to reduce actual teen pregnancy rates for participants, compared to those programs without a service-learning element. Likewise, Muscott and O'Brien (1999) found that service-learning programs increase social skills, such as cooperation and communication, as well as problem-solving skills, among participants with behavioral and learning disabilities.

Rosenberg, McKeon, and Dinero (1999) also found many positive outcomes for students who were previously disengaged and alienated from school. Participants showed marked improvement in attitudes toward school and greater initiative than those students in control groups. Studies have found that students who are actively involved in school activities such as school accreditation processes and school reform conferences are less cynical and apathetic about their schools and learning (McCall, 2000). Students who participate in other school-related projects, such as membership on school boards, hiring teachers, school planning, curriculum, and policy, show likelihood of increased learning and more positive attitudes toward school (Fletcher, 2003; Hackman, 1997; Kaba, 2000; Marques, 1999; Patmor, 1998). Participation in service-learning projects can also result in heightened participation in class-rooms (Loesch-Griffin, Petrides, & Pratt, 1995).

The benefits are not restricted to participants alone. Like any meaningful form of social intervention, service-learning benefits many parties. Stukas, Clary, and Synder (1999) found, in their review of the literature, that the benefits of service-learning extend to communities and institutions. When service-learning is school based, teachers have a greater tendency to use cooperative teaching methods, conduct more student self-assessments, and show more of a willingness to view education as a contextualized process involving communities than do teachers who do not use service-learning as a method of instruction (Toole, 2000). Weiler, LaGoy, Crane, and Rovner (1998) found that service-learning results in greater mutual respect between teachers and students, greater cohesiveness, and more positive peer relations among students. These positive feelings, in turn, impact the general school climate (Billig & Conrad, 1997). A shift in viewing students as allies rather than as passive in the learning process also assists teachers in becoming more effective at teaching (Berg, 2004; Cervone & Cushman, 2002; Chin, 2004).

Finally, service-learning also has a positive and far-reaching impact within communities (Irby, Pittman, & Tolman, 2003). Community members who work in partnership with youth on service-related proj-ects get an opportunity to see youth as valued resources and positive contributors to their communities (Billig & Conrad, 1997; Johnston & Nichols, 1995; Kingsland, Richards, & Coleman, 1995; Kinsley, 1997; Melchior, 1999; Weiler et al., 1998). The community of youth, in turn, ultimately benefits from research by being able to participate in programs geared toward their expectations and needs. Community service-learning provides youth with an opportunity to enter into colle-gial roles with adults, moving them out of what Hamilton (1981) calls an "adolescent ghetto." Not surprisingly, collaborative adult-youth partnerships have the potential to make important and lasting contributions to society.

Characteristics of Typical Service-Learning Projects

Although it can be effectively argued that there are rarely two service-learning projects that are alike, there certainly are clusters of types that are commonly found throughout the country and have implications for youth-led research. Sigmon (1996), for example, developed a four-stage typology on service and learning that identifies the major perspective that can be taken on this educational intervention, and assists in categorizing these efforts based on the emphasis: (1) *service-Learning* places the greatest emphasis on learning goals; (2) *SERVICE-learning* places the greatest emphasis on service goals; (3) in *service-learning*, the goals are separate; and (4) *SERVICE-LEARNING* makes both of equal weight, with each enhancing the other. The difference between these four types is much more than semantics. Each of these perspectives toward service-learning embraces its own set of values, beliefs, activities, and roles, for youth and for adults.

Johnson (2002) effectively argues that service-learning projects, regardless of type, must actively address the following components: (a) making connections that hold meaning; (b) self-regulating learning; (c) doing significant work; (d) collaborating; (e) thinking critically and creatively; and (f) nurturing the individual. Some readers may argue that the components identified by Johnson should be a part of any learning endeavor and not restricted to service-learning. Nevertheless, service-learning projects do lend themselves to these critical components, allowing each component to increase or decrease in importance depending on the goals of the project, the age of the student/participant, and duration of the project.

Service-learning projects can usually be differentiated along six dimensions: site origination, scope, project duration, goals, degree of adult involvement, and youth roles. However, service-learning must ultimately involve students as evaluators of the projects either through self-assessment, peer evaluation, or the use of tools or questionnaires that focus on broader goals (Fletcher, 2002). It is this very dimension that will help propel these projects into the realm of youth-led research. It is best to conceptualize the range of learning involved with service-learning as multilayered (Strand et al., 2003).

Eyler and Giles (1999) identify the features associated with "high-quality placements" as places where students can engage in work with meaning, initiative is valued, activities are varied and considered important, work has a direct relationship to learning goals, and the work involves quality interactions with the community. The goal of finding a balance between service and learning must never be lost sight of in development of service-learning activities.

As already noted, in the evaluation of outcomes, it is important not to lose sight of the ultimate beneficiaries of service-learning projects, such as the community (Jacoby, 2003; London, 2000; D. Schensul, 2004). Mullahey et al. (1999) note that the use of service-learning to address community needs effectively transforms the community into a learning laboratory; this shift in paradigms involving youth brings them into collaborative partnerships with adults, instead of having adults view youth as the source of problems and lacking the maturity and competencies to achieve positive social change.

It is critical that service-learning, however, not embrace a "missionary ideology," wherein those undertaking service-learning projects are there to save other youth and communities (Weah, Simmons, & Hall, 2000). This type of ideology is counterproductive to the goals of service-learning and creates barriers between learners and their communities. It also further alienates the institution sponsoring these projects from the community it wishes to engage and positively change. As a result, adults and institutions sponsoring service-learning with a community focus must embrace a set of values that stresses mutual respect and learning as a means of minimizing potential bias toward community.

Service-learning projects can define a "service" activity as research. Research does not have to be defined as a narrow, "academic" exercise. Research can also be defined as a means of furthering the goals of social change and empowerment, embracing social and economic justice themes (Delgado & Staples, 2005). Bringing research as a viable activity within a service-learning perspective effectively broadens this perspective and further grounds this activity within a community context, helping to ensure "concreteness" to the outcome (Hart Leadership Program, 2003). It further serves to make research an activity with meaning and purpose, rather than an activity with the sole purpose of uncovering knowledge. Social change resulting from research gives a sociopolitical meaning to this activity.

Last, the settings that sponsor service-learning influence how this form of activity gets conceptualized and implemented. If the setting is a school, then this activity is closely tied to academic learning (Berg, 2004; Chin, 2004). If the setting is a community-based organization, then service-learning is tied to the primary mission of the organization (Naughton, 2000; Schensul, LoBianco, & Lombardo, 2004). The former may find it easier to recruit youth for these projects because they substitute for more formal classroom time; the latter may have a greater challenge because the activity transpires during nonschool hours. Schools may experience greater restrictions pertaining to the service-learning project because of school policies and schedules; community-based organizations, on the other hand, can be more flexible in designing projects.

❖ THEORIES SUPPORTING SERVICE-LEARNING

The theoretical underpinnings supporting service-learning, as to be expected, are ever evolving and encompass a variety of elements and perspectives. A number of scholars have specifically focused their expertise on developing theories to explain and support service-learning in youth within and outside of school. Each scholar brings a unique perspective on this type of activity. Giles and Eyler (1993) strongly advocate for the development and refinement of theory guiding service-learning as a means of generating a research agenda. Regardless of the rationale for theory development, there is no disputing its importance to helping shape the direction of future interventions and bringing greater clarity as to what constitutes the field of service-learning, its elements, boundaries, and uniqueness. Theory shapes how research is conducted and how we interpret the findings, and it can also shape research as a method of intervention. Systematic reflection and comparison of theories foster the better understanding of behavior (Egan-Robertson & Willett, 1998).

Morton and Troppe (1996) note that service-learning theory "begins with the assumption that experience is the foundation for learning; and various forms of community service are employed as the experiential basis for learning" (p. 21). McAleavey (1997), in turn, comments on the basic premise of service-learning: "One learns as well or better by doing as reading and listening. Education is not only a function of books, but a function of experience and connecting what one reads and hears with ongoing observation and experiences" (p. 1). These theorists emphasize the importance of learning being contextualized, having real meaning for the learner, and they stress activities and action as the primary vehicles for ensuring that learning takes place alongside some form of social change, even if it occurs along individual rather than collective realms.

John Dewey's theories on knowledge and action are close to seventy years old and yet are still widely acknowledged to be the primary theoretical sources for this field (Carver, 1997; Giles & Eyler, 1993; Kolb, 1984; Kraft, 1996; Nicholls & Hazzard, 1995; J. E. Smith, 1983). Harkavy and Benson (1997) identified four propositions that can be directly and indirectly traced back to Dewey:

1. Reflective thought is an active response to the challenge posed by the environment.

2. Learning is enhanced when the learner participates in a meaningful way in learning activities.

3. All individuals have the potential to contribute meaningfully to knowledge.

4. The primary purpose of knowledge should be the betterment of human welfare.

Deans (1999), in turn, brings together Dewey's theories and Paulo Freire's critical pedagogy theories to support service-learning, further reinforcing an educational foundation to this activity and the important role communities play in the educational process. Freire emphasized tying education and learning to social action, bringing an implicit "political" dimension to service-learning, and effectively creating a sociopolitical context for informing how social interventions must be created to reach and involve youth.

It is important to pause and make a statement pertaining to who should engage in service-learning; that is, is it reasonable to expect every youth to participate, enjoy, and learn from service-learning projects? Although I would like to think that the number of youth who would not benefit from service-learning, and in this case youth-led research, would be very small, this may not be the case. Strand et al. (2003) identify three key considerations: (1) familiarity with and sensitivity to the community, (2) the understanding and embracing of principles integral to community-based research, and (3) relevant research skills and substantive knowledge related to the issue or problem being researched. I would add a fourth consideration: youth unwillingness to enter into hands-on projects. Each of these considerations requires serious thought, strategic preparation, and adequate time to reach a consensus.

❖   EMERGING SUPPORTING PARADIGMS

A service-learning perspective or concept can easily be incorporated within a social paradigm such as the three that I address in this section. In many ways, these paradigms not only serve to reinforce the goals and philosophy behind service-learning, but they also lend themselves to generating empirical validation. The inclusion of service-learning within a broader and more encompassing paradigm also ensures that this concept can enjoy greater appeal and usability and further serve as a bridge between school and community settings. The inclusion also serves to broaden the number of professions that can come together to collaborate in support of and with youth.

Although there are many paradigms that can serve as the basis for advocates of youth-led research, I present only three significant social paradigms here. Empowerment and capacity enhancement illustrate the potential broad reach of youth-led research. The third paradigm of youth development, however, has the greatest potential for setting the conceptual foundation for youth-led research because of its explicit focus on youth, and it is the one enjoying the tremendous popularity within the field of practice and in academic circles. Further, it is the only paradigm that specifically focuses on this population age group.

London, Zimmerman, and Erbstein (2003) strongly advance the importance of a youth development paradigm as a means of maximizing youth's potential to learn, grow, and serve their community:

> When isolated from community (and organizational) development, youth development efforts are stunted [in] their ability to impact institutional and community change. Youth are "developed" through [a] set of controlled activities rather than as active participants in real world experiences and projects. At best, the objectifying model deprives youth of valuable learning opportunities and relationships; at worst it leads to young people's alienation and resentment of the implied low expectations and the cultural and political disconnect from their communities. (p. 3)

Each of the following paradigms brings a distinctive perspective on youth, their assets, and need for involvement in decisions affecting their lives. These three paradigms actively seek to give voice and power to the "voiceless" (Tienda & Wilson, 2002b): "Being voiceless is particularly egregious for poor people who are doubly marginalized because of their economic status and age" (p. 272). Youth must be provided with meaningful opportunities to help shape policies and programs that wield tremendous influence in their lives. It is not just providing them with a voice but also the decision-making power to influence all aspects of programming. An asset orientation toward youth and community is predicated on a bottom-up perspective toward initiatives; a deficit perspective, in turn, relies on a top-down orientation that invariably is controlled by adults, who also happen to be professionals (Benson, 2003a). The former approach is capacity enhancement driven; the latter approach is problem reduction driven (Delgado, 1999).

Lorion (2000), however, raises a cautionary flag pertaining to the use of the concept of wellness, so that it does not become a proxy for another deficit in need of being addressed:

> Whether conceptualized categorically, statistically or dynamically, wellness has the potential to become yet another parameter by which people are categorized and differentiated. If that were to occur, levels of wellness other than the idealized end-state could be interpreted as another index of relative deficiency. Inevitably, then, the "less-than-well" could be deemed in need of repair. (p. 11)

Some readers may consider Lorion's caution to be too cynical. However, the author raises a very important point, such as the tendency of professionals to focus on problems, needs, issues, and concerns, since society is willing to pay for services addressing these elements and is less inclined to pay for enhancement and development. Funding can be a very powerful incentive in skewing how professional providers and educators view youth and their communities.

The connection between service-learning, research, and community service has been made by a number of scholars in the field (Strand et al., 2003). Service-learning, however, is not without its potential drawbacks. "Live projects," for example, may encounter significant barriers in the process of implementation: Projects require a considerable commitment of time on the part of all parties, high levels of ambiguity are often a part of projects, and failure of a project can have long-range implications within the community. In essence, failure has an impact far beyond the student-learner and the academic year.

Empowerment

An empowerment paradigm brings to any discussion on youth as researchers a perspective on what attitudes, knowledge, and skills are necessary to effectively have youth as decision makers within all social domains. Interestingly, these same three elements are also critical to any definition of competence, including this definition by Garbarino (1985):

> a set of skills, attitudes, motives, and abilities needed to master the principal setting that individuals can reasonably expect to encounter in the social environment of which they are a part, while at the same time maximizing their sense of well-being and enhancing future development. (p. 80)

An ability to influence one's circumstances is at the heart of any definition of empowerment and ultimately shapes any initiative premised on this principle.

M. A. Zimmerman (1990) raises an important distinction to be made within an empowerment paradigm. Is empowerment conceptualized as individual oriented or as a form of psychological empowerment? Individual-oriented empowerment is founded on a contextualized understanding of empowerment as a "personality" variable; the latter focuses on an individual level of analysis but takes into account ecological and cultural influences. Community empowerment, in turn, represents a collective (community, group, institutional) construct (Rissel, Perry, & Finnegan, 1996).

The need to contextualize empowerment is also well argued by Rappaport, Swift, and Hess (1994):

> Empowerment is easy to define in its absence: powerlessness, real or imagined; learned helplessness; alienation; loss of a sense of control over one's own life. It is more difficult to define positively only because it takes on a different form in different people and contexts. (p. 3)

Consequently, how conditions of powerlessness get carried out on a daily basis is very much determined by the context in which they are perceived and acted on.

Not surprisingly, empowerment and competence are positively correlated. Having the belief, knowledge, and skills to influence the direction of one's life necessitates believing in oneself, having the knowledge to assess and problem solve, and possessing the requisite skills to initiate and complete an action plan directed at an explicit set of goals. Harter (1993) identified empowerment as critically important in the lives of adolescents because empowerment effectively leads to competence, and competence is closely linked to self-esteem. The introduction of an empowerment paradigm at a critical stage of development cannot but help ward off particularly damaging experiences and substitute them with potentially positive and powerful experiences.

Youth empowerment takes on greater prominence within schools and communities. School settings have historically been considered very difficult places for youth to exercise a great deal of decision-making power. The absence of youth in decision-making roles is considered significant because of the length and amount of time they spend within educational institutions during the first eighteen years of their lives. The multiple developmental stages that transpire during this time period are significant and effectively serve as a foundation for eventual transition to adulthood.

The professional literature on after-school programs is quick to note that these programs offer incredible opportunities for youth to exercise decision-making powers, use their authority, and participate in a meaningful manner: in short, to be empowered. Schools, unfortunately, have generally not shared this observation and commitment to placing youth in decision-making roles within these institutions. This missed opportunity effectively transfers this responsibility to other institutions in the lives of youth. If there are no other institutions involved with youth, particularly in the case of those who are marginalized, then the missed opportunity takes on greater magnitude.

Empowerment, not surprisingly, is either an explicit or implicit central element in the other two paradigms covered in this chapter. In an extensive review of the literature on youth empowerment, Holden, Pendergast, and Austin (2000) note:

Youth empowerment initiatives represent a new paradigm in applying the understanding of youth development to field work in social and community interventions. Prior to this shift in paradigms, there has been a long history of examining issues through a variety of perspectives, many of which tend to examine the factors that place groups of individuals at risk for a particular social problem . . . in order to understand the risks that need to be reduced or eliminated. (p. 4)

The centrality of youth empowerment in most social paradigms that are focused on social change brings to the fore how important it is to have youth in decision-making roles, particularly when collaborating with adults. Harley et al. (2000) advocate the use of empowerment research, in this case evaluation-focused, as a means of achieving change "through" rather than "in" communities. This is achieved through purposeful involvement of community residents in all facets of the research process.

Empowerment is not associated with any one particular age group, however, and can be actively pursued in a wide variety of settings and among a diverse group of individuals regardless of their age (Bowes, 1996). The youth participation or youth-led movement, however, must endeavor not to use this movement for what Prout (2000) refers to as social control of youth. This movement can concentrate on improving the future of youth when they achieve adulthood rather than focusing on their present well-being and social participation (Scottish Parliament, 2002).

Too much emphasis on preparation for future roles is intuitively counter to how youth may view the benefits of participation in activities; regardless of how much adults favor this perspective, present-time orientation and immediate gratification are still powerful motivators in the lives of many youth. A focus on the present can be relegated to the foreground, while the future becomes the background. Neither time orientation is lost; one takes on precedence, while the other takes on a secondary importance, but importance nonetheless.

Chinman and Linney (1998) developed an empowerment model specifically tailored to adolescents and their developmental stage, by emphasizing identity development and incorporating the experiences of assuming meaningful and decision-making roles. Hodgson (1995), in another rare publication specifically addressing youth empowerment or the opposite of social control, identifies five critical conditions that must be met in order for youth to become empowered: (1) unimpeded access to those who hold power; (2) open access to relevant information; (3) an opportunity to exercise a range of behavioral options; (4) access to support from trusted and independent sources where applicable, a representative; and (5) an opportunity to exercise an appeal or complaint when necessary. These elements all play a critical role in youth-led initiatives and show the importance of how context shapes youth empowerment on a daily basis, and the significance of participation in the decision-making process.

Huebner (1998) specifically addresses the potential pitfalls of youth empowerment:

> Too often youth workers assume that "empowering" is a synonym for relinquishing all guidance, control, and responsibility for a project to the young people with whom they work. Typically, this approach is met with failure on the part of youth, frustration on the part of the youth development professional, and more evidence that the notion of "empowerment" is a concept that looks good on paper but does not work in the real world of youth work. (p. 6)

Huebner's warnings highlight the role adults can play in either facilitating or hindering youth empowerment. Youth empowerment cannot, as a result, transpire within a vacuum, free of adults. The empowerment that can result from participation in youth-led research necessitates discussions led by senior researchers, most likely adults, about youth perceptions and understanding of the forces, overt and covert, that create positive change within a community (Kincheloe & McLaren, 2000).

Since the birth of the youth development movement, there have been numerous concerted efforts at tying together youth development with youth empowerment (Denner, Kirby, & Coyle, 2000; Holden et al., 2000; Kim, Crutchfield, Williams, & Hepler, 1998). Blanchard, Carlos, and Randolph (1996) identified three significant ways that empowerment of youth can transpire, each requiring a different degree of support and commitment to empowerment by adults and institutions: (1) free and open sharing of information, (2) creation of autonomy through boundaries by use of clear rules and limits, and (3) examination of the role of youth development professionals in helping youth exercise power and decision making. These three ways, in turn, are greatly influenced by the developmental stage of youth and the trust adults have for youth and their abilities to make positive contributions to society. When youth become empowered, so do their communities (Camino, 1992; Hart, 1997; James & McGillicuddy, 2001; Sabo, 2003b).

There is a tremendous need to empirically understand the characteristics and conditions of the larger community that can foster youth empowerment (Susskind, 2003). DiBenedetto (1992) conducted a study in which adolescents were asked to identify what factors made them feel empowered. Eight factors were identified:

1. Adult leadership that was not authoritarian

2. Experience and exercise power

3. Being the recipient of quality education and training

4. Actively engaging in critical thinking

5. Being in an environment where they felt physically and emotionally safe, appreciation, and a sense of belonging

6. Embracement of diversity values

7. Having a voice and feeling that it is welcomed and respected

8. Being able to initiate action

Youth empowerment cannot systematically include or exclude one or more of these factors; all of these factors must be embraced to achieve the goal of youth empowerment.

The range of types and factors that influence youth empowerment is impressive. I sincerely doubt that a similar study of adults would uncover the same outcomes. DiBenedetto's (1992) study highlights the need and importance of taking age into consideration when discussing youth empowerment, and the need to hear the voices of youth on this subject. Empowerment as an abstract concept is quite powerful. However, without an ability to make it specific, it loses much of its potential impact to bring about transformation in individuals and communities.

Community Capacity Enhancement

The emergence of community as a feature of social paradigms has served to incorporate other types of paradigms that have been focused on particular special groups, but lend themselves to a broader perspective (Aspen Institute, 1997; Homan, 2004; P. W. Murphy & Cunningham, 2003). Community capacity enhancement is based on a very simple premise (Dorfman et al., 2001):

In each community, within each person, is a capacity to achieve something of worth. How we recognize and encourage such capacity will have a great impact on how we build strong ties and communities. Building on existing capacities for growth and achievement also helps us avoid turning to outside experts for help. Communities have the capacity to develop themselves. (p. 154)

The degree to which community plays a prominent role is dependent on how the paradigm conceptualizes community and on its role in a social change effort. Community capacity enhancement, for example, has community as a central feature with its being the target, vehicle, and context for change. A social and economic justice set of lenses influences how social change gets conceptualized and implemented for youth and all other groups.

It has been only during the late twentieth and early twenty-first centuries that the paradigm of community capacity enhancement has emerged and attracted greater attention in academic and practitioner circles (Delgado, 1999, 2003; Poole, 1997). This paradigm, because its focus is on communities, has served as an umbrella for bringing together other social paradigms that stress community assets and participation. I define community capacity enhancement as the systematic identification and mobilizing of community assets as part of any intervention (Delgado, 1999). How these assets get manifested, however, is very much dependent on particular group circumstances, with age being one possible consideration as in the case of youth (Richmond, 2000).

Whitlock (2003) has proposed looking at social capital from four different perspectives as a way of better understanding assets that can be mobilized in service to children and youth. Family, neighborhood, school, and community represent arenas through which social networks can be assessed and mobilized. This perspective does not mean that communities, particularly those that are marginalized in this society, must ultimately "pick themselves up by their bootstraps" without any assistance of outside forces (Aspen Institute, 1997). This could be considered "blaming the victim." However, it does mean that collaborative partnerships with external sources are possible, as long as the community dictates the change agenda and is able to identify and mobilize its internal assets in response. Control of the process must ultimately rest in the hands of the beneficiaries of these changes, namely, the community.

Community capacity enhancement represents an overarching view of communities, of which youth are instrumental members along with countless other groups (Delgado, 1999). This paradigm focuses on the goal and process of identifying community assets and seeks to uncover ways of mobilizing them in service to community. Community capacity enhancement is premised on the question "What are community assets?" rather than "Are there any community assets?" Community capacity enhancement requires social change to occur at two levels: individual residents and the physical environment. These changes are synergistic, with one influencing the other. Social interventions have historically been focused on individuals, families, or communities. Bringing these three arenas together within an intervention serves to maximize existing resources. Community capacity enhancement does this while also stressing collaboration across special-interest groups.

Community-based research is particularly attractive for community capacity enhanacement and youth-led community research because of its emphasis on social change (Chow & Crowe, 2004):

> Community-based research relies on the same set of technical skills as other forms of research. Unlike other research, however, community-based research aims to produce findings that are practically relevant to community members, local political actors, and funders. Because the interest of community research is to enhance community functioning, most community-based research pertains to designing interventions based on community identified needs and resources. (p. 616)

Community capacity enhancement and community-based research are a natural fit in youth-led community research, broadening the potential beneficiaries of these types of initiatives.

Strand et al.'s (2003) model for community-based research fits well within a community capacity enhancement paradigm by emphasizing collaboration, multiple sources of knowledge and use of multiple methods of discovery, and the importance of social change with the goal of achieving social and economic justice. Democratizing and demystifying knowledge represents a critical cornerstone of community research, and this can be accomplished only by challenging conventional views of who has the legitimacy to produce knowledge and who ultimately owns the outcomes of the research. Strand et al. (2003) sum up the value of demystifying knowledge:

> The demystification of conventional knowledge helps students to understand the nature and production of knowledge and challenges

the notion that there is any objective or neutral knowledge. This perspective validates knowledge that is rooted in people's— including students'—own lives and experiences. (pp. 130–131)

Research undertaken within a community capacity enhancement paradigm explicitly acknowledges that the community is the primary stakeholder. This translates into the community's assuming a decision-making role in dictating the nature, process, and outcome of the research, resulting in research with a focus on identifying the most pressing issues and needs—concrete results rather than answers to questions of great relevance to scientists, which is usually the case in investigator-driven research (American Association for the Advancement of Science, 2003). A community capacity enhancement paradigm, as a result, seeks to create a culture that stresses the rights of residents not only to participate in research that affects their lives but also to control all facets of the process. This makes the research process transparent, accessible, and productive (Shrestha, 2000). In essence, it makes it relevant.

Informed decision making within a human rights and social justice context guides all key assessment and strategic actions. Evaluation of capacity enhancement initiatives is also informed accordingly. The research endeavor cannot help but be demystified in order for it to serve the greater public good. A community capacity enhancement paradigm is a viable paradigm for guiding community-based research. Unlike the youth development paradigm (which I discuss later in this chapter), capacity enhancement is not age-specific to youth; it does bring youth within an intergenerational partnership perspective. This does not preclude youth-centered research from transpiring alongside other types of research addressing non–youth-related agendas, however.

Community capacity enhancement actively lends itself to a philosophy of inclusion and participation from all sectors of a community. Projects can involve people who do not share the same language or cultural background. Community gardens, for example, can bring together residents from disparate backgrounds who share an interest in agriculture. These projects, in turn, can foster intergenerational relationships between senior members in the community working closely with youth. The former may not have the physical dexterity to garden but possess wisdom and knowledge on gardening; the latter may have the physical dexterity but not the knowledge of growing plants.

Gardens serve as a vehicle for engaging community residents that normally would not work together and in the process significantly altering their environment. A garden then becomes a symbol of what is possible when a community comes together in pursuit of a common set of goals.

Achieving concurrent changes at these two levels makes a community capacity enhancement paradigm unique. Physical changes can be manifested through murals, community gardens, community-built playgrounds, and sculptures, to list but four types. Community involvement in these types of projects, for example, serves as a vehicle for personal transformation to occur while physical changes to the environment can be viewed as artifacts of these transformations (Delgado, 2003).

The Asset-Based Community Development Institute (2001) draws a close connection between individual residents and the broader community capacities:

> In each community, within each person, is a capacity to achieve something of worth. How we recognize and encourage such capacity will have a great impact on how we build strong ties and communities. Building on existing capacities for growth and achievement also helps us avoid turning to outside experts for help. Communities have the capacity to develop themselves. (p. 154)

Youth as a community resource, as a result, cannot be overlooked in any community capacity enhancement initiative, and they can rightly take their place alongside adults as equal important members of any team of collaborators (Benson, 2003b; Rhodes & Roffman, 2003).

Youth Development

I have purposefully saved youth development as the final paradigm to discuss because of its particular applicability to youth and youth-led initiatives. The other two paradigms addressed earlier can be quite significant in guiding practitioners interested in youth-led initiatives. However, youth development stands out for its potential to transform the lives of one age group in particular and its community. The values and principles that form the foundation of this paradigm bring together a disparate group of advocates in search of common goals, and do so in partnerships with youth in positions of leadership (Hughes & Curran, 2000). Richmond (2000) notes, "Giving youth responsibility and expecting accountability is at the core of most successful community youth development initiatives. . . . Young people are learning by doing and the community and its youth are experiencing positive ripple effects" (p. 24).

Practitioners focused on youth might not like a paradigm that does not specify this age group as a target for mobilization and change. Nevertheless, a community context has the advantage of fostering collaborative partnerships across age groups and community-based institutions, both formal and informal in scope (Farrell & Johnson, 2004; Pittman, 2000). In addition, it broadens the paradigm's appeal to increase its presence in the field, allowing many different disciplines to come together by using community as a common social arena. Social paradigms that stress collaboration at various levels and across professional boundaries have great potential for achieving social change.

To say that the field of youth development is riding an incredible wave of popularity in the past decade would be a gross understatement (Eccles & Gootman, 2002; Spano, 2003). To say that there is a concensus definition of youth development would also be a gross misstatement. It is arduous to find any major national foundation or youth organization that has not embraced a youth development paradigm as a guiding force in policy development (Benson & Saito, 1998; Hein, 2003). This paradigm has found its way into a wide variety of fields, including juvenile justice (Schwartz, 1998). Readers can rightfully ask to what extent can, and should, a youth development paradigm intersect with other paradigms such as empowerment and community capacity enhancement? Is more better, or does it simply dilute existing resources?

A youth development paradigm brings a specific focus on youth and the role their assets can play in undertaking social change in this society. Youth do have needs and issues that they struggle with, and this paradigm does not seek to avoid these aspects. However, it does so within a context of youth possessing strengths and attributes that are expected to be beneficial to socially navigating their way through life. Thus, assets must be identified and enhanced in any initiative to meet current and future youth needs.

My definition of youth development incorporates many of the key features or elements commonly part of most definitions (Delgado, 2002):

Youth development . . . views youth both as partners and central figures in interventions. These interventions systematically seek to identify and utilize youth capacities and meet youth's needs. They actively seek to involve youth as decision makers and tap their creativity, energy, and drive; and they also acknowledge that youth are not superhuman—that they therefore have needs that require a marshaling of resources targeted at youth and at changing environmental circumstances (family and community). Positively changing environments that are toxic and antithetical to youth capacity enhancement requires the use of a wide range of strategies—tailored to fit local circumstances ranging from advocacy to consciousness raising and political mobilization. (p. 48)

The reader may consider my definition of youth development to be too wordy and expansive. However, the field of youth development is one that is expanding by leaps and bounds and defies any "simple" definition that can do justice to its potential reach within this society and internationally (Pittman, Irby, & Ferber, 1998). These changes make any definition of youth development incomplete because of the dynamics of the field. It seems that the moment a definition is developed to capture the process of youth development it becomes dated immediately. This does not mean that we should not endeavor to develop a definition; it does mean, however, that we need to be cognizant of the dynamics of the field and be flexible as to what constitutes the field of youth development.

Regardless of the definition of youth development subscribed to, and there certainly are countless such definitions, the theme of facilitating youth transition from school to the world of work or adulthood is central to this paradigm (Delgado, 2004; Zeldin, 1995b). The reader may ask, "How does youth-led research relate to youth development and more specifically to successful transition to adulthood?" Simply, the competencies and discipline required for understanding and conducting social research can easily be applied to any other realm. Work habits such as attendance, response to supervision, participation in training, tardiness, being a team member, effective communication skills, and time management are also applicable to the world of career (Delgado, 2004). Youth not only learn important job and life skills but also benefit from increased self-awareness and self-esteem, which effectively facilitate the transition to adulthood and benefit them in the present as well (Goggin et al., 2002). Further, this is accomplished within a team context that also necessitates the development of interpersonal skills.

Youth-led research is an employment experience in the truest sense of the word, with a set of expectations that relates to the world of work. It so happens to be work undertaking research, and when work is meaningful, it not only enhances competencies but also promotes psychological well-being (Mortimer, Harley, & Staff, 2002). Nevertheless, expectations related to work performance in research are no different than those related to employment in recreation, service, or even manufacturing. The far-reaching implications of research, however, make this type of employment experience very significant for the life of the institution such as a school, a community-based organization, or a community. Providing youth with decision-making opportunities within organizations has translated into practice outcomes for youth as well as adults, although benefits to communities have yet to be systematically explored (Ruth, Brooks-Gunn, Murrey, & Foster, 1998; Zeldin, McDaniel, Topitzes, & Calvert, 2000a). Youth development has had a fascinating ascent as a paradigm over the past decade or so. It has slowly embraced a wider social arena that now goes far beyond youth themselves to embrace family, peers, and community (Armistead & Wexler, 1998; Connell, Gambone, & Smith, 1998; Hughes & Curran, 2000; Pittman, 2000; Zeldin & Camino, 1998). With this expansion comes challenge, as noted by Connell et al. (1998):

> Our basic premise is that, as a *field* of practice, youth development is defined so narrowly that it excludes key settings in which youth develop. At the same time, we have allowed youth development as an *approach* to practice to remain far too broad. (p. 283)

Youth assets are not nonorthognal, with changes in one type reverberating in others simultaneously or sequentially as the case may be (Lorion & Sokoloff, 2003). The field of youth development has entered into a number of prominent social arenas since its initial focus on youth themselves (Kahne et al., 2001). An embrace of an ecological orientation has shifted the field to include families, peers, school, and community (Delgado, 2002; Eccles & Gootman, 2002; London et al., 2003; Whitlock, 2003). Each of these arenas, in turn, can be a subject of interventions stressing capacity enhancement or development. The goal of balancing "people" versus "places" in initiatives is ever present in any social paradigm, and youth development is no exception (Spano, 2003).

The goals usually associated with youth development generally get translated into a set of core elements. These core elements cover moral, emotional, spiritual, cognitive, physical health, and social elements (Delgado, 1999, 2002; Pace, 2003). In their research on service-learning outcomes, Eyler and Giles (1999) identified a set of twelve personal, interpersonal, and cognitive outcomes that correspond to the six core elements integral to youth development practice. These core elements are addressed as if they were separate from each other, although it is artificial to do so. Doing so, however, allows the reader to develop interventions that highlight or focus on one or a particular set even though all elements are interrelated.

Unfortunately, as I already noted, one of the major stumbling blocks to youth engaging in significant decision-making roles is that adult perceptions of their abilities very often do not match their actual capabilities (Huber et al., 2003):

> One of the reasons that youth are not often involved in community decision making is because adults often question whether or not youth will possess the capacities needed to be involved in important decision making. . . . Adults have often underestimated the capacities of youth . . . and their desire to participate in decision making. (p. 306)

When these doubts are focused on youth-led research, they can easily translate into numerous questions about youth's follow-through on assignments, behavior in the field, maturity to handle emotional content, confidentiality of information, and ability to problem-solve and avoid potentially compromising or dangerous situations.

Together with Jones and Rohani (Delgado, Jones, & Rohani, 2005), I raise a series of concerns about how a paradigm such as youth development cannot be applied to all youth without serious considerations pertaining to their ethnic and cultural backgrounds. We add that even though a youth development paradigm can be quite powerful in helping youth become empowered and ultimately influential in decision making within institutions and communities, newcomer youth (immigrant and refugee) may face additional challenges because of cultural considerations that militate against these youth's having decision-making power within their respective cultural groups. Nevertheless, this does not mean that a youth development paradigm is not applicable with these youth. It does mean, however, that the paradigm must be modified to take into account their unique set of circumstances regarding gender, cultural heritage, and values (Huebner & Betts, 2002).

The continued expansion of the field of youth-led research necessitates that efforts be made to unite communities and organizations sponsoring these types of research (Sabo, 2003a, 2003b; Wingspread Symposium on Youth Participation in Community Research, 2002; Zeldin & Camino, 1998). Linking community and youth development represents a synergistic effect that benefits youth as well as their immediate surroundings (Zeldin, 1995a). Just as significantly, it also brings together the fields of youth and community practice (Spano, 2003). The linkage of youth-led research to youth and community development has been advocated by a number of practitioners and scholars (London et al., 2003). For practice to be effective in achieving its goals and maximizing resources, it must unite youth with organizational and community development. Youth-led research, as a result, can be a vehicle for bringing together arenas that have historically been separated and need to be combined.

Spangler and Teter (2002) comment that both the service-learning and the youth development fields have evolved to embrace the importance of community in service-learning and youth development projects. Huebner (2003) rightly notes that youth development and community development are intertwined endeavors and that it would be artificial to separate one from the other. Community, as a context, target, and vehicle for youth-led initiatives, opens up avenues for youth to undertake projects that have great relevance to them, the institutions serving them, and their community. In instances where these projects are initiated out of a school-based curriculum, the potential for inclusion of academic subjects is increased dramatically. This does not mean that "academic" learning cannot transpire from community-based organizations that sponsor service-learning projects, however.

❖ YOUTH-LED INITIATIVES

The goals of the youth-led movement are ambitious and significant in how they target changing power dynamics between those with a voice in shaping this nation's policies and those without a voice. This shift in power brings with it an increased recognition of youth with rights and corresponding responsibilities (Delgado & Staples, 2005). One of the most powerful rationales for youth-led research is that the conclusions of the research are enhanced when those ultimately affected are actively involved. Some critics may well argue that this type of research lends itself to the introduction of bias. Advocates would argue, in turn, that research by the unaffected is also biased by the lack of insight into the lives of those being studied.

Successful youth participation, however, does not mean that youth are not meaningfully involved in interactions with adults. In fact, some advocates of youth-led projects would go so far as to argue that these projects are primarily about collaboration between youth and adults and not exclusively youth-led (Rhodes & Roffman, 2003). The ability to foster these collaborative relationships helps to ensure the success of the project and also equips youth and adults with experiences, or tools, to draw on in future projects. Adult-youth relationships based on mutual trust and respect can be quite powerful and transformative in changing institutions, communities, and eventually society.

The field of youth development has addressed the importance of adult-youth partnerships, with adults playing instrumental and supportive roles in youth activities (Spano, 2003). Save the Children (2000) specifically addresses this key point:

> Children and young people's participation does not mean that adults cease to be involved in the research, or give up their share of responsibility. Nor does it mean that whatever young people say will be taken on board and acted on immediately. Participation is a process of partnership between young people and adults, whereby they share ideas and come to common solutions. (p. 7)

Jones and Perkins (2002) developed a five-stage continuum of youth-adult relationships and partnerships that helps conceptualize potential adult involvement in youth-led research and other types of youth-led initiatives (see Figure 2.1). The first type (Adult-Centered Leadership) typifies the most common form of practice and has adults leading with youth following. The second type (Adult-Led Collaboration) has youth involved in limited decision making. The third type (Youth-Adult Partnership) is categorized by equal chances in utilizing skills, decision making, and mutual learning. The fourth type (Youth-Led Collaboration) has adults assuming limited supervision. Finally, the fifth type (Youth-Centered Leadership) places youth in decision-making roles with limited or no adult involvement.

Jones and Perkins's (2002) continuum reflects a shifting of power and decision making from adults to youth, along with a shifting in roles

Figure 2.1   Youth-Adult Partnership Continuum

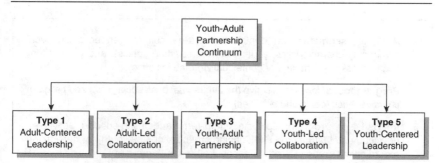

SOURCE: Jones and Perkins (2002).

for adults. This conceptualization helps organizations develop measures for assessing their mission and corresponding programs and activities. Finally, this continuum facilitates the development of interorganizational partnerships sharing the same stages of youth-adult partnerships. The lofty potential of youth-led initiatives is contingent on the ability of sponsoring organizations to work together.

McCall and Shannon (1999), in turn, propose a framework for youth-led health promotion that can also easily be applied to youth-led initiatives in general. This framework consists of six stages (see Figure 2.2) and takes a multifaceted perspective to the planning and implementation of a youth-led initiative and stresses the importance of specificity in all aspects of the initiative.

Youth in Focus (2002) summarizes the key goals and elements of youth-led initiatives:

> Youth REP [youth-led initiatives] is fundamentally about sharing power and democratizing knowledge-production and decision-making. By including young people as effective partners, Youth REP advances participatory models of institutional and community improvement; empowers young people to become critical thinkers, effective leaders, and active change agents in their organizations and communities; and demonstrates and builds on the tremendous capacity of young people. (p. 6)

As I already addressed in Chapter 1, youth-led initiatives get manifested in a wide variety of realms. However, youth-led research is but

Figure 2.2   Youth-Led Health Promotion Framework

---

1. **Audience segmentation:** identification of age, culture, gender, ability, local community characteristics, youth cultures (psychographics), and youth situations (at-risk) as a means of contextualizing the initiative

2. **Program focus:** focus of initiative (health, recreational, social, etc.) and program characteristics (goals and activities)

3. **Intensity of program:** episodic (short-term and issue-specific activities), developmental (structured and ongoing organizations for youth), or networking (coordinating group of youth to connect other youth groups)

4. **Purposes of intended outcomes:** desired attitudinal and behavioral changes

5. **Sites/settings to deliver programs and activities:** sponsors of initiative (e.g., community sites or settings, school sites, parents or adults as delivery mechanisms)

6. **Interactive media:** type of media to be targeted

SOURCE: McCall and Shannon (1999).

one of several prominent ways that this movement has shaped youth-involvement practice.

A total of ten key categories of youth-led initiatives have been identified, with some having several subcategories (see Figure 2.3). The reader can no doubt identify additional categories. The extensive range of the types of youth-led initiatives is not an exhaustive list and clearly illustrates the broad reach of this field, which is ever expanding. The reader cannot help but see that youth-led initiatives, with some exceptions, can easily fall into multiple categories. This observation is quite accurate. The central goal of a youth-led initiative is the determining factor in whether a project falls into one versus another category. Its primary focus dictates where it is lodged, although it can be acknowledged that there may be multiple secondary foci.

A close examination of the youth-led initiatives presented in Figure 2.3 highlights the important role that social and economic justice plays in helping to shape the thrust of youth-led initiatives, as well as the ever-expanding nature of these types of initiatives. Youth-led initiatives will no doubt continue to expand into formally "uncharted territory" as this decade progresses. Nevertheless, the importance of social and economic justice will be a central and unifying feature of these types of initiatives.

Figure 2.3   Youth-Led Initiatives

1. **Philanthropy:** Youth philanthropy has emerged within the past five to ten years, representing an exciting expansion of the youth-led movement. Youth philanthropy places youth in decision-making roles pertaining to the assessment and allocation of funds for youth programming (Bjorhovde, 2002; Falk, 2002; Swanson, 2002). Although a number of foundations have encouraged and funded youth philanthropy, the Kellogg Foundation is probably the most prominent foundation in this arena.

2. **Courts:** The increased prominence of youth within the judicial arena reflects the increased importance of this field for youth (D. S. Anderson, 1999). This field, too, is broad in scope and can encompass a number of subareas, such as court-led youth initiatives, conflict resolution, and various forms of mediation within and outside of school settings. Youth-led neighborhood policing can also be placed within this category (Burg, 1998).

3. **Social Enterprises:** Business enterprises that combine social and economic goals are classified as social enterprises. These initiatives intertwine these two goals throughout all facets of the initiative. Youth-led social enterprises effectively address these goals for the purposes of assisting youth and the communities they live in (Delgado, 2004). Profits are funneled into social projects such as scholarship funds or underwrite community-focused projects such as food distribution and microenterprise development. The lessons learned cover academic subjects as well as socially focused ones that stress the interrelationship between youth and their broader community and the importance of never losing sight of how one's individual behavior, positive or negative, impacts the broader community.

4. **Community Organizing:** Activism, as represented through organizing and related to social and economic justice themes, is without question one of the most vibrant areas of the youth-involvement movement (Delgado & Staples, 2005; Terry & Woonteiler, 2000). Mullahey et al. (1999) do a splendid job of describing youth-led initiatives that have as a central focus social change:

    > Youth-based initiatives for social change are those in which young people define the issues that they work on and control the organizations through which they work and the strategies they use. In this form, youth employ a variety of strategies, including advocacy, social action, popular education, mass mobilization, and community and program development, to achieve their goals for social change. (p. 5)

    Ecological, civic activism, antiracism, gender equality, peacemaking/conflict resolution, political reform, and education reform can all be cast into youth-led economic and social justice initiatives (Delgado & Staples, 2005).

5. **Recreation:** The field of recreation has embraced youth-led initiatives as a means of making services more relevant and attractive to youth, particularly those who, as a result of ethnic or racial and low socioeconomic backgrounds,

(Continued)

Figure 2.3 (Continued)

have not historically availed themselves of formal recreational services and activities (Caldwell & Baldwin, 2003; Dworkin & Bremer, 2004). Extracurricular activities not only serve to engage youth but also serve to impart important social and academic lessons in the process.

6. **Prevention:** The field of prevention has an illustrative history that can be traced back to the early 1970s in the United States. However, it has not been until relatively recently in its history that youth-led initiatives have found their way into the prevention field (Roth, 2004). Some social historians would even go so far as to trace the origins of the field of youth development to the field of prevention, including noting how many staff from this field eventually found their way to the field of youth development. Initiatives such as crime patrol, drug abuse prevention, and peer support have played an integral role in youth-led prevention initiatives.

7. **Media:** The role of media in shaping the lives of youth cannot be underestimated, particularly when they are subjected to targeted campaigns by advertisers and programmers. Youth utilize the media to educate the public about issues of great relevance to them (Kinkade & Macy, 2003). In the process, youth undergo personal growth and acquire competencies to succeed in other aspects of their lives. Media-related activism can encompass newspaper articles, newsletters, radio and television programming, video, and Web sites to advance social causes pertinent to youth. Media expertise and social change agendas make a powerful combination for affecting the lives of youth.

8. **Transportation:** There are few social systems that effectively limit youth physical mobility more than public transportation. Youth reliance on public transportation systems makes this system a prime target for change when it does not respond to their needs or actively discriminates against them. Youth-led transportation initiatives have sought to make these systems more accountable to their age group by pointing out inequities and recommending more inclusive policies.

9. **Health and Health Promotion:** In their review of the research literature, McCall and Shannon (1999) identify numerous youth-led efforts at addressing mental and physical health concerns and health promotion for youth. The field of youth-led health has focused on sexually transmitted diseases, mental health (with particular attention to depression), nutrition, and smoking cessation. Youth play instrumental roles in shaping curriculum and delivering content to a wide range of audiences. However, these audiences invariably consist of other youth.

10. **Research:** Finally, the field of research has become a part of the youth-led movement and has quickly expanded in scope over the past several years. What constitutes youth-led research is no longer restricted by national boundaries and can rightly be viewed as an international movement.

A successful youth participation or youth-led movement rests on at least six factors, each of which is significant onto itself yet becomes that much more powerful when in combination with the others (McCreary Centre Society, 2002; see Figure 2.4).

The factors identified by the McCreary Centre Society (Canada) inherently incorporate a vision and a set of values of a new society that

Figure 2.4   McCreary Centre Factors

1. The availability of an atmosphere predicated on the respect of youth and seeking of inclusiveness and activities welcoming to them is central to youth participation. Organizational climate can either facilitate or hinder youth-led movements. Effective youth-led initiatives rarely occur in organizations that do not value youth, and their climate does not occur by chance.

2. Youth can expect to enhance their competencies rather than develop them. The former acknowledges that all youth have competencies that can be enhanced; the latter does not, and it views youth as in need of development or having these competencies put in place. The central question guiding this feature is "What are youth competencies?" rather than "Do youth have any competencies?"

3. Youth participation cannot be a random activity based on the whims or opportunities that happen to be present at a particular point in time. Although this is a model that is sufficiently flexible to allow local circumstances to contextualize how youth participation can be conceptualized and operationalized to guide youth participation, it cannot be taken for granted. Much thought, effort, and commitment is essential to foster meaningful youth participation and decision making.

4. Youth participation is very often premised on them having activities that are meaningful and over which they have decision-making powers. This does not mean, however, that adults have no significant decision-making role in this process; adults may still be called on throughout a decision-making process to provide a wide range of instrumental, expressive, and informational support.

5. Youth participation can only be enhanced when there are a variety of activities that can lend themselves to various interests on the part of youth. A variety of activities lead to a variety of experiences, increasing the likelihood of engagement on the part of all youth, and making their experiences meaningful.

6. Youth, although possessing high energy, creativity, interests, and motivations, can still benefit from receiving instrumental, expressive, and informational support from adults. Youth participation does not mean that adults disengage; it does mean, however, that they are prepared to provide support when appropriate, and to do so in a manner that stresses respect and mutual trust.

SOURCE: McCreary Centre Society (2002).

welcomes and sustains youth in positions of authority and actively seeks to prepare them for adult roles with a civic-mindedness that will benefit society. There is no society where such a set of values is not meaningfully operative. However, that does not invalidate the importance of having a vision and a corresponding set of goals to guide current and future actions in helping to realize this new society.

❖ CONCLUSION

In this chapter, I have provided a variety of ways of grounding youth-led research so as to appeal to youth, adults, and a wide professional audience. The different perspectives that lend themselves to youth-led research are by all means not exhaustive. However, some perspectives lend themselves particularly well to youth-led research and bring with them a higher likelihood of achieving success with youth, such as is the case with youth development and youth-led interventions.

There certainly is no dearth of paradigms, perspectives, orientations, constructs, theories, or concepts to help better explain the appeal and potential of youth-led initiatives, regardless of how they are labeled. The youth development/youth-led movement is certainly impressive and only highlights how youth-led research is part of a broader and very powerful family of initiatives, which bring with them countless numbers of youth and adult advocates. Youth-led research can be appreciated only when grounded within a broad canvas with a set of values and vision that is inclusive and empowering. It has a long and well-respected history based on the rights and privileges that go with meaningful participation within a democratic society.

The conceptualization of youth-led research within a broad and encompassing paradigm such as empowerment, youth development, and community capacity enhancement, and more specifically within a service-learning context, sufficiently sets a foundation for any form of youth-led initiative, research or otherwise. This foundation, in turn, helps guide practitioners in developing appropriate activities and tasks for increasing youth decision-making roles within settings such as schools and community-based organizations. Further, the field of youth-led research will not suffer from a lack of theoretical foundation on which to expand in the future.

The youth-led movement, for example, is so dynamic and evolving that a book or a series of books devoted to this movement is very much in order. Each of the youth-led initiative types identified in this chapter can easily provide sufficient material for a book specific to that initiative. Each of the youth-led movements can exist in isolation from each other or in combination with each other. Several of the case illustrations covered in Chapter 10 illustrate this very point. The reader, I believe, should be sufficiently well grounded and versed to conceptualize youth-led research within a broad set of similar value grounded initiatives and is no doubt ready to focus specifically on youth-led research, to which the rest of the book is devoted.

PART II

Youth as Researchers

Approaches and Considerations

3

Guiding Goals, Principles, Objectives, and Outcomes of Youth-Led Research

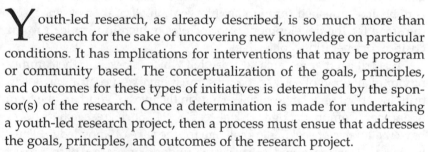

Youth-led research, as already described, is so much more than research for the sake of uncovering new knowledge on particular conditions. It has implications for interventions that may be program or community based. The conceptualization of the goals, principles, and outcomes for these types of initiatives is determined by the sponsor(s) of the research. Once a determination is made for undertaking a youth-led research project, then a process must ensue that addresses the goals, principles, and outcomes of the research project.

As I have already addressed in the previous two chapters, youth-led research can best be understood and appreciated when placed against a backdrop of paradigms that are asset-based, embracing the importance of youth developing a voice and actions that actively and systematically tap their potential for social change. Once this stance is embraced, what follows represents a systematic effort at concretizing and operationalizing this point of view. There are multitudes of ways that this can be accomplished through youth-led initiatives. These principles help practitioners navigate through the difficult waters of practice. As the saying goes, "To practice is human. To implement is divine!" Practitioners rely on principles for guidance in developing interventions under a wide variety of circumstances and settings.

In this chapter I provide a foundation for youth-led research by focusing on its primary goals, principles, objectives, and potential outcomes. Each of these areas represents an important dimension of the planning and implementation process that goes with an intervention such as youth-led research, and brings with it a range of potential approaches. Thus, practitioners and organizations sponsoring this form of research have a high degree of flexibility in how to conceptualize and carry out youth-led research. This is a very important quality because "one size" does not fit all organizations and communities.

❖ GOALS

Youth-initiated research and the corresponding values and questions guiding it must be firmly grounded in the reality of what is important in the lives of youth at a particular point in time, and not in what adults think should be important to youth. Thus, a goal, or set of goals, serves to motivate and guide interested parties or constituencies toward using positive social change as a guide to developing research questions. A goal can be defined as a vague and inspirational statement of what is to be accomplished through an intervention. A goal, in essence, sets the stage for the development of principles, which in turn lead to the creation of operational objectives.

It is critical that research, at least that which is based in the community or evaluation of social programs, must have as a central purpose a bringing about of positive social change in the lives of youth in one form or another (Campbell, Edgar, & Halstead, 1994). Social researchers never have the luxury of seeking knowledge for the sake of knowledge. Thus, having a clear focus and purpose for undertaking a research project serves as a beacon or guide for youth-led research. The process of answering research questions (as well as the actual answers), as a result, must have significant meaning for those undertaking the research and those willing to answer the questions and be a part of the research. The more significant the questions being asked are, the higher will be the likelihood of instilling motivation in all parties to engage in the research. However, this also results in higher expectations for positive and significant change to occur once the research has been completed.

Interestingly, as adults we expect outstanding behavior from youth, yet have very little confidence in their abilities to meet our expectations. In many ways, we expect more from them than we do from ourselves (Hine, 2000):

> We seem to have moved, without skipping a beat, from blaming our parents for the ills of society to blaming our children. We want them to embody virtues we only rarely practice. We want them to eschew habits we've never managed to break. Their transgressions aren't their own. They send us the unwelcome, rarely voiced message that we, the adults, have failed. (p. 3)

Howard et al. (2002) comment that those who work with a human rights focus and with provision of services to marginalized youth have shown the greatest enthusiasm for youth-led research. This embrace is probably due to the need to empower youth while generating data and information on how best to engage them in the process and achieve important social changes in their lives. Research becomes a political method that emancipates and transforms rather than one that emphasizes scientific integrity and maintains the status quo. Embracing a rights perspective naturally influences the nature and purpose of any social investigation.

The goals of youth-led research, in essence, are grounded in the belief that society can be made better only through the partnership of all sectors of the country, including our youth. Cheshire and Edwards (1998), for example, note that the involvement of children as researchers has a relatively long and distinguished history in the United Kingdom, dating back to the 1960s. Steinberg and Kincheloe (1998) effectively argue that students must play a central role in the creation of knowledge within the classroom; knowledge acquisition must be accompanied by a high level of critical understanding and competencies in the search for a more socially, politically, and economically equitable and fair society. Steinberg and Kincheloe go on to define student researchers as those individuals "who possess a vision of 'what could be' and a set of skills to uncover 'what actually is'" (p. 2). Thus, student as researcher within a school classroom should be competent in critiquing "mainstream" knowledge and institutions, and the effects of power relationships and privilege.

The goals of research are further grounded in the belief that all age groups are capable of undertaking research. Research does not, as a result, have to be complicated, expensive, or technologically centric. Research has over time been conceptualized and operationalized as resting in the hands of a few, who in turn have transformed the knowledge, science, and technology generated by research into an industry that has served to disempower those for whom it was intended to benefit (Shrestha, 2000).

Shrestha (2000) argues that research must not be viewed as the exclusive domain of any one age group:

> Research is a natural behavior of all persons. An infant explores, interacts, experiments, learns and adapts or makes changes in one's biophysical and psychosocial domains alone with others and [the] environment. This way, the people survive, grow, develop and make innovations and changes throughout their life individually as well as collectively. . . . Research is thus a common medium of perception and development in establishing dynamic relations in and around the total niche of people and environment. Historically, too, throughout the period of human development some tried to put research in straight-jackets in order to monopolize research and research technology to harvest benefits and exploit others and nature. (p. 1)

Having students' voices influence their educational activity involvement is sometimes much easier said than done. The quest to foster youth voices has its challenges:

> It is tempting to think if you pay attention to students' voices, you will hear what you already know. Secretly, adults—outside schools as well as in—generally believe that they know best. Just as tempting is to take at face value the quick responses students often give when asked for input. As we know but too often forget, some students feed back what they think adult listeners want to hear. Some feel ill-qualified to render an opinion, and some fear reprisal for speaking what they believe is true. Hardest of all, some students, even when encouraged, keep their feelings under wrap. (Cervone & Cushman, 2002, p. 97)

It may be unreasonable to expect youth to feel comfortable in articulating their opinions when asked to do so because of countless numbers of years when their opinions were not valued or even sought. Thus, the process of getting youth to voice their opinions may take a lot longer and require greater effort than most adults are willing to acknowledge. It may be best to view this process developmentally, with an understanding that it will take time and accomplishment of various stages to get youth to the point where they feel empowered enough to give voice to their opinions. Patience and persistence assume added importance in bringing about changes in youth behavior; the same can be said about adults.

At minimum, youth-led research should accomplish four primary social-related goals, all of equal importance (see Figure 3.1). Each of these four goals, in turn, addresses immediate and future needs and systematically builds on the capabilities of youth and the goals they possess for their future. Building on or enhancing competencies is one of the most direct benefits of youth-led research in addition to getting youth-generated data and recommendations.

The process by which to achieve these goals within a research arena cannot be overly stressed (Save the Children, 2000):

Participatory monitoring and evaluation (PME) is a process shaped primarily by stakeholders—in this instance children and young people. . . . As with all participatory research, children's participation in PME starts with negotiating with those who control children's time, their freedom to travel, to have information, and have and express opinions. The key to negotiating children's

Figure 3.1   Social-Related Goals

---

1. Ultimately increase the effectiveness and efficacy of youth programs and services.

2. Create an organizational and community climate conducive to civic involvement by youth by tapping their expertise.

3. Provide youth with meaningful learning opportunities that will result in competencies that can be translated to other spheres in their lives (Males, 1996, 1998).

4. Provide youth with meaningful opportunities to engage in dialogue among themselves and with adults about their perceptions of their social reality. There is a wide agreement that there must be a meaningful link between the inquiry, researchers, and the audience (Alcoff, 1994; Schwandt, 1996). This dialogue can result in new understandings pertaining to issues and possible solutions; it also can generate enthusiasm for the process of research by highlighting its worth and potential contribution to positive social change.

freedom to participate is clarity about what is expected from their participation. It is vital to stress that participation is based on equality and not on privilege. (p. 30)

❖ PRINCIPLES

Principles play an influential role in helping us to negotiate our way through life's difficulties as well as life's more pleasant periods. Consequently, it should not come as any great surprise that they also play a significant role in professional interventions. In fact, principles play a monumental role in helping to guide any form of social intervention. They act as a vital bridge between the world of the academics and theories and the world of the practitioners. In essence, they connect theory to the "real world." Principles should never be meant to restrict practitioners. Instead, they are meant to provide license to individualize practice by taking into account local circumstances (issues, resources, goals) in devising an intervention (Delgado, 2002). It is necessary to create a set of principles that specifically applies to engaging youth in a research role within communities and programs.

Earls and Carlson (2002) put forth a value or vision that should guide any form of youth-involved research, which is that youth-led research must embrace youth participation in order to create a more valid and useful product or outcome of the research: "In the process, social science achieves a closer approximation to reality. We claim that youth participation in research adds significantly to substantive validity and adds another dimension to the research (and policy implications), namely, democratic legitimacy" (p. 63). In essence, researchers must not only concern themselves with reliability and validity, but they must also add democratic legitimacy. Principles must embrace elements of Earls and Carlson's (2002) emphasis on participation.

A number of researchers have drawn on their experience in conducting youth-led research, lending the field an opportunity to draw on these lessons to establish a set of guiding principles (Schensul, Berg, et al., 2004). Earls and Carlson (2002), for example, share some observations of their experience in Chicago conducting a study of youth well-being:

First, adults must provide some structure to kindle that motivation and provide incentives for children to initiate. In the context of our research study the purposes and design of the work provided sufficient structure. Second, we discovered the importance of having an adult present. Good guidance, like good nutrition, had to be a regular and engaging affair. Somewhat surprisingly, we learned that it was too easy to over estimate the children's readiness to keep activities moving forward when an adult partner was temporarily absent. Another surprising aspect of this experience was the frequency of absenteeism, despite the children's loss of salary. Apparently, the need for free time was more important to them. (p. 74)

In discussing their experience initiating participatory action research with Latino youth with disabilities, Balcazar, Keys, Kaplan, and Suarez-Balcazar (1998) highlight the consciousness-raising aspects of such research. However, this type of research is not without its set of challenges, such as relinquishing control of the research endeavor, settling for a short-duration project rather than one that is extended in time and goals, and the lack of literature reporting on the outcomes of youth participatory action research.

It is important that a set of guiding principles for youth-led research be presented. It is tempting, although not very useful, to present an exhaustive list of principles and allow the reader to select nine principles that best meet his or her interests and needs. However, I have elected instead to select nine principles that, I believe, establish a core that must guide any youth-led research project regardless of its goals, context, and circumstances (see Figure 3.2). These principles span a variety of arenas. Like all sets of guiding principles, this set embraces a set of values. These values are empowerment, inclusiveness, rights, and equality across all sociocultural groups.

In addition, this set of principles is grounded in the professional literature, representing a compilation of principles developed by a variety of organizations and practitioners, including myself. I will utilize practice examples throughout this book as a means of illustrating their significance for use in development of youth-led research.

❖ LIMITATIONS AND CONCERNS
REGARDING YOUTH-LED RESEARCH

Youth-led research brings with it numerous advantages for sponsors, participants, and the community at large. However, youth involvement in research has limitations that must be acknowledged and

Figure 3.2   Principles for Youth-Led Research

1. Research must ultimately benefit youth researchers, participants, and communities (Lau, Netherland, & Haywood, 2003; London et al., 2003; Mead, 2003).
   The ability of youth-led research to maximize benefits across social arenas and
   constituencies, particularly those that have historically directly or indirectly
   resulted from research, is critical to the ultimate advancement of the field and
   its ability to play a vital role within community capacity enhancement initiatives.
   Clarifying the benefits that result from the research will increase the quality of
   the results by getting youth to believe in the importance of their work.

2. Research must be timed to maximize the participation of youth as both the foci
   of the research and as researchers themselves (Schensul, LoBianco, et al.,
   2004). No research stage is exempt from youth participation and decision
   making (Matysik, 2000; Youth IMPACT, 2002). Every effort, in turn, must be
   made to increase the participation and responsibility of youth to assume
   greater decision-making powers in the project.

3. Children and youth have the right to be at the table discussing research alongside adults and are entitled to engage in a process that encourages giving
   them a legitimate voice (Checkoway, Dobbie, & Richards-Schuster, 2003;
   Voakes, 2003). Milner and Carolin (1999) argue that adults must actively
   endeavor to really listen to the voices of children and youth in a manner that
   they are unaccustomed to. Youth must be viewed as possessing rights, opinions, and ideals that are as equally valid as those of adults, although they
   certainly represent a departure from those of adults (International Youth
   Foundation, 2000).

4. Youth-led research must not violate the rights of those being asked to participate in a research undertaking, youth or adult. As in adult-led research, ethical
   considerations are prominent and must be developed with specific procedures
   clearly articulated to ensure the protection of subjects, data, and researchers.
   These rights must be prominently addressed in the training of youth researchers
   and available to all research subjects and the community at large to see. These
   rights must always be written so that they are comprehensible to whomever
   reads them, and in multiple languages when necessary.

5. Research methods must stress inclusion by taking into account any physical,
   emotional, or cognitive challenges children or youth subjects may have
   (Checkoway et al., 2003). No individual can, or should, be excluded from participation in a research project because of a disability or an inability to read or
   write. This applies to both those being researched and those doing the
   research. Communities consist of multiple types of groups, and research must
   endeavor to include their voices to ensure that findings are representative of
   the community.

6. Youth bring a unique perspective to the research process that must be taken
   into account in financially compensating them for participation. Local and self-
   knowledge have equal if not greater legitimacy than knowledge obtained from

(Continued)

books and formal classroom instruction. Thus, youth should not automatically be considered "minimum wage" staff simply because of their age or need for training and support. Adequately compensating youth, particularly in the case of those from marginalized communities, is another way of supporting these communities indirectly, and not just through an accurate assessment of their needs, issues, and assets.

7. Because children and youth are not a monolithic group, youth-led research must strive to recognize the power of diversity within this age group. Thus, there is a tremendous need to make findings reflect the impact of diversity in the lives of both the subjects of research and the team of researchers (Delgado, 1979). Social and economic justice themes must ultimately find their way through all phases of a research project, particularly the recommendations in the final report.

8. Youth-led research must embrace social change as the primary and ultimate outcome of any research undertaking. This change goal will be arrived at through a participatory process that results in a consensus decision pertaining to target and process to be utilized (Fetterman, 2003). It must also serve to mobilize a community and provide it with a detailed road map for what strategic changes are recommended as the next steps.

9. Youth-led research must never be conceptualized as episodic; instead, it must be viewed as an ongoing process that is integral to an organization's mission (Checkoway et al., 2003). This form of activity needs to be valued equally alongside other forms of programming that have as a central goal improving the life of youth within schools and communities (Brase et al., 2004).

systematically addressed. As in adult-led research, these limitations can be minimized but not totally eliminated (Delgado, 1981, 1995; Save the Children, 2000). The following twelve limitations, as the reader will quickly note, are not easily overcome. This list, I might add, is not in any particular rank order pertaining to importance or challenge:

1. Although youth can have a profound understanding of events and conditions in their lives, asking them to draw social policy implications, for example, may be asking too much of them because of their limited understanding of the broader world. High expectations of youth, but not unrealistic ones, must guide youth-led research. The danger of expecting and demanding too much is offset by expecting and demanding too little. Finding the delicate balance between the two is an ever-constant challenge, but one that must be addressed head-on in any youth-led research venture. Developmentally and

experientially, older youth may be in an advantageous position, when compared to younger and less experienced youth, to draw policy conclusions.

2. The concept of power, although usually associated with adults, is also a critical factor in youth interactions. Some youth may find it too arduous to share or hand over power to other youth involved in the research process. Effort must be made throughout the research endeavor to identify power differentials and help youth recognize these situations and develop appropriate ways to redress them. Some of the power differential may be based on sociocultural factors such as gender. Heightened awareness of how decision making occurs and how responsibilities are assigned can prove important in facilitating the growth process for youth researchers and can help them better understand their own biases.

3. Youth researchers may encounter situations that parallel conditions that they, too, may be experiencing or have experienced, making for potentially difficult interviews or seriously compromising their participation in a research project. Although this subject is usually a part of any well-designed training program, it can easily re-emerge in an interview when the subject matter is one that has had, or currently has, profound meaning in the life of the researcher. Such situations not only increase the likelihood of youth obtaining information that may be skewed, but they can also cause severe discomfort or even trigger an emotional response that can eventually lead to youth dropping out of the research team.

One study involving youth interviewing key informants in Latino-owned botanical shops (culture-based pharmacies) is such a case in point. Two interviewers absented themselves from this phase of the research project because of fears they had about botanical shops. Both interviewers had had negative experiences with this type of nontraditional setting (Delgado, 1996).

4. Parental concerns over the safety of their children conducting interviews may seriously limit the selection of the geographical area being studied. A process exploring parental concerns needs to be a part of any youth-led research, with the understanding that parents may insist on logistical changes to ensure the well-being of their children. Seeking ways to inform parents of youth researchers directly and indirectly (e.g., through newsletters) is one way of minimizing concerns parents may have about the safety of their children.

A meeting of the parents or guardians of the youth researcher prior to initiation of the actual research is highly recommended, to help allay concerns and build strong community support for the project. This meeting can be cast in a variety of ways. However, a "celebration" of the inauguration of the project provides an uplifting forum for issues to be raised and for validation and support to be expressed.

5. The gender and age of the researcher influence the nature of a research study. It is almost never advisable, for example, to have female youth researchers interviewing male respondents. The reverse is also true. Pairing male and female interviewers minimizes this potential barrier, although it is costly to implement. Having field interviews conducted in certain sections of a community may raise safety concerns on the part of parents as well as youth, as already noted. Sometimes these geographical areas develop reputations of violence because there is an excessive probability of violence occurring there. Sometimes this is not the case, but reputations persist. Parents may restrict youth participation in a study due to safety concerns.

6. Question types and study foci are influenced by the age of the researcher. When youth are entrusted to interview adults, for example, the nature and types of questions must be carefully chosen. Questions pertaining to stigmatizing adult problems, such as unemployment, substance use or abuse, and health conditions, may not be considered "legitimate" for youth interviewers to ask. Limitations on the type of questions that youth can ask adults limit the nature and scope of youth-led research projects.

7. Youth undertaking studies involving other youth who speak a language other than English as their primary language must be sufficiently bilingual to be able to record responses, particularly when interviewers code-switch (change languages within a sentence). This situation is not that unusual when the content of the interview elicits an emotional response, causing respondents to switch to their primary language even though they may be fluent in English and may have started the interview in English. These types of interviews can be very demanding on youth researchers. It necessitates not only that they, too, switch languages but also that they be able to record the responses in the primary language of the respondent. In situations where the interviews are tape-recorded and later transcribed, the expense of doing so can be quite formidable because of the kind of language expertise needed on the part of the transcriber.

8. Confidentiality is the cornerstone of any good research and practice. Thus, breach of confidentiality takes on added significance in cases where youth live in the same community in which they are conducting research. This point is ironic because youth possession of local knowledge allows them to bring much-needed expertise and perspective to a research project. Because of these concerns, parents may not grant permission for their children to be interviewed. As adults, we know how difficult it is, or impossible, as the case may be, to keep a "secret." The challenge is just as great for youth, no more so than when they come across the individual they have interviewed in a social situation or in school.

9. Research undertaken by youth may not be given the respect it deserves by other youth and adults because of the notion that if the project is considered "important," then adults must carry it out. This point may resonate for adults. However, it also applies to youth. Youth researchers are in an excellent position to undertake research on topics that are particularly relevant for youth. It becomes ironic that other youth may be reluctant to participate because they do not believe the research to be serious because adults are not in the positions of power in the research. Youth researchers must be prepared to have their expertise and legitimacy questioned by other youth, difficult as this may be to accept.

10. The "scientific merits" of youth-led research findings will undoubtedly be challenged as youth seek to disseminate their findings to professional audiences and key community stakeholders. The blurring of the lines between researcher and subject will often be the focus of this criticism. Park (1993) addresses this very point in a critique of positivist research:

The gist of the criticism is that not maintaining a proper distance between the researcher and the researched, as in the policy in participatory research, seriously compromises the objectivity of the data, thus destroying its validity. This charge, however, derives from a misguided emulation of natural science methodology [that] has maintained the separation of the subject and the object in controlled experiments. The arguments concerning this shortsighted methodological stance in the social sciences are overwhelmingly on the side of the practice prevalent in participatory research. (pp. 16–17)

Scientific merit is not absolute and therefore is highly subject to sociopolitical factors in its determination. No research is perfect, but there are ways to minimize criticism and increase the chances that the results do, in fact, represent the views of the community. There are critical lessons to be learned that have applicability beyond research. Youth, for example, must accept that achievement of perfection can be a goal, but one that cannot be achieved in everyday life. Making an honest effort to minimize bias and do the best job possible are goals that will serve youth well in life, however.

11. The general rule of 50/50 has been applied to youth development projects and is also applicable to youth-led research (Goggin et al., 2002). What is 50/50? Simply, 50 percent of the time is devoted to formal activities, such as training and work, that serve to engage youth in purposeful activities that stress some aspect of educational learning. The remaining 50 percent is allocated for informal interactions and activities that stress fun and entertainment. This does not mean that learning is not taking place, however. It means that a causal atmosphere allows learning to transpire in ways that engage youth. This perspective often flies in the face of most conventional research projects that stress the seriousness of the undertaking at the cost of fun and purposeful learning.

12. There are a number of concerns, or considerations, that must be taken into account in using certain visual-focused research methods, although these methods offer much promise in the field of youth-led community research (Boyden & Ennew, 1997; Save the Children, 2000):

1. Drawing as a means of communication is very much dependent on drawing abilities and not everyone has these abilities, adult or youth.

2. Depending on the age of the respondent, drawing may not be an activity associated with other children or youth, and they may consider it "child's play."

3. In the case of youth who draw frequently, their images may be the result of stereotypical images that are based on past teaching and discussions rather than current perspectives.

4. Interpretation of images by adults can be the result of misinterpretations.

Visual-focused methods are not panaceas for situations where youth are illiterate or have difficulty expressing them in youth-led research. They must be considered part of a wide array of methods that can be tapped when appropriate to both the content being researched and the local circumstances.

The twelve limitations outlined above should not come as any great surprise to those who have participated in youth-led research. Any form of research would be fraught with limitations. Biases inherent in losing objectivity are more than offset by the "reliability" of the results from being closer to the phenomenon being studied (B. Williams, 1996). However, youth-led research brings with it a set of limitations that directly corresponds to the age of the researcher, which is not the case in adult-led research.

❖ INNOVATIVE METHODS
   OF YOUTH-INVOLVED RESEARCH

Community-based research according to Strand et al. (2003) encourages development and application of "unconventional criteria" for determining the most appropriate research methods, and avoids discipline-bound methodologies. These innovative approaches can encompass video, art, theater, or quilting activities, for example, that seek to tap local knowledge, making this form of research particularly appealing to youth. Any discussion of youth-led research is not complete without attention to the use of innovative research methods. The openness of the field to new ways of gathering information makes this field very attractive to youth, practitioners, and academics alike.

The seemingly constant introduction of innovative methods and research designs makes vigorously staying abreast of the field arduous for most practitioners and academics alike; innovation by its very nature brings with it a set of challenges. Getting detailed information on an innovation is one example, particularly when it occurs in a foreign country that does not share the English language. Relying on academic publications takes too long because of the peer-review process and potential extended publication lag time. Access to reports and the language that is used can also hamper publications. Scholarly publications by their very nature are not intended for public consumption and require a considerable amount of decoding and rewriting to make the content useable for the general public.

Youth-led research has expanded dramatically over the past decade and, in the process of doing so, has embraced numerous innovative and fun approaches to undertaking research. The introduction of nonwritten and visual-based methods, for example, has broadened the reach of this type of research to include youth with disabilities who would normally not be able to participate and various age groups of children (Kirby, 1999; Morris, 2000; Ward, 1997). Further, an emphasis on visual methods has allowed youth who are illiterate to also share their voices with the world. A stress on inclusion in creating methods naturally involves careful consideration of who can and who cannot participate in a purposeful manner.

Theis, Pickup, Hoa, and Lan (1999) do a wonderful job of describing the use of photography as a research tool by young Vietnamese youth with visual impairments, and show how participation is not restricted because of a disability. The use of photography, with the proper training, support, and equipment, allows youth to capture a perspective that may not initially lend itself to the conventional use of written or verbal language. It also provides them with a vehicle to involve the broader community through possible exhibits in public venues.

Save the Children (2000) has issued a challenge for youth, particularly in their role as researchers, that no age group should be ignored because they are too young. This organization has played an international influential role in bringing forth new research methods that place youth in all research roles, particularly the roles of participant and researcher.

The use of innovative methods de-emphasizing written and spoken techniques can allow researchers, in this case adults, to involve even those as young as 3 or 4 years old. The use of felt boards to draw pictures, role-play, and play, for example, can tap children's views and feelings about particular subject matter. In fact, many of the research methods used in participatory research depend on visual techniques that can be modified according to the developmental stage of children and youth. These techniques, as I've already noted, also have the advantage of being able to enlist the opinions and perspectives of youth who have experienced great tragedies and trauma in their lives but have not been afforded a meaningful opportunity to share their experiences with others.

Cameras can be an effective method through which youth can record what is good about a community, what is missing, or what needs to be altered to make a community stronger. Pictures, in addition, can be used to establish baselines and monitor conditions over an extended period of time, thus recording positive or negative changes. Photography, as a result, can be an effective vehicle through which youth can use a set of "lenses" to record their perceptions and lend themselves to comparisons, dialogues, and archival retrieval for future reference. The peers, parents, and elders of the community, in turn, can attend exhibitions of these photographs, allowing youth to effectively "show off" their talents and work, making an exhibition a community-unifying and -validating event. In some communities across the United States, there are relatively few such events, and when they occur, they become that much more significant.

The introduction of digital cameras will no doubt revolutionize the use of photographs as qualitative data–gathering tools. Although considerably less expensive than digital cameras, conventional cameras, particularly those that are disposable, can end up costing more, due to the time and expense required for film development. Photographs taken with digital cameras can facilitate comparative assessment within and between communities across the nation and internationally. Youth in one city can share and have access to photographs from youth in another community several thousand miles away and be able to dialogue more easily with their counterparts. Compared with conventional photographs, digital pictures can be more easily manipulated to allow for more critical analysis; for example, sections within a photograph can be enlarged to highlight key findings. Finally, digital pictures lend themselves to wide-scale national and international dissemination through the use of the Internet and computers. This allows youth to exhibit their work in a manner that can influence other youth thousands of miles away, unlike conventional photograph exhibitions that almost exclusively target a local audience.

Lau et al. (2003) report on a middle school project where youth researchers, as part of an interview team, spent two weeks interviewing and photographing students, teachers, staff, and parents, with focus on the prevention of violence and what action steps are needed to address it within their school. The authors report on another school project where seventh- and eighth-grade boys utilize video and scripts to interview youth, school district employees, school staff, and foundation representatives and make a movie about what elements make for a good after-school program.

Like digital cameras, video cameras have emerged as research tools that can be used effectively by youth. The continued decrease in the costs of video cameras and the widespread availability of such equipment has increased its attractiveness as a method for undertaking research. As Howard et al. (2002) report, the use of video has become a method for successfully engaging youth in the research process:

> Video is an important medium; it is easily transportable, inexpensive and is congruent with many young people's "culture reading" skills. Unlike live performance (i.e., music, drama, dance, etc.), it can be viewed more often than once, and can reach a potential audience larger than any auditorium maximum capacity. It was important that the medium for this project was video, given that it is a relevant cultural medium for the participants and for the intended audience. (p. 7)

Howard et al.'s (2002) observations of the attractiveness of video within youth circles suggest that this method of research can also serve as an attractive recruitment tool.

Faulkner (1998) reports on the use of video cameras as a means of increasing the participation of youth in documenting and communicating about their lives and the challenges they face in meeting their basic needs. Youth were able to integrate drama by re-creating scenes from popular Brazilian soap operas about the life of the wealthy. Youth assumed the roles of reporters and decision makers of who best represented this perspective. They, in turn, developed technical expertise in producing, directing, filming, acting, and editing their own documentary. Adults provided assistance when solicited to do so. However, the final product was shaped and owned by youth themselves.

The following testimony of Hayley, 16 years old, on the benefits of using video as a research tool illustrates the multiple gains that are capable through youth-led research (Howard et al., 2002):

> I just want to say that participating in the video project was one of the best things I have ever done. I have gained heaps of experience and a better understanding of myself, youth and society. It has really opened my eyes to the career pathways I might choose in the future. (p. 7)

Hayley's transformative experience is not unique to this individual. This type of experience can play an important role in helping to guide a young person along a career path that may not involve research, but may entail the use of videos and the communications field, for example.

My experience with video cameras and youth-led research occurred in the mid-1990s when a group of Latino (Puerto Rican) youth in Holyoke, Massachusetts, undertook a project developing a video of Latino community needs (Delgado, 1995). This needs assessment represented a visual assessment of their community and how adults in authority were neglecting youth needs. Youth selected the scenes, chose background music, developed narrative, videotaped, and edited the video. The project was focused on drug prevention because of the source of funding, and as a result, youth had this as a central organizing theme. Afterward, a premiere, which involved parents, peers not in the program, and community leaders, was held and allowed youth to showcase their accomplishment. Each youth, in turn, was provided with a copy of the video to be shown in their homes and in the institutions that they felt needed to be educated. Some of the youth participants showed the video within their high school classrooms and in the houses of worship they belonged to.

Participation in video production is an effective way of generating excitement in a research project. There is a certain Hollywood aura associated with the creation of a video and a premiere showing. The excitement can be positive in getting a community to coalesce with youth and generating momentum toward achieving social goals. A visual report, if you wish, unlike conventional written reports, brings the potential for engaging community residents because it allows groups to share information, even if members are illiterate. Just as importantly, however, video reports lend themselves to engaging youth who would otherwise not bother with a written report or summary. Unlike written reports, videos provide youth with a chance to see themselves and hear their own voices. This certainly personalizes the research process for youth.

Based on their assessment of participatory evaluation methods used in Nepalese children's clubs, Hart and Rajbhandary (2003) identify a number of promising approaches for encouraging research participation from youth. Their central guiding principles include (a) making research methods "simple and clear" for use by youth who are not formally schooled, (b) putting data analysis and interpretation in the hands of youth researchers, and (c) taking into account time restrictions and attention spans.

In community mapping, youth were encouraged to do the following: use yarn, pieces of cardboard, and crayons to identify nonclub members in all households (understanding patterns of social exclusion); categorize and rank participation in activities using the movement game and card sorting; arrange cards into diagrams as a means of developing an understanding of organizational structure and decision making; use skits of preferred activities to establish categories for a preference-matrix; and use Venn diagrams for identification of the people and organizations that have any influence on the running of clubs.

Innovations in research methods are not limited to visual approaches. When children and youth are literate, there are various ways of eliciting responses that do not involve the usual question-answer format, which may work well with adults but may be considered too limiting for use with youth. Participatory methods used with literate respondents can include essays, poetry, diaries, recall, and observations (Save the Children, 2000). Storyboards or comics have been used to assist youth in describing scripts of common events in their lives. Typically, figures are presented, and the respondents are asked to fill in a blank narrative to help them express a scene or event in their lives. This method utilizes visual cues as prompts for narrative and does so in a way that does not embarrass youth in the process.

The importance and use of semistructured or unstructured interviews are well acknowledged within the field of youth-led research (Save the Children, 2000):

> One of the best ways to build up an understanding of children's lives, their interests and needs is to interview them. Interviewing is one of the most fundamental approaches to research and both semi-structured and unstructured interviews are vital to any participatory work. If done sensitively, they can elicit a great deal of qualitative information. Children, too, can have a reasonable amount of control over the process and the issues covered. Adults can carry out the interviews with children, or children themselves can interview one another. These interviews can cover life stories, testimonies of an event or specific topics. (pp. 23–24)

A search for innovative methods does not necessitate discarding conventional approaches, however. Although the field of youth-led research certainly lends itself well to the introduction and use of innovative methods, there are many appealing elements in the "old-fashioned" methods when they take into account the age of the respondents and researchers and are sufficiently flexible to take into account local circumstances. The combination of conventional and innovative methods provides researchers with the flexibility of designing research agendas that capitalize on local conditions and strengths, therefore allowing research questions and local circumstances to dictate research design rather than the reverse. A mixture of conventional and innovative methods also brings diversity to a research undertaking, increasing the likelihood of keeping youth researchers engaged and highly motivated.

❖ OUTCOMES OF YOUTH-INVOLVED RESEARCH INITIATIVES

The "best practices" movement has provided a rationale and framework for documenting the effectiveness of youth-led research and other youth-led initiatives. Although best practices have emerged in virtually every aspect of human services, it has only recently made its way into the youth development and youth-led fields (Delgado et al., 2005). Best-practice challenges related to making youth development and youth-led research relevant to nontypical youth provide an exciting opportunity for evaluators to influence the field of practice.

Any in-depth appreciation of youth-involved research outcomes by necessity must take a broad and multifaceted perspective, helping ensure relevance and direct applicability to this field. The benefits to be derived from youth-involved research are many and so are the challenges of researching them. Calvert, Zeldin, and Weisenbach (2002) note that these positive impacts need to be explored and detailed. The potential expansiveness of the field of evaluation brings with it a host of specific challenges related to identifying and measuring a research project's impact, particularly when changes do not occur immediately. The establishment of a foundation from which positive social change can occur is a major achievement, although difficult to measure when it is initially established.

The outcomes of youth-led research, as a result, must be placed within a developmental framework that facilitates their identification and measurement (Moore & Lippman, 2005). McCall and Shannon's (1999) framework for investigation of youth-led initiatives, in this case youth-led health promotion, can help us better understand the effectiveness and sustainability of youth-led research. McCall and Shannon developed a six-stage framework to categorize the developmental stages of research (see Figure 3.3):

Figure 3.3   Developmental Stages of Research

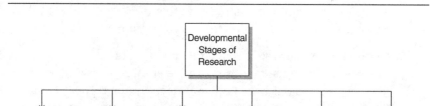

SOURCE: McCall and Shannon (1999, pp. 4–5).

1. **Case Studies:** The cases are generally qualitative in nature and rely heavily on participant feedback and observations. Data primarily raise issues and are used to create linkages between activities and apparent results. Case studies bring an inherent advantage of providing a detailed and vivid rendering of a phenomenon, and therefore make for relatively easy access to practitioners and scholars alike. In addition, they attempt to develop a holistic picture that facilitates the adaptation of an intervention that takes into account how local circumstances played a role in shaping outcomes.

2. **Inventories:** Efforts to catalogue various types of programs and activities based on established criteria play an important role within the field. Data, in turn, are used to advance theories and explanations based on said groupings. Inventories allow researchers and practitioners to establish a better grasp of the key elements involved in an intervention.

3. **Quasi-Experimental Designs and Studies:** Empirical observations are derived utilizing quasi-experimental designs and studies. The results are considered summative but not generalizable to other settings and situations. The attractiveness of quasi-experimental designs and studies is unquestioned in research because it facilitates the isolation of key factors at play in bringing about a studied change.

4. **Meta-Analyses of Case Studies:** The goal of developing explanatory theories is served through the analyses of case

studies. Meta-analyses, however, are predicated on the availability of numerous studies with sufficient details to allow comparisons along a variety of key dimensions.

5. **Comparative Studies:** Once theories are developed they then lend themselves to large-scale comparative studies, allowing scholars to draw conclusions based on empirical findings. These comparisons can cut across national and international boundaries, making their appeal that much greater in the scientific community.

6. **Knowledge Dissemination:** Knowledge development and dissemination represent the final stage in any research endeavor; policy development ensues for this increased awareness. (pp. 4–5)

Youth-led research, like its youth-led health promotion example, is best categorized as stage one (case studies), at this point in time. This stage is the most rudimentary of the six identified by McCall and Shannon (1999). However, this categorization by no means should be considered a slight on this movement. All movements such as youth-led research go through an initial stage that, at times, can best be described as confusing or ambiguous, but one that generates considerable excitement and imagination. Youth-led research falls into this stage, but has the potential to make its way up the ladder, so to speak, and reach the stage of *knowledge dissemination*. This progression may take years if not decades to achieve, however.

Youth-led initiatives effectively cast youth into a spotlight that focuses on their capabilities and contributions to community and society. These types of initiatives, in addition, engage youth in dialogue and create opportunities to enhance their skills and encourage their participatation in social problem-solving strategies (Burgess, 2000). Such initiatives also represent a creative way of employing youth that would otherwise be excluded from the labor market, and they help circulate money within the community (Israel, 2000). Opportunities to earn money in ways that stress positive civic contributions directly benefit youth, their communities, and society in general. Youth involvement in research also results in youth becoming more self-confident and developing a belief in their power to create their own future; their empowerment also empowers their community, which is especially important in cases where the community is undervalued (Marsh, 2002).

Further, youth-led research can provide valuable insights into how schools and community-based organizations can develop structured means to involve youth in decision-making roles that most significantly influence their lives (Fletcher, 2003). This type of research provides youth with competencies and insight into how organizations effectively disempower them. One youth member notes the following benefits of participation in decision making (qtd. in Goggin et al., 2002): "Young people felt that they had become more aware of their own community . . . its laws, its people, its youth, and what they need. They feel that education works in both directions: they educate the community and are educated by it" (p. 33). The benefits of empowerment can be far-reaching and life-altering for youth and their communities.

Youth IMPACT (2001) youth program evaluators in San Francisco comment on their various forms of growth: "The things we enjoyed from the whole process were learning presentation, writing, and critical thinking skills. We also had the opportunity to learn more about San Francisco and all the wonderful CBOs [community-based organizations] serving children and youth" (p. 7). According to Sabo (2003b), the competencies youth may acquire as researchers are quite impressive (survey development and analysis, focus group facilitation, logic model development, program development, and qualitative and quantitative data analyses) and complement those identified by Youth IMPACT.

The following six youth testimonials from the Youth IMPACT evaluation project illustrate the range and types of benefits youth derive from participation and how they broaden this vista of the world around them. This broadening of their world can only be a positive outcome in the course of their lives (Youth IMPACT, 2001, pp. 20–21):

I believe this is a once in a lifetime opportunity for youth to genuinely improve the programs of San Francisco. (Lily Onovakpuri)

I think my experience was very interesting. It was interesting seeing all the different programs and meeting different people. I learned a lot about different places in the city and a lot of CBOs that I never knew about. (Marvin Rivera)

I learned about evaluation and planning. I had the opportunity to learn about things other kids my age would never have the opportunity to do. By us being youth ourselves we know what youth want and need and through that we'll be able to work towards providing better services for the youth. (Khalillah Hill)

The things that I learned will be beneficial in life because they will help me further my skills as a person and as a worker doing evaluations in the future. (Kenisha Roach)

I think that Youth IMPACT is giving back a lot to all of the funded CBOs. We are giving them a voice to speak up about the important things that they are doing. We are also giving them a voice to let the government know the help they need to improve their CBO. (Jamie Golden)

I like doing the evaluation. It made me more aware and more interested in politics and things that go on in the city so it can help me in the future. (Kamael Burch)

Branda Robertson's (Columbus, Indiana) observations on her growth as a result of participating in a community youth mapping research project further highlights the multifaceted gains possible in this type of research (Community Youth Development, 2000):

Not only did it give me something productive to do over the summer months, but it opened up so many opportunities and possibilities for me. It gave me more incentive to keep working for my community, especially for youth. I learned what the real world is like. I was able to interact with adults on a one-to-one basis. I improved my communication skills greatly and gained more self-confidence. I learned what is and is not out there for young people. (p. 1)

Checkoway and Richards-Schuster (2002) identify five prominent benefits for youth researchers: (1) a method for acquiring knowledge for social action; (2) enable the exercise of political rights; (3) sharing in the democratization of knowledge; (4) preparation for participation in a democratic society; and (5) strengthening social development (pp. 3–4). Youth in Focus (2002), in turn, identify three critical outcomes of youth-led research: It (1) facilitates good youth development, (2) strengthens organizational development and capacity building, and (3) catalyzes youth involvement in community change (pp. 2–3).

Benefits go far beyond making youth competent researchers. In fact, these benefits easily translate into the domain of civic participation, with society being the ultimate beneficiary. London et al. (2003) present a very compelling argument on how youth-led research can effectively transform the lives of youth participants and the organizations sponsoring the research. The nature and force of social action resulting from the research findings can only be possible by what the authors label "careful investment" in youth.

Schensul (1994) identifies three steps that are necessary to transform a research project into an intervention project that has applicability for youth-led research:

1. Determine which causal factors can be altered and which will resist, given the constraints of time and resources.

2. Anticipate what changes are feasible in the causal factors.

3. Anticipate what changes might result in the dependent variable. (p. 3)

The transition from research to social change requires a process of decision making and brokering of competing interests to achieve a consensus on the direction and target for change. The research team in collaboration with outside forces enters into this deliberative process.

Youth researchers must take a multifaceted perspective on their research study experience in order to fully appreciate the impact of their work. Sustain's (2000) community mapping project elicited youth responses along four dimensions: (1) What have I learned? (2) What will I take with me? (3) What did I love? and (4) What will I throw away? These four questions, in turn, divide the experience into attitudes, knowledge, and competencies for each of these dimensions. Just as importantly, experiences do not all have to be positive. Negative experiences, particularly when discussed and the reasons uncovered, can prove just as transformative as positive experiences. Learning, after all, can occur from both positive and negative experiences, although I, like the reader, prefer positive experiences.

D. L. Miller et al.'s (2001) summary of the skill sets developed through participation in research illustrates the benefits youth can obtain through engaging in research:

facilitating interviews, framing open-ended questions, probing for depth, listening, analysing and interpreting data . . . through active participation in real-life research projects. Successful collaborative experiences may also increase high school students' self-efficacy and give them confidence that they have something to contribute to their peer group and the adult community. (p. 23)

These benefits, not surprisingly, cover a wide variety of types with high levels of transferability to other arenas.

Another benefit rarely talked about is the potential therapeutic outcomes youth researchers experience. The discussion of transformative experiences and outcomes has generally focused on attitudes, knowledge, and skills. Clacherty and Kistner (2001) report on a highly innovative youth-led research project based in South Africa. They report that the research project not only generated important data but also served as a therapeutic intervention for the adolescent male researchers (ages 12 to 16 years old) involved in criminal activity. The research project focused on youth on the "edge of crime." The primary research tool in the initial stages was a disposable camera.

The boys took photographs that illustrated the "lives of boys in Kathrorus." The time was spent labeling the photographs and talking about them, all the time with the boys in the role of "objective" researchers. The discussion was tape-recorded and became the qualitative data that the adult researcher used to develop a picture of the reality of boys on the edge of crime and what pushed them into crime. (p. 1)

South African youth researchers were able to explore and develop new insights into their own struggles and challenges by recording the experiences of others; the distancing achieved through the research role allowed youth to maintain their defenses while concomitantly beginning to own their own past. Eventually, these youth undertook similar research projects on school issues, substance abuse, and gun violence. The positive experiences in one realm served as a foundation for experiences and research in other realms. Although they constitute an emerging area within youth-led research, youth with histories of receiving mental health and social services have generally been unexplored and warrant further in-depth attention from the field.

Perkins and Jones (2002) specifically tie youth development to youth-led research through the Comprehensive Community Assessment of Youth Development Opportunities (CCAYDO), a yearlong assessment and planning project. The primary goals were (Perkins & Jones, 2002):

> (1) creating a community taskforce and youth action teams; (2) conducting an assessment of the opportunities for youth in terms of skill development, recreation, and engagement in risk behaviors; (3) identifying the needs and desires of youth, parents, and youth professionals in terms of the enhancement of existing positive youth development opportunities and the creation of new positive youth develop opportunities; and (4) employment of the information gathered from strategies two and three to develop a community mobilization plan to address the identified needs. (p. 2)

Perkins and Jones (2002) have clearly taken the research process far beyond research into the realm of action, illustrating the potential of youth-led research to socially enhance youth lives, their communities, and adult-youth relationships. Further, youth are provided with a viable and meaningful opportunity to learn and serve their communities in the process. Benefits of research, as a result, extend in an ecological manner to a wide range of audiences, both immediately and in the long term, and social arenas. Any concerted effort to better comprehend the outcomes of youth-led research will necessitate the development of longitudinal efforts of both output and impact objectives on communities.

In my experiences with youth-led research (Delgado, 1996, 1998), I found that youth are the primary, although certainly not the only, beneficiaries of youth participation. Based on a community asset assessment undertaken by Latino youth in a New England city in 1994, I identified four benefits the research yielded to the youth and their community:

1. It provided a greater sense of control over the youth's lives, family, and community.

2. It instilled important research skills and knowledge that would serve youth and their community in the future.

3. It provided the community in general, and the Latino community in particular, with a perspective that youth can be, and

are, vital and contributing members of the community, thus counteracting pervasive views that are deficit-based.

4. It resulted in youth serving as role models for other human service organizations.

Like the benefits or skill sets identified by D. L. Miller et al. (2001), youth, in this case Latino, were cast into roles that are positive, and they were considered contributing members of the community just like adults.

Youth can play leadership roles within their respective adult communities and not just with other youth. When these communities do not share English as their primary language and have cultural values that are distinctively different from those of the host nation, in this case the United States, leadership roles can take on important brokering or bridging functions between the host nation and the newcomer community (Delgado et al., 2005). As this nation continues to undergo rapid changes in demographic composition because of the influx of refugees and immigrants, youth's potential to aid their communities and the host society in better understanding and appreciating each other's similarities and differences may well be a critical key to how well this nation competes in an increasingly global society.

For the Harvard Family Research Project, Horsch et al. (2002) identified three goals commonly sought in youth-run research projects: (1) Enhance the individual development of participating youth and encourage their meaningful involvement in the decisions that affect their lives; (2) contribute to organizational development and capacity enhancement; and (3) provide youth with a vehicle and purpose to create significant and sustainable community change efforts. These goals stress capacity enhancement of individuals, institutions, and communities, and actively unite these three realms together in pursuit of common goals.

The Triumph and Success Peer Research Project (France, 2002), based in England, shares the sentiments that youth researchers benefit tremendously from participation in research: "Peer research clearly has a future as a method of engaging young people in project work. Not only does it create opportunities for young people to learn new skills but also for them to gain personal benefits from being involved" (p. 4). These benefits are not restricted to any particular core element. It is entirely possible for youth to benefit socially, emotionally, spiritually, morally, cognitively, and physically. The core element(s) emphasized can vary depending on the primary goals of the project.

Finally, Matysik (2000), in summing up the benefits for youth program evaluators, notes how youth involvement can be a positive and possibly tranformative experience:

> Youth self-reported that their involvement in the participatory projects impacted them personally in the following ways: by learning about the process of research, gaining experience in solving problems, becoming more able to accept new and different ideas, recognizing that it is acceptable to ask for help, experiencing teamwork, feeling more confident in their own abilities, and realizing that the learning process can be enjoyable. (p. 18)

Sabo (2003b) has observed that youth can rise and meet the challenges of assuming a researcher role, and in effect "growing" into this role and becoming "who they were not" (p. 17).

Personal impact goes far beyond changes in attitudes or perceptions; it also includes changes in behavior related to relationships, learning, and the development of productive work habits. Measuring how these areas have benefited from youth involvement in a research project can be quite challenging. Changes may not be immediately apparent and may evolve over an extended period of time, or they may be only minor at first and take on greater prominence at a later period. Failure to note these benefits, however, seriously shortchanges the impact of participation.

Youth-led research, particularly when youth are paid for their time and expertise, also serves to provide youth with money that is often in short supply within undervalued communities. When the research project shares a community capacity enhancement perspective, every effort is made to rent space and purchase supplies, food, and expertise from the community being studied as a means of circulating funding (Delgado, 1998, 1999). Youth researchers are paid, and so are the research participants or subjects. Having research projects based within the community where youth live increases community accessibility to staff and helps break down potential barriers between researchers and community (Delgado, 1998; Israel, 2000). The research process thus becomes a part of daily life within the community and serves to demystify this activity; it also provides other members of the community with an opportunity to enter and find out what is going on if they wish to do so.

As I address in greater detail in Chapter 7, youth-led research costs can be considerably lower than conventional research endeavors, because personnel with many academic degrees and years of experience are quite costly. Youth-led research, in addition, tends to be more cost-effective because youth know their community (local knowledge) quite well; this saves time and resources that often go toward orienting an external community research team or engaging local stakeholder support for the research project. Regardless of how well an orientation program is crafted, it will never approximate the knowledge youth possess of their own communities and peer groups. In essence, youth-led research makes sense philosophically, conceptually, and financially.

Horton, Hutchinson, Barkman, Machtmes, and Myers (1999) developed a five-phase model that can be used effectively in conceptualizing and presenting youth-led research and its potential benefits to youth and their communities: (1) Experience the activity; (2) share the experience by describing what happened; (3) process the experience to identify common or cross-cutting themes; (4) generalize from the experience to create principles and guidelines for use in other real-life situations; and (5) apply lessons learned to other spheres and situations. This framework, although developed specifically for service-learning, nonetheless has relevancy for youth-led research and helps influence how learning about research can transpire without alienating youth in the process. This is no small undertaking since learning is often associated with boring lectures, dull books, and meaningless assignments in the eyes of many youth, particularly those representing undervalued groups in this society.

Finally, it would irresponsible to think that the benefits of youth-led research are restricted to youth, their organizations, and communities. Adults as a group, too, benefit tremendously from their involvement with youth, particularly when they consider themselves to be in partnership with them. Zeldin, McDaniel, Topitzes, and Calvert (2000b) specifically emphasize the synergy that is created between youth and adults when they work together. Adults cannot help but get caught up in the energy that youth bring to an enterprise and the creativity that is often displayed in problem solving, particularly when it involves reaching out and engaging other youth. These persistent efforts to engage youth offer an abundance of opportunities for all youth to develop a better sense of how the world is (not just for adults but for themselves as well) and to play an influential role in shaping it.

The continued evaluation of the effectiveness of youth development programs and the lessons learned in the process will undoubtedly serve as an important step in helping demonstrate the value of youth-led research and other youth-led initiatives (Catalano, Berglund, Ryan, Lonczak, & Hawkins, 2002; Eccles & Gootman, 2002; Leffert, Saito, Blyth, & Kroenke, 1996; Lewis-Charp, Yu, Soukamneuth, & Lacoe, 2003; Moore & Lippman, 2005). The Harvard Family Research Project's (Horsch et al., 2002) findings of the key elements associated with a successful youth-involved research project are no doubt relevant to other types of youth-led initiatives: (a) organizational and community readiness, (b) adequate training and support for involved youth, (c) adequate training and support for adult staff, (d) selecting the right team, and (e) sustaining youth involvement.

❖ CONCLUSION

It is relatively easy for practitioners to develop a set of operating goals and objectives to guide their youth-led research projects. There is no aspect of social life that does not lend itself to systematic investigation. Some elements, however, lend themselves particularly well to these types of interventions. Research that integrates fun into work cannot be overlooked in any form of youth-led initiative. However, having "fun" takes on added significance when discussing research. Unfortunately, fun is rarely part of any discussion of adult-led research projects, although adults can no doubt enhance their experiences with some fun along the way.

The evolving nature of youth-led research brings with it a set of challenges in defining what youth-led research is and how we can develop boundaries to explain this approach without effectively limiting its potential reach. Further, as this chapter has indicated, this form of research must be thought of as benefiting youth and their communities in both the short and long run. Thinking of youth-led research as a form of community service compounds a process that is challenging to begin with and makes it more challenging. Nevertheless, the fact that it is challenging should not discourage such efforts; it should make us more cognizant of why it is arduous and why it is so significant in the lives of youth and their community.

Ideally, youth-led research must successfully achieve a delicate balance between generating generalizable knowledge, benefiting the community that is the focus of the study, and improving research protocols for future use on these types of initiatives (Macaulay et al., 1999). Success in achieving all of these articulated goals is never guaranteed.

Nevertheless, rarely will these projects fail completely because of an emphasis on engaging and giving back to the community.

The need for studies specifically focused on identifying the range of benefits or outcomes associated with youth-led research is obvious. As this form of youth-led initiative continues to become more viable within organizations and communities, so, too, will the cry for research to demonstrate the effectiveness of this form of intervention. The field should welcome such a cry because evaluation of youth-led research can only reflect on its importance and help move this field forward. Research findings will identify what aspects of youth-led initiatives lend themselves to maximizing benefits and which aspects require further modifications. Further, research that is context driven (namely, that which takes into account a range of sociodemographic factors such as race, ethnicity, gender, sexual orientation, and physical and cognitive abilities) is complex and does not lend itself to "cookie-cutter" forms of analysis. We must not let this dissuade us, but rather challenge and motivate us to be inclusive and creative in designing research studies because this is important for youth and society, now and in the future.

4

Youth Research Competencies

Attitudes, Knowledge, and Skills

The question "What does it take to make it as a successful youth-led researcher?" is closely tied to the question "What does it take to make it as a successful researcher?" There is obviously a core set of attitudes, knowledge, and skills that are central to this success. However, bringing the dimension of age to the answers adds a critical, yet elusive, quality to any response regarding youth-led research. The reader may well argue that answering the question related to youth has significance because youth bring the innate curiosity and skills needed in a research endeavor. Others might argue that not every adult is capable of being a researcher, and why should youth be any exception?

Any form of social intervention, be it research, educational, or service focused, must be based on a solid foundation of knowledge and competencies. Anyone who undertakes research, as a result, must possess requisite research competencies. It is not unusual for the field of research to also require some form of specialization in research methods, as well as population-specific knowledge. The tendency to specialize, although not restricted to the social research field, is nevertheless highly valued and thus rewarded when putting together a research team.

It is important to pause and make note of the potential drift in the field of social research that historically has consisted of two camps. Although the field of research has slowly moved toward acceptance of both quantitative and qualitative methods, for example, it is rare to find someone with equal background and competencies in these two areas. Those involved in youth-led research will also encounter these historical divisions, issues, and sentiments, thus requiring an open discussion of the advantages and disadvantages of each approach, and the importance of the research question dictating approach rather than the other way around. It is not unusual to have these differences translate into heated and rigid positions on the virtues of one approach versus another, making for tense moments and challenges in carrying out a research project.

Steinberg and Kincheloe (1998) developed a definition for student as researcher that captures the essence of competencies any researcher, adult or youth, must possess: "a vision of 'what could be,' and a set of skills to uncover 'what actually is'" (p. 2). This definition eschews taking sides on the merits, or demerits, of any one approach or method and emphasizes the need for research questions dictating the most appropriate approach based on consideration of the context in which the research is being undertaken. This is the way it should be, rather than a research method dictating research questions.

This chapter consists of four sections, each taking a different perspective on youth research competencies: (1) Self-/Local Knowledge; (2) Developmental Perspectives; (3) Youth Research Competencies; and (4) Qualities That Make for an Excellent Youth Researcher. This foundation serves to better prepare youth to assume the role of researcher within a youth-led research perspective. The goal of this chapter, however, is not to provide an exhaustive review on this subject matter. Nevertheless, I hope that the reader develops a better appreciation of what it takes for youth to lead or be a part of a research team and that the reader also will come to understand the capital that youth bring to the field. R. Campbell's (2002) description of key approaches to ensuring maximum participation on the part of youth is also quite applicable to youth-led research:

The task of workers is also to generate a whole range of tools for working with young people that helps them to think, challenge, create and express themselves. . . . However, to emphasize, the approach taken should not only suit the aptitudes of the young people involved, but also the issue they are interested in pursuing. (p. 6)

Youth engagement serves many different goals in addition to carrying out a research project in a manner that is sensitive to the needs of those being questioned as part of the study.

❖ SELF-KNOWLEDGE AND LOCAL KNOWLEDGE

Before delving into a description of the requisite attitudes, knowledge, and skills youth need to possess to be effective researchers, it is necessary to pause and note that youth bring much to the table. First and foremost are their self-knowledge and their local knowledge. The concept of expertise within the scientific world generally serves to uplift a set of competencies and knowledge specialties. This form of expertise is integrally tied to structured coursework or advanced hands-on experience. This effectively translates into a career path that takes the expert through a university setting. If expertise is defined in such a narrow manner, then youth and other community residents without formal training in research can never participate in a research project in any meaningful manner, thus limiting their potential quest for answers to key issues in their lives.

The role and importance of self-knowledge has been well addressed by a number of researchers, most notably Howard Gardner, and as a result, I only touch on this topic in this section. The construct of self-knowledge can be traced back to a considerable period of time (Gertler, 2003). Pointing out the importance of self-knowledge for youth is an effective means of empowering youth in a research undertaking. In philosophy, self-knowledge is generally used to convey knowledge of one's particular mental states such as beliefs, desires, and sensations. Further, it can also refer to knowledge pertaining to a persisting self (its ontological nature, identity conditions, or characteristics). Self-knowledge is considered significantly different from knowledge of the external world (Gertler, 2003). Some scholars would go so far as to argue that self-knowledge is a prerequisite for satisfaction and success in all significant aspects of life.

Self-knowledge, or what Gardner (1993) calls intrapersonal intelligence, can be defined as

> knowledge of the internal aspects of a person: access to one's own feeling life, one's range of emotions, the capacity to effect discriminations among these emotions and eventually to label them and to draw upon them as a means of understanding and guiding one's behavior. A person with good intrapersonal intelligence is a viable and effective model of himself or herself. (pp. 24–25)

This perspective has enjoyed considerable currency in the past decade because it advances the position that intelligence can consist of many different types. Gardner (1993), probably the leading proponent of multiple types of intelligence, identifies eight types: verbal linguistic, logical/mathematical, spatial, body/kinesthetic, musical, naturalist, interpersonal, and intrapersonal.

In turning to local knowledge, this concept has not received the attention it deserves although it has recently emerged as a powerful construct within youth-led research (Goodyear & Checkoway, 2003). An extensive search of the professional literature and the Internet did not uncover any articles or documents devoted to the subject of local knowledge. In addition, although I found references to the importance of local knowledge, I found no formal definition of it. Thus, it is incumbent to provide one.

Local knowledge refers to information or insights that are generally obvious or only available to community residents. This knowledge is obtained from observations or other informal sources during the course of daily life within the community. Specific dimensions of local knowledge are developed by groups sharing similar sociocultural characteristics. The acquisition of local knowledge is not an intended goal of residents, but rather a by-product of typical interactions and occurrences.

This knowledge can encompass a variety of spheres related to beliefs, values, customs, history, behaviors, and interactional patterns, which can prove useful in planning and implementing an intervention with research being one such example. Thus, the construct of local knowledge is not widely understood by "outsiders" to the community. Either this information is not considered important enough to report through local news channels, or it necessitates having someone living within the community to acquire it, or both. Its accessibility is severely limited to outside of the community, as there are no standard sources for acquiring this knowledge and no central repository for retrieving it. Murals are a good example (Delgado, 1999, 2003). The symbols used in the body of the mural very often have meaning to only the local community, because of the cultural background they tap. Local residents, as a result, are in the propitious position of having to translate these messages to the external world, making them "experts."

What are the types of local knowledge that can be useful to a research endeavor? What are the historical changes within a community that have not been captured by external sources such as the media or data-gathering entities such as the U.S. Census Bureau? What enters into those decisions? Where do youth congregate and who are these youth? Who are the youth that by their reputations can be considered to be "in the know" and would make excellent key informants or consultants on a research project? How is leadership defined within the local context? How do youth view local institutions, particularly those that are not engaged in formal participation? Integration of local knowledge into research questions and design is essential to minimizing research bias and increasing the likelihood of achieving success in collecting answers to the research questions.

Youth-led responses to HIV/AIDS in Kenya, Africa, provide an excellent example of how youth (in this case, 18- to 20-year-olds) utilize local knowledge to assess needs and develop culturally appropriate interventions such as sporting activities, plays, songs, role plays, and celebrations (G. Williams, Ng'ang'a, & Ngugi, 1998). Their participation in all facets of research and program design and implementation increases the likelihood of these interventions being accepted by the local community and of meeting the most pressing issues/problems within a sociocultural context.

Youth-led research actively seeks to make extensive use of self-knowledge and local knowledge and serves as a cornerstone for any effort to engage youth in the research process. If "expertise" refers to knowledge that is specialized and not within easy grasp without "formalized" ways of obtaining and retrieving it, then youth definitely can be considered to possess expertise that adults do not possess, and this must be formally recognized. The premise that "youth are the experts on their own lives and circumstances" then becomes the central point that must be acknowledged to help ensure that a project can be successful, whether research focused or otherwise. Thus, those possessing the greatest amount of local knowledge about youth are youth themselves, and they are the ultimate arbiters of the status of youth within a community (London et al., 2003; Matysik, 2000; Shaw, 1996; Wallerstein, 1998).

By training and supporting youth in the undertaking of a research project, adults obtain an opportunity to exchange expertise with youth. These forms of expertise should not be placed in a hierarchy. Instead, they need to be conceptualized as areas of knowledge that are necessary in the accomplishment of a project. Thus, broadening the definition of what constitutes "legitimate" knowledge opens up who can be considered an expert within this field and provides an arena for the exchange of information that effectively minimizes hierarchy based on formal educational credentials.

Checkoway et al. (2003) make this observation and advocate for a wider conceptualization of expertise:

At a time when expert, technical knowledge predominates over knowledge derived from everyday experiences and active citizenship, new strategies are needed to allow traditionally underrepresented groups to develop their knowledge resources as part of the broader movement for democratization. This has potential to break the monopoly on knowledge development and enable young people to gain knowledge and skills for active participation in a democratic society. (p. 10)

A critique of self-knowledge and local knowledge reinforces the importance of the perspective obtained by tapping this form of knowledge and attests to the need for obtaining "buy-in" for the purpose of developing an intervention plan. The entire field of participatory research places the importance of self-knowledge as central to the appeal of this type of research because it represents the voices of those individuals generally overlooked by society as having no insight into their circumstances (Chow & Crowe, 2004; Pennell et al., 2004).

A central negative criticism, however, is that this form of knowledge is biased or of limited usefulness because it lacks a broader perspective in which to ground it. In essence, local knowledge may be a perspective that is too limited. Advocates of self-knowledge and local knowledge would argue that this bias is, in fact, a strength, which must be acknowledged and tapped. Bringing together a diverse group of individuals and systematically gathering and synthesizing this knowledge allow for the development of a broader perspective and increase the value of the findings and possible development of new concepts, constructs, and theories. Any substantial and comprehensive effort to develop any form of social change initiative must be based on the foundation that local knowledge provides.

There is much that youth can learn through participation in a social research project. Youth, for example, must possess some degree of knowledge pertaining to the substantive area they wish to study. This substantive grounding will necessitate an assessment of their knowledge and a systematic effort to build on it through some form of instruction. Thus, obtaining knowledge and skills related to research methods and design represents only a portion of preparedness. Substantive knowledge on a social problem, need, or issue serves to ensure that the research is focused and relevant to the goals on hand.

❖ DEVELOPMENTAL PERSPECTIVES

It would be irresponsible for any organization or community undertaking youth-led research to ignore a developmental perspective on youth as researchers. A developmental perspective applies not only to the age of the interviewer but also to their skills and the totality of their experiences as researchers. An inexperienced researcher would never be put into a position of leadership within an adult-led research project. Thus, this factor, or consideration, must also find its way into youth-led research.

The matching of research roles with skills is well recognized in the field (Horsch et al., 2002):

> Youth need to be given evaluation and research roles that are appropriate to their level of development and expertise. For some, the gradual approach . . . is successful. . . . Youth are given initial, well-defined tasks and gradually take on more, depending on their motivation, their time, and their ability to take on tasks by themselves. . . . While age level can be an important consideration in determining how much direction students need, their level of independence and maturity is also a factor. (p. 3)

A developmental perspective brings with it an explicit understanding that there certainly is no universal set of stages in a child or youth's development; instead, there is an embrace of a hierarchy of

s a
earn
e com-
pervisors

and, some
be challenging
enting this form
rations for organi-
d no more so than in
utsiders. When youth
arch, the challenges take
isting of groups that tradi-
ity, for example, youth face
ly in this newly found role.

wledge related to the research proce
overwhelm any experienced professio
this knowledge can best be conceptuali
ch stage or phase addressing specific g
ematically building on the previous stage.
n is thought of in this way, it becomes conside
youth and provides trainers and facilitators
de in how best to impart knowledge to youth.
ion of knowledge can transpire in a variety of fo
I noted earlier in this book, youth do not ente
deavors totally blank about research. Their self-kno
knowledge must be recognized and integrated throug
(training) of acquiring knowledge about research des
The weaving of new knowledge with existing knowl

evolving competencies that get manifested in ways that are s
each individual (Mullahey et al., 1999). Creation of such a
serves as an important tool in helping research project le
and develop appropriate training and support mechan'
into account a developmental stage. This, too, in tur
researchers to better assess their status within a resea
then take necessary steps to move on a continuum

❖ YOUTH RESEARCH AND SERVICE-LEA
ONE VEHICLE FOR ACHIEVING CO

The acquisition of research competencie
accomplished through the use of a ser
element in most youth development
1994). Service-learning as a meth
to incorporating numerous goals
capacities but also aid institut'
Service-learning, in addition,
as schools and community-'
can serve as an excellent ve
munities in pursuit of c
learning can serve as a
youth as a central for

    The profession
youth-led researc'
edge, particularly L.
nities while engaging in
not about getting youth to lea
integral part of these endeavors. 'I.
on helping youth make important conn
the real world. Lessons learned, as a conse
academic subject matter, and they can find their v.
for youth, thus increasing their meaning and significa.

    Bloome and Egan-Robertson (1998) put forth a chai.
field of research that effectively serves to empower youth and b.
their horizons:

> Research then, can never be bounded by classroom or library
> walls, the walls of teacher knowledge, or even the walls of extant
> disciplinary knowledge. As researchers, students—like any

prove quite powerful in preparing youth for the demands that go with assuming a research role within a youth-led research model.

The general consensus is that knowledge should be presented in a variety of formats other than didactic, which, in many ways, is what is typically stressed in research courses. Further, having youth assume instrumental roles in presenting this material brings an added, yet critical, perspective, namely, the legitimacy of the experiences and knowledge of the teacher or facilitator. Leadership development occurs over an extended period of time and through the use of a variety of methods. Thus, having youth assume positions of experts is just another way of helping them develop leadership skills for future endeavors, be they research or otherwise focused. Assuming this role also results in a research project being more grounded within a community context, increasing the likelihood that the results will have greater relevance.

Critical Skills

Finally, the ability to actually carry out key research functions represents the final aspect of any preparation for youth to assume a research role. This aspect very often represents the culmination of a long training and support process. Phillips et al. (2001) raise a cautionary point concerning the broker role youth researchers can be expected to play in helping young people access appropriate services and resources, without the expectation that they must always have this information available at their fingertips. Youth researchers, in turn, need to be informed and have the ability to ask for assistance from staff.

One skill that is often overlooked as critical, particularly in qualitative research, is the ability of the researcher to be able to connect with the respondent by being able to share of themselves (S. Howard et al., 2002):

> Peer researchers are often used because of their knowledge and experiences of the particular area being researched. As such, this type of research is about obtaining rich, detailed information and this, it is argued, requires the need for the participant to feel comfortable with the researcher. . . . Accordingly, the researcher needs to be able to share their similar experiences, in this way demonstrating their personal understanding of the issues. The role of personal sharing should be facilitative, not the major focus of the interviews. (p. 14)

A youth's ability to make a respondent comfortable and feel respected, regardless of characteristics and circumstances, facilitates the research process and increases the possibility that the information gathered is reflective of the respondent's experiences and feelings about a particular subject.

Listening Skills

It may seem unusual to think of listening skills as particularly important in a research undertaking. Listening skills are usually relegated to counseling and peer-support interventions that stress the importance of a relationship based on mutual trust. However, on closer scrutiny, listening skills do play such a critical role in any form of research undertaking, and they take on greater prominence in qualitative studies because of their emphasis on dialogue and providing participants with a chance to share their stories or voices. For participants from undervalued communities, it may well be their first opportunity to share their stories. A researcher's abilities to be patient, identify nonverbal cues, and clarify an important point made by the respondent are all examples of good listening skills.

Communication

Communication skills, like listening skills, regarding youth-led research, must be approached from a multifaceted perspective to take into account verbal and nonverbal, written and nonwritten approaches. As I address in the following section, effective communication skills are predicated on a researcher's ability to be flexible and take into account local circumstances, adjusting methods of communication accordingly, and the researcher's ability to convey the central purpose of a question or a research study. Communication skills also come into play when disseminating the results of the research; researchers need to reach the broadest audience possible and do so with very targeted messages.

❖ QUALITIES THAT MAKE FOR AN EXCELLENT YOUTH RESEARCHER

This final section seeks to identify what qualities, or factors, need to be present in youth to help ensure that they have a higher likelihood of succeeding in a research role. Not unexpectedly, there is no research that I could find that highlighted these qualities for youth. Sonnichsen (1994) identifies five attributes for successful adult evaluators that, with certain considerations and modifications, can also be applied to youth: (1) the belief that positive social change is not only desirable but possible, (2) the ability to think critically, (3) possession of credibility, (4) objectivity, and (5) understanding how decisions are made and implemented (pp. 537–538). The reader can rightfully argue that the attributes identified by Sonnichsen (1994) can also be applied to any other form of helping and are not restricted to research. Nevertheless, these attributes take on a particular form when discussed within a research context, and, more specifically, within a youth-led project.

Based on my experience in the field and conversations with youth, I believe that the following eight qualities are essential and do incorporate those identified by Sonnichsen (1994). In many ways, the same qualities that make adults "good" researchers are also those required of youth. Nevertheless, there are certain qualities that stand out for youth in particular. These qualities, not surprisingly, are closely interrelated with the abilities I addressed in the previous section of this chapter.

Embrace of Innovation

Youth who are not afraid of trying something "new" bring a much-needed bravado and spirit of adventure to a research team. These youth are not afraid of failing, and this advantage can be contagious within a research team. Youth-led research, after all, is not just about research, important as that may be in its own right. This form of research is also about learning and setting the stage for positive social change within a community. The very fact that youth exhibit a willingness to be a part of a youth-led research venture separates them from those who are more interested in a sports activity, for example.

Engaging in innovative practice is challenging, exciting, and even fun and provides youth with an opportunity to witness firsthand engaging in a career path that is not associated with economic stagnation and is full of promise for the future (Ferrari, 2003). It also serves to empower them to venture out into new arenas that they may not have seriously considered prior to their involvement in research. Exploration becomes an essential part of the experience, and this will no doubt aid them as they socially navigate distinct worlds, so to speak (Delgado et al., 2005).

Sense of Humor

A sense of humor is a quality that is vastly underrated and, as a result, overlooked in the research field or any other field of practice. A sense of humor goes a long way toward making research fun, particularly when youth encounter situations in the field that no one could have predicted. These situations can result in embarrassing moments. When these experiences are shared with the team, it can open up the team to a willingness to laugh at the experience, which I believe is critical to the research process. The openness that results from this type of process is quite healthy for a research project and for youth who participate in it. It takes on added significance when adults involved in these efforts are also willing to share experiences with youth that can be quite humorous.

Research teams with high numbers of youth who possess a good sense of humor allow the research process to occur in what seems to be a rapid and highly efficient manner. Youth with a sense of humor are excellent in helping to plan events that uplift the morale of the team and thus help diffuse potentially difficult situations. They invariably have a knack for identifying the irony in situations and for helping a research team to stay focused on the tasks at hand. Further, the combination of having a sense of humor and critical insights provides a research team with an opportune situation to learn without suffering assaults on self-esteem. An ability to laugh at oneself can represent a critical aspect of humor.

Critical Thinking Skills

Having an inclination for questioning the world around them and being able to follow through with appropriate questions, use different sources and experiences, and be open to new meanings and interpretations of existing events are very attractive qualities in youth researchers. These skills, in combination with the use of reflection, place youth researchers in the enviable position of making important and highly innovative contributions to theory development and creating services to meet specific youth needs. Further, it legitimizes the process of inquiry and the importance of being open to new ways of looking at circumstances and life itself.

Adults in positions of authority in the lives of youth, however, may not appreciate the very qualities that make for an excellent researcher. Adults may interpret youth's propensity to question as passive-aggressiveness or hostility, a continuing search for new ways of interpreting phenomenon as avoidance of work, and a willingness to use unconventional sources for information as an unwillingness to follow directions. In short, context will be the ultimate determining factor in how these qualities are viewed and embraced by adults.

Patience and Persistence

The qualities of patience and persistence are essential to good research. The process of research is predicated on researchers having a great deal of patience, particularly if they are interested in achieving social change. Although youth invariably bring a great deal of energy and enthusiasm, which can be both positive and negative qualities, a research project is not one that lends itself to researchers who are impatient with the progress of a research project, particularly one that has not been implemented according to plans.

Persistence is a quality that can be labeled in a variety of ways, for example, "dogged," "stubborn," "purposeful," and "tenacious." The embrace of an attitude that the job is not complete until it is complete serves youth researchers quite well in helping them to stay the course during difficult times. Persistence is a quality that can be quite useful in other social arenas in the lives of youth. Nevertheless, it certainly has a home in youth-led research.

Eagerness to Learn About Others and Their Communities

The undertaking of social research provides researchers with an excellent opportunity to venture outside of their immediate world and learn about other worlds. Youth who possess a willingness or, even better, a desire to do this will be better situated for eventual success as a researcher. This natural inquisitiveness is a quality that cannot be easily taught; some would argue that it cannot be taught at all. Depending on the type of research and its goals, youth will be thrust into asking questions and learning more about people outside of their family and immediate peer network.

The process of learning about other cultures will also expose youth to opportunities to learn about themselves. What do I mean by this? When youth are provided with a safe forum from which to ask questions of each other without feeling defensive, and in this interchange youth share about themselves, they become more cognizant of themselves and their cultural traditions, values, and beliefs. This newfound knowledge translates into a more informed research process, and a researcher is better prepared to confront new experiences later on in life that involve various types of people.

Flexibility to Work Alone and in Groups

A research undertaking, youth-led or otherwise, must be staffed by researchers who possess sufficient flexibility in how they carry out their functions on a daily basis. Youth-led research requires youth who can be competent working alone or as part of a team. This does not mean that youth may not have a preference; it does mean that they must step forward regardless of circumstances and operate in a forum (individual or team) that will facilitate the completion of necessary tasks in a project. This quality increases the likelihood that a research team will consist of members who are not fixed in their way, and it opens up the possibility of learning new approaches and experiencing new experiences.

Youth researchers must be willing and able to socially navigate these two worlds and to assume different roles depending on the tasks that need to be accomplished. It also serves as an excellent learning tool for youth because of the varied skills that are necessary when working alone or in a group. Researchers never have the luxury of working in one particular mode. Youth researchers, too, must possess this flexibility and the interpersonal competencies to do likewise.

Resiliency or Tendency to "Bounce Back"

Research undertakings invariably consist of both successes and failures. It is always a pleasure to complete a research project without any serious setbacks or need to significantly readjust some aspect of it. However, this occurrence is rare. Learning to deal with failures is also part of an experienced researcher's repertoire. Extremely valuable lessons learned from negative experiences will ultimately make the researcher that much more competent.

As adults, we realize that setbacks are part of life in professional, as well as personal, life. Youth, however, do not enjoy this perspective. Consequently, possessing the steadfastness or resolve to weather these types of experiences is a quality that takes on significant meaning in youth-led research. This does not mean that provision of a supportive environment is not necessary. However, innate resiliency will go a long way toward helping youth navigate life's unexpected and expected challenges.

Communication Skills Across Audiences

An ability to communicate across age groups is a skill that is comparable to being bilingual. In this case, it makes reference to competencies in language that allow youth to not only converse with peers but also converse and formally present to an adult audience. It should be noted that youth with bilingual language capabilities can be an asset in all aspects of the research, particularly in situations where the community being researched consists of residents whose primary language is not English.

An ability to communicate across disparate audiences and settings takes on significant importance in a research endeavor. Communication, however, must cover both written and verbal spheres. Youth, as a result, must be able to write with two audiences in mind: their peers and adults. Getting the central message across to both audiences is critical in helping to translate research findings into social change. Yet each audience requires a different set of written messages. The same can be said for verbal communication. Presenting to a youth audience takes on different dimensions than presenting to an adult audience. Youth researchers must be able to socially navigate between these two worlds at all times.

❖ CONCLUSION

What makes for an excellent youth researcher? The answer to this question is complex yet no mystery. The influence of attitudes on knowledge acquisition, and then knowledge acquisition on skill development, is well accepted in the field. If youth do not believe in their abilities or the ultimate power of research, it is impossible for them to acquire the requisite knowledge to be able to participate in or lead research projects, regardless of the lofty goals of the project.

The role youth feel most comfortable with because of past experiences and competencies also plays a part in answering the question "What does it take?" Youth who gravitate toward assuming a role such as interviewer or focus group facilitator versus data entry, for example, require a different set of interpersonal qualities to help them carry out their responsibilities. It is important to note, however, that a successful project requires youth with a wide range of qualities, and no one quality can be considered the most important. It takes a team to successfully carry out a research project.

The length of time that it takes to turn out a consumable youth research project will obviously depend on the youth researchers' innate abilities and willingness to learn new roles and techniques, as well as the specific learning opportunities presented to them. In short, numerous factors and considerations will influence the journey. Nevertheless, it would be unreasonable, and even irresponsible, to view this journey as consisting of weeks or months rather than years. A career ladder is one way of thinking about youth as researchers, and like any career ladder, we can expect that reaching the top will take years for those who decide that they see their future as a senior-level researcher or even as an independently funded research scientist.

5

Continuum of Youth Involvement in Research

How best to classify youth-led research efforts presents a conceptual challenge for the field. Classifying youth-led research efforts that are not monolithic in character or "one size fits all" is a challenge not for the faint of heart. Being able to select the most appropriate model based on a series of considerations will result in a higher likelihood of success. It is best to conduct youth-led research projects utilizing a model that effectively identifies the roles and expectations of both youth and adults. Calvert, Zeldin, and Weisenbach (2002) note that the field of youth development will benefit tremendously from further research into a variety of areas and arenas. Youth can play significant roles in defining questions, collecting and analyzing data, and disseminating results. Before they can achieve this, however, there must be a vision in place.

Woods's (1990) vision for youth places them in contributing roles in society, both now and in the future:

> We need young people as democratic citizens . . . (who) will have the ability to use academic skills to make a difference in the world; a sense of the importance and value of their contribution to their

community; a commitment to fundamental values such as equity, justice, and cooperation; and the self-confidence tempered with empathy that it takes to act on behalf of the common good. (p. 34)

Woods's expectations of an active citizen within a democratic society are certainly lofty but well within the grasp of all societies.

Use of a continuum that takes into consideration degree of youth involvement and in decision-making roles along the research path can be an effective tool in helping youth, practitioners, and academics better conceptualize youth-led research. Jones and Perkins's (2002) continuum of youth-adult partnerships is such an example (see Chapter 2). A continuum facilitates the creation of markers or indicators that lend themselves to assessing the progress of the research along distinct stages (Save the Children, 2000):

Before any project begins it is very important to carry out a situation analysis, which is also known as a needs assessment. Central to this process should be the participation of children and young people, as well as other stakeholders. These analyses should focus on the change the project is aiming for and the main barriers to reaching change. Setting indicators for a project in this way is central to any participatory monitoring and evaluation process. (p. 32)

Any serious effort to better understand the role of youth as researchers will necessitate that this vision also involve adults in some manner or degree, depending on the model being used. Adults can fulfill a variety of roles, such as providing expert advice on research-related matters, motivating youth during difficult phases in a research project, role-modeling democratic decision making, validating experiences, helping youth reflect and tie learning experiences to other areas of their lives, and providing advice on personal or social aspects of the lives of youth (Matysik, 2000). Youth-led research, as a result, can take on a variety of forms depending on the setting and the goals that have been established for the research. This flexibility in model selection makes youth-led initiatives, such as those utilizing research, easier to embrace. Rigid models invariably have very limited shelf life. Flexible models, in turn, do not.

In this chapter, I provide the reader with several continuums currently in use from which to compare the various models that can be used in youth-led research and program evaluation. Fortunately, there are various prominent frameworks that focus on increasing youth participation, each lending itself to particular organizational and community considerations. I do not endorse one framework over the others because they all have value. Instead, readers can select the model that best suits their circumstances and purposes.

❖ POTENTIAL PITFALLS OF YOUTH-LED RESEARCH

It is very easy to view youth-led research from a perspective that highlights its potential contributions and ignores its potential limitations. Eschewing potential limitations, however, will only serve to set the field back rather than successfully promote it forward. Consequently, I begin this chapter by discussing limitations, so as to ground the reader in the factors that must be considered prior to conducting youth-led research.

Seven critical areas have been identified that must be seriously considered when advocating for youth-led research. This list is far from exhaustive. Nevertheless, these areas signify important factors or considerations that cannot be ignored in the process of advocating for and initiating youth-led research. The field's willingness and ability to address these issues in an open and fair matter will bode well for the future of youth-led research.

First, youth-led research is not a panacea for all the ills confronting children and youth in this society. Although it clearly has elements of an intervention, it is not an intervention in the same category as other social interventions with a youth focus, such as youth-led community organizing (Delgado & Staples, 2005). I would never recommend research as the only activity in helping youth develop. Youth development programming, for example, is very often highly time and resource intensive with the use of many youth engaging in activities over a prolonged period of time that is best measured in seasons and years rather than weeks or months. Youth-led research would make an excellent corollary to other forms of youth programming, but it should not stand alone as a way to enhance youth competencies. Thus, youth-led research can best be conceptualized as part of a broader field of practice, one that includes other programming dimensions.

Second, although research must ultimately lead to social change, it is important that youth do not overreach and look to research as the primary means of achieving significant social change. Research is the first step. However, major social change is a lengthy and labor-intensive process that cannot be easily predicted and will necessitate youth entering into partnerships and coalitions with adults to achieve success (Delgado & Staples, 2005). If youth enter a research project thinking that once findings are disseminated change will automatically follow, they will be disappointed and may eschew any future role in a research undertaking. This action may well prove to be a terrible disservice to any youth-led movement, but it has particular relevance for youth-led research.

Third, like any tool, youth-led research must be placed in the right hands. Youth-led research can achieve its potential only when planned and implemented by knowledgeable and committed youth and adults. Organizations and communities cannot simply assume that these types of projects can be carried out without the requisite expertise and the willingness to put the time and effort into their planning. To do so will only increase the likelihood of failure. In situations where organizations or communities wish to undertake youth-led research but do not have the necessary expertise, they may wish to collaborate with other institutions and communities that do have the expertise. Youth-led research, like any other form of research, cannot and should not be done by the "seat of one's pants." A healthy respect for the intricacies associated with research will convey to youth the seriousness of their endeavor.

Fourth, youth-led research must be viewed from a broad perspective, and researchers must be willing to integrate innovative methods when the goals of the research warrant it. Innovation for the sake of innovation often results in a lack of focus and the dissipation of valuable energy and commitment; in this case, conventional approaches may be more suitable for the project. Research projects are hard enough to plan and implement without making the process that much more challenging because of a "need" to be innovative when the situation at hand does not require innovation. Innovation brings with it a sense of excitement. Nevertheless, it also brings with it immense responsibility; researchers must be deliberate and sensitive to the inherent nuances of the research.

Fifth, like other forms of participatory research, youth-led research will necessitate considerably more time and energy when compared to conventional research models. This will make the estimation of financial costs more difficult. Youth-led research projects need leaders competent in research, education, and activism—a tall order under most circumstances (Maguire, 1993). In an extended project relying on participatory principles, researchers may well be tempted to use short-cuts. No facet of the research project must be subject to shortcuts regardless of demands on time and expertise. Youth researchers, as a result, must temper their energy and impatience and allow participatory research to run its natural course. It is imperative to emphasize that the process is as important as, or even more important than, the outcome. Shortcutting the process serves to shortcut youth, undermining the very principles on which youth-led research is based.

Sixth, research methodologies that stress participatory goals are not without controversy and debate surrounding the generalization of sociological knowledge. Thus, it can be expected that the findings from youth-led research will undergo more than their rightful share of scrutiny. If, based on the findings, researchers recommend significant change within an organization or community, intense resistance might follow and a harsh critique of research methods and data analysis might ensue. Youth researchers may be disheartened by this reaction and turn away from a possible promising career in research. Youth researchers must be properly prepared for this possible reaction. Reactions such as these may not then be construed as a setback but rather as "natural," effectively relieving tensions and feelings of disappointment.

Seventh, maintaining youth in a research project is a challenge not normally encountered in adult-led and -staffed projects (Anyon & Naughton, 2003):

> Consistent participation was a particular problem. For example, only eight students in the first cohort of sixteen youth researchers met the expected yearlong commitment. Several left because the program was not what they had anticipated. But more troubling were the students forced to leave for reasons unrelated to the project, such as their arrest or their family's eviction. Barriers to full participation came from multiple arenas of the youths' lives, from their school environment to their families' background. (p. 3)

Thus, the realities faced by youth from socially and economically marginalized communities can also find their way into the best-designed project.

The seven considerations that I have outlined here are quite formidable. Nevertheless, these limitations must not hinder the use of youth-led research, as adult-led research, too, has its share of limitations, particularly when it addresses youth-related issues and needs or marginalized communities in general. Each of these limitations or considerations touches on a variety of dimensions pertaining to the research process, those carrying it out, the organizations sponsoring it, and the ultimate beneficiaries of the research, such as youth and the community at large.

❖ FRAMEWORKS FOR YOUTH-LED RESEARCH

There are a number of frameworks that have originated out of the youth-led movement that can easily be used or modified to fit a specific project. These frameworks spell out not only the role of youth but also the role of adults. Norman (2001) does a very good job of capturing the essence of what is meant by youth-adult partnership:

> A true partnership is one in which each party has the opportunity to make suggestions and decisions and in which the contribution of each is recognized and valued. A youth-adult partnership is one in which adults work in full partnership with young people on issues facing youth and/or on programs and policies affecting youth. (p. 1)

To achieve this partnership, however, adults must eschew the propensity of engaging in what is commonly referred to as "adultism." Stoneman (1988), as cited in Mullahey et al. (1999), in what is probably one of the earliest references to the concept of adultism in the professional literature, defines it as

> the attitudes and attendant behaviors that result when adults presume they are better than young people and that young people, because they lack life experience, are, therefore, inferior to adults. . . . As a result young people are talked down to and not seen as contributing individuals with valuable opinions and ideas who are capable of making responsible decisions. Many become passive recipients of information rather than people who assert themselves to voice their particular concerns or viewpoints. (p. 7)

Probably the most widely cited youth-led framework is the one developed by Hart in the early 1990s. Hart (1992) developed an eight-step framework, or ladder, that specifically focuses on the degrees of youth participation, with manipulation of youth by adults on one end and complete youth empowerment on the other end. The first three steps can best be thought of as *nonparticipatory*: (1) *manipulation*; (2) *decoration* (appearances); and (3) *tokenism* (adults include youth but do not act on their suggestions or provide meaningful opportunities to exercise power). Steps four through eight focus on *degrees of meaningful youth participation*: (4) *assigned but informed*; (5) *consulted and informed*; (6) *adult-initiated, shared decisions with youth*; (7) *youth-initiated, shared decisions with youth*; and (8) *youth-initiated, shared decisions with adults*.

Although Hart's framework was not created specifically for youth-led research, it lends itself to this youth activity when taking into consideration the importance of inclusion (Canadian Health Network, 2001; Children's Society, 2001; Edwards, 2000; Scottish Parliament, 2002). This framework specifically addresses the relationship between adults and youth in the decision-making process. In addition, it highlights different key stages regarding youth roles and responsibilities. Each stage represents a distinctive perspective on how adult and youth collaborate and engage in decision making.

R. Campbell's (2002) critique of Hart's (1992) framework brings to the fore a different set of considerations that must be weighed when discussing youth-led initiatives:

> Participation should be able to encompass a wide range of approaches without necessarily presenting a hierarchy of approaches—for example, that an entirely youth-initiated and led activity is automatically superior to one in which adults contribute to initiation and supporting the process. Hart's ladder, although useful in identifying different stages young people might go through in a participation process, unfortunately tempts people to see the highest rung as the holy grail. This concern is particularly important in terms of social inclusion—means of participation must be open to young people who do not necessarily have the personal or social skills, or physical abilities to do things without adult support. (p. 3)

Youth participation, at least the model advocated by R. Campbell (2002), can take on various approaches, all of equal importance, and can accommodate youth of differing abilities and, one could argue, interests and commitments. The balance of youth-adult relationships is influenced accordingly. Merrifield (1993) identifies four critical questions that must be asked and answered before undertaking any form of research:

- Who determines the need for the research?
- Who controls the process of research and makes decisions along the way which affect its outcome?
- Who controls the dissemination of results?
- Where does accountability lie? (p. 83)

The answers to these questions will set the foundation for any research endeavor. However, they take on added prominence within youth-led research because youth are not only possessing but also answering these questions.

The Hart (1992) framework, unlike the other frameworks I discuss in this chapter, specifically sets collaboration between youth and adults as a central goal of any initiative. Other frameworks seek to place only youth, and not adults, in leadership positions and thus represent a more encompassing perspective of youth development. Adults in these frameworks, however, can still be involved in roles dictated by youth needs, and this represents a more encompassing perspective of youth empowerment. Their ultimate role is dependent on how youth define it and not the other way around, which is usually the case in youth initiatives.

Youth in Focus (2002), however, developed a seven-step framework specifically for assessing institutional capacity and readiness for youth-involved research (see Figure 5.1):

- Step 1—No Youth Involvement. This step, unfortunately, represents the prevailing mode in the field of youth services.
- Step 2—Little Youth Involvement. This step typically focuses on viewing youth as an important source of information but does not involve them in any other way.
- Step 3—Low Involvement. Youth assume roles in collecting data but not in conceptualizing or leading the study.
- Step 4—Medium-Low Involvement. Youth play an active role in providing feedback and input into adult-designed questions.
- Step 5—Medium-High Involvement. Youth design and carry out research instruments but do not analyze findings or write reports.
- Step 6—High Involvement. Youth are active throughout the entire research process.

Figure 5.1   Institutional-Youth Readiness Continuum

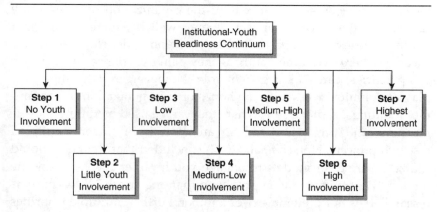

SOURCE: Youth in Focus (2002).

- Step 7—Highest Involvement. Youth not only are involved throughout all facets but are also acting as peer trainers, and the youth-led research is institutionalized as part of an organization's planning cycle.

The importance of organizational readiness and competence cannot be minimized in determining the ultimate success of any youth-led initiatives, including those that are research focused.

Checkoway and Richards-Schuster (2002) present a very good framework consisting of four dimensions for looking at youth research roles: youth as subjects, consultants, partners, and directors. Each of these roles, in turn, is examined in relation to discrete research tasks. There is a need, however, for a broader conceptualization of roles for youth-involved research, along with a more detailed examination of their relationship to research tasks. For example, one possible continuum would have at one end youth as subjects and playing no other role in the research. At the opposite end of the continuum would be research projects that are totally conceptualized and implemented by youth with consultation and advice from adults only when requested. Projects co-led by youth and adults fall just before this latter category. Other models can be placed on the continuum based on the degree of control exercised by youth and the functions they serve on projects. Each of these models would rely on adults stepping back but not disengaging from the research process (Earls & Carlson, 2002).

This continuum helps readers conceptualize what model best meets their needs and the needs of the organization or community sponsoring the research project. It may well be, for example, that youth-led research can best be thought of from a developmental perspective where over time youth, as they gain experience and develop competencies, can play a greater role. However, initially they may play only limited roles with the hopes of an organization or community building a cadre of researchers that can be used by different organizations and projects. Based on an analysis of fifteen youth-led research projects, Horsch et al. (2002) concluded that the field should utilize a variety of models to engage youth rather than rely on one model: "We conclude by emphasizing that one approach to youth as researchers is not preferable over another. Further, multiple priorities can be met in the same youth-involved research and evaluation project" (p. 7).

This flexibility has both advantages and disadvantages for the field. It allows local circumstances and goals to dictate the most optimal research approach. Nevertheless, this flexibility places a tremendous amount of pressure on organizations and communities to recruit, train, support, and sustain a cadre of youth researchers with the necessary research competencies—no easy task, particularly in socially and economically undervalued communities.

❖ CATEGORIZING YOUTH-LED RESEARCH PROJECTS

Categorizing youth-led projects represents an important conceptual step in explaining the nature and expansiveness of the field. The reader, as a result, must be prepared to embrace an expansive view of social research when it includes youth-led research. This expansive conceptualization of research can prove quite exciting from a practice perspective because of the endless possibilities for youth to use new and highly imaginative methods. Conversely, the expansive perspective can create a tremendous amount of confusion and anxiety in deciding what research is and how it relates to more conventional and widely embraced methods.

Is there such a thing as a typical youth-led research initiative? Based on an extensive review of the field, J. C. Smith (2001) found that there is no typical research and evaluation project or initiative:

There seems to be no "typical" evaluation and research project that involves youth. Most of those we talked to grounded their work in youth development practices that are asset-based, incorporating a possible youth development focus within the context of evaluation and research work. They mentioned different frameworks for this work including youth development, risk and prevention, participatory action research, community development, and empowerment evaluation. Those who engage in this work focus on establishing youth as partners or leaders in the research and evaluation endeavor, involving youth in determining the right questions to ask, designing and conducting the study, and engaging with the community and other decision-makers in a discussion of findings and action steps. (p. 1)

This flexibility in conceptualizing youth-led research, as already noted, can be both a reward and a challenge for the field (P. Campbell et al., 1994).

There are numerous examples of youth-led initiatives. However, regardless of type, they are usually founded on one basic premise that connects each of these diverse endeavors by a common purpose (Youth Research Institute, 2002). This premise, broadly speaking, seeks to identify youth assets, commitments, visions, and barriers that either facilitate or hinder the completion of key developmental tasks or stages. Completion of these stages is a prerequisite for opening up opportunities for career advancement and personal growth.

It is best to think of youth-led research methods and approaches as falling into three distinct arenas represented by concentric circles, such as an inner circle that is referred to as "Conventional," a surrounding circle called "Emerging," and the final outer circle referred to as "Unorthodox" (see Figure 5.2).

Conventional methods and approaches signify highly accepted and utilized research designs and methods that are widely covered in the professional literature, in the field of practice, and in academic training programs. Emerging methods and approaches are exciting and slowly are being considered conventional research. Oral histories, a qualitative research method that recognizes the importance of data emerging from interviews, are probably the best example of a research method working its way into the mainstream of research.

Unorthodox methods and approaches represent innovations in the field that have found places within research agendas, but most

Figure 5.2   Youth-Led Research Methods and Approaches Circles

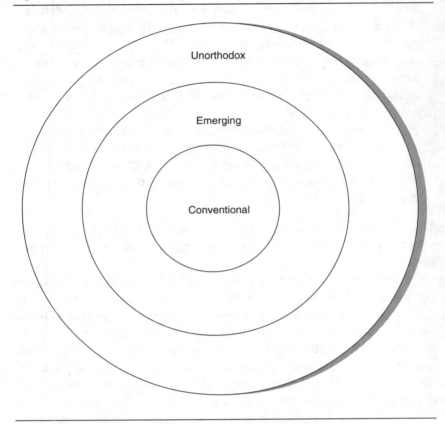

researchers either have not heard of them or, if they have, do not have an in-depth understanding and appreciation of what they entail. Whether these methods eventually find their way into emerging methods and approaches or achieve a conventional status will be determined in time. Use of photographs or sketches done by youth, analysis of community murals, videos, and art projects typically fall into this category.

Distinguishing between a project that can be categorized as "art" (such as a photography exhibit by a group of youngsters) and a research project using photography requires examination of the (a) goals of the project, (b) degree of collective effort in the training and implementation of the project, (c) level of analysis of findings incorporating individual and collective interpretation, and (d) evaluation process and outcomes. These four dimensions help the process of determination.

The final product that is often an artifact of a conventional research project does not have to be a written report. It can be a video, photographic exhibit, or an actual social change that can be measured. The ultimate success of researchers undertaking "emerging" or "unorthodox" research rests on their methods for communicating the results of their research to each other and to those doing conventional research, and providing documentation of the effectiveness of these methods to the "scientific" world (Brydon-Miller, 1993).

Whether one method or approach transcends a category is very much determined by the interplay of a variety of key factors, such as the degree of academic support and funding. I suggest youth researchers be open to using innovative and therefore controversial research tools and approaches in the field. The development of new ways to solicit answers to research questions effectively opens up new population groups that can participate in research. The effective inclusion of these groups may well represent the hallmark of youth-led research. Organizational and community support for or against certain methods will ultimately dictate the best match between research methods and goals.

❖ CONCLUSION

The field of youth-led research is certainly not suffering from the absence of frameworks influencing the conceptualization and implementation of research. As I have shown in this chapter, the importance of research frameworks is not to be underestimated, as frameworks serve a variety of important roles, not least of which is to inform scholarship. Nevertheless, frameworks play an instrumental role in helping to shape practice by helping practitioners organize their goals and tasks along developmental lines and thus helping youth researchers acquire a better understanding and appreciation of how research projects bear similarities and differences with the planning of a program or service.

Further, from my standpoint and that of other advocates, the field of youth-led research is still very much in its infancy and will no doubt enrich the general field of social research before the movement is no longer considered a "movement" but part of the establishment. There are numerous highly innovative ways that youth can carry out the role of social researcher, and this certainly bodes well for the future of this field. Determination of how and when these methods are embraced by the broader field of social research is impossible to predict, although it is hoped that a responsible and systematic process is followed. Anything short of this would be a great disappointment and would limit the potential of the youth-led research field to progress.

6

Youth-Led Research
and Methods

The previous five chapters have served to prepare the reader
for examining youth in their role as social researchers within a
youth-led context. It is a role that, I believe, is well suited for several
asset-based paradigms, not least of which is youth development. The
conceptualization of the research process is similar for youth as it is
for adults, with significant modifications to take into account the age of
the youth and the goals of the project (Hill, 1997). Because youth-led
research unites youth from latency to late adolescence to early twen-
ties, it is appealing to youth-centered programs. Youth-led research is
arguably the only youth-led movement that can encompass such a
wide age distribution.

It is important to pause and note that the role of researcher cannot
be performed by just anyone. Specific and significant considerations
related to character, competencies, and attitudes influence who is best
suited for undertaking research. Or there may be circumstances where
youth are best suited for particular roles within the research process but are not comfortable with or competent to fulfill other roles.
Assessing the proclivities and competencies to match role expectations

with youth is but one dimension, although a critical one, of youth-led research.

I have divided this chapter into three categories for the purposes of discussing how youth-led research is and can be incorporated in an organization's research and program evaluation agenda: (1) research methods, (2) quantitative research methods, and (3) qualitative research methods.

❖ RESEARCH METHODS

It is important to make sure that the reader is exposed to both quantitative and qualitative forms of youth-led research. In discussing the latter, however, I focus on the use of ethnographic-specific research. I provide an extensive review of research methods and how they have been, or can be, modified to take into account the age and background of youth. I pay particular attention to how cultural factors and considerations influence research method selection.

Social research offers an abundance of perspectives, approaches, and methods through which to answer important social questions. These broad possibilities are not restricted to adult-led research but are also applicable to youth-led research. The "best" method, as a result, is contingent on a series of considerations, such as time, funding, organizational capacity, sources of legitimacy (expertise, institutional, ethical, and consumer), and the importance of creating momentum for achieving social change. Lengthy discussion and deliberations must be structured toward making decisions. This requires time, but it is time that is well invested for orienting and guiding research team members.

The Youth Justice Coalition/Free LA organization (McGillicuddy, 2003), in commenting on a juvenile justice youth-led research project, brings up other factors and considerations that necessitate the expenditure of time:

> You are often engaged in developing, conducting, transcribing and assessing surveys, interviews and personal stories. You learn to avoid bias in the development of questionnaires and interview techniques, as well as the importance of both valuing others' experiences and opinions and selecting a representative sample of people to reach out to. (p. 3)

Stubbs (1996) notes that the discussion of the "best" appropriate research method is often limited by a rather narrow interpretation of methods:

> Discussions on evaluation methodology are often limited to a discussion of "methods"—tools to be used for data collection. But methodology is much more than methods, it is about human behaviour, attitudes, principles, beliefs about knowledge, power relationships, and ultimately it depends on our own deep-seated beliefs about why we are involved in an evaluation. (p. 12)

Although Stubbs's observations are related to program evaluation, they are still applicable to community-based research in general and serve as a warning for those advocating one specific approach toward youth-led research. A narrow interpretation of what is "best" does a serious injustice to the field.

The universe of social research is so vast that it is virtually impossible to truly comprehend it, let alone define its parameters. Further, it is ever expanding in all directions. Youth-led research lends itself to both quantitative and qualitative approaches. The nature of the research question, just as with adult-led research, must ultimately determine the preferred methods. Both research approaches necessitate that youth receive high-quality training: Some of the training is core regardless of methods and some training is specific to a particular method (I address this later in the chapter).

Research and program evaluation can be broken down into a series of developmental steps that in turn lend themselves to specific goals and planning activities. This breakdown not only facilitates the carrying out of the research but also facilitates the training and supervision of staff. The following ten-step framework represents a common way of operationalizing a research undertaking:

1. Preplanning

2. Recruitment, orientation, and team building

3. Study design

4. Staff training

5. Data collection

6. Data analysis

7. Report writing

8. Press conference/community meetings

9. Celebration

10. Next research/action steps (Youth in Focus, 2002, pp. 28–30)

Each of these steps brings with it a multitude of primary and secondary goals, objectives, and tactics. A developmental approach to research necessitates that each step must be addressed sequentially before movement to the next step can transpire.

Youth-led research, like community-based research as conceptualized by Strand et al. (2003), can incorporate conventional, emerging, or unorthodox methods such as community forums, video documentaries, legislative records, shared testimonies, public art, and mural creation and analysis.

The use of multiple techniques and methods in youth-led research is exciting from a research standpoint. However, multiple methods are rarely done concurrently, as each is based on a sequential time frame, which requires one stage to be completed in order to inform the questions and subject selected for the following stages. Delays in one stage have immediate and long-range implications, often resulting in a set of frustrations for researchers. The multifaceted research approach, nevertheless, offers much potential for youth to get their questions answered and provides them ample opportunities to experience different forms of research, including identifying the one(s) they are most comfortable with. Finding their niche within the research field is important in the case of adults and is that much more important in the case of youth. Some research approaches fit well with the personality, goals, and competencies that youth possess and other do not. Finding the right one can go a long way toward encouraging youth to pursue research careers.

When these types of research initiatives are undertaken, a tremendous amount of training, supervision, consultation, and field support is required, not unlike that experienced in youth-involved research. Despite all of these challenges, multifaceted research approaches seem to be the norm in youth-led research. Such approaches lend themselves to the flexibility to take into account resources, goals, and youth proclivities and competencies.

❖ QUALITATIVE/ETHNOGRAPHIC METHODS

Qualitative research focused on children and youth has its set of challenges (Grave & Walsh, 1998). These challenges manifest themselves throughout the research process, including interpretations and reporting of findings. Greig and Taylor (1999) also note the unique challenges and ethical considerations of research focused on children and youth. Nevertheless, qualitative research offers the field of youth-led research a tremendous potential to make significant contributions to research methods. Qualitative methods, challenges notwithstanding, encourage exploration and generally refrain from a priori judgments. Youth, as a result, bring a fresh perspective to interpretation of findings, although youth certainly are not perfect (Perry-Williams, 1998).

There is general agreement in the field that qualitative methods are particularly attractive for use in youth-led research (Horsch et al., 2002). Curry and Bloome (1998), for example, extol the many virtues of ethnography as a research tool and as a means of teaching students how to write. Ethnographic research also offers youth the benefits of addressing themes of diversity and learning about diverse cultures within their communities. An ethnographic research project, as a result, can easily incorporate a range of educational and social goals. Curry and Bloome's (1998) project incorporated three goals: (1) legitimize community knowledge; (2) acquire an ethnographic framework regarding knowledge, learning, and writing; and (3) apply an ethnographic framework to academic writing.

Mercado (1998) sees the value of ethnographic research as a vehicle for students from marginalized backgrounds to learn how to scribe (obtaining and taking notes), plan, reflect, and share. These educational skills are fostered through the use of observations and interactions, which are also skills of utility for students in other realms or arenas. The concept of "authentic purposes" gives increased power to the above listed competencies.

Cheshire and Edwards (1998) document the use of small-scale projects in which children record in a notebook the different phrases that they hear in the course of a day for greeting, thanking, or taking leave of people. Another project entailed children recording dialect vocabulary used within their respective communities that may not be understood by outsiders. Expanding the linguistic awareness of children through research helps students understand how words and phrases are influenced by context, thereby helping them navigate between different social worlds. The classroom, in essence, has been transformed from a setting for text reproduction to workshops for conducting inquiry (Cheshire & Edwards, 1998). Finally, Andrade (1998) sees tremendous value in using ethnographic methods for elementary school children in ascertaining how children experience, and perceive, their lives within and outside school. These ethnographic reflections help teachers be better able to instruct and also place children in a teacher role in and out of school.

Ethnographic tools, which can consist of a variety of types, lend themselves to the goals of the research and to the inclinations and competencies of students carrying out the research. Use of participant observations, dialogue journals, and oral histories can become effective vehicles for youth to transmit knowledge and can also serve purposes in other dimensions of their lives not related specifically to a research undertaking. Ethnographic research can serve as an effective vehicle for demystifying knowledge and modes of inquiry and, in the process, empower youth.

Qualitative research offers the tremendous advantage of humanizing and personalizing the research process. However, this very advantage can also be considered a disadvantage (Patton, 1990):

> Because qualitative methods are highly personal and interpersonal, because naturalistic inquiry takes the researcher into the real world where people live and work, and because in-depth interviewing opens up what is inside people—qualitative inquiry may be more intrusive and involve greater reactivity than surveys, tests, and other quantitative approaches. (p. 356)

Perry-Williams (1998), for example, found in a youth-led research project that youth, even after extensive training in the use of research techniques, still displayed an unsympathetic view toward the children they were interviewing even though these children shared the same circumstances as the evaluators. Evaluators tended to dominate discussions and generally rushed through the interview sessions, effectively displaying behavior that could be construed as aggressive. After further training using role playing to demonstrate the importance of empathy, youth evaluators grew increasingly more sensitive and matured as interviewers.

Even though screening and training can go a long way toward selecting and preparing youth to become researchers, follow-up is needed to ensure that youth, like their adult counterparts, are carrying out their responsibilities in a professional and sensitive manner. This field assessment must not be construed as "spying" on youth, but rather, it is a method of helping to improve their understanding of the challenges inherent in social research, and it is a method that is used with adults as well. Research methods can consist of an extensive variety of types, depending on organizational preferences and the nature of the research/evaluation questions being addressed. Some of these methods, in turn, are more labor intensive (training, field support, consultation) and expensive than others. These methods, in addition, can be used in combination with each other and can be conducted strategically to build on study findings. Based on the number of professional publications and presentations on the subject, qualitative, and particularly ethnographic, research has certainly found a prominent role within youth-led research. Like its quantitative counterpart, qualitative research, ethnographic in particular, has its vociferous advocates, including this author.

Qualitative research, particularly when researchers put undue emphasis on the verbal abilities of the respondent, also has its share of critics. Biklen and Moseley (1998), for example, raise warnings about how some forms of qualitative research place too much emphasis on verbal language abilities: "The dependence of the qualitative researcher on language and the image of the ideal informant as an articulate person may call for some creative tactics in the face of an informant who cannot verbally inform" (p. 156). Qualitative research, nevertheless, does not have to be dependent on verbal competencies. Observational techniques can play a critical role in helping to address the concerns raised by Biklen and Moseley (1998) and lend themselves very well to youth-led research.

Key Informants

The key informant, or the systematic use of an expert judgment method, has enjoyed a considerable amount of popularity within all phases of a research study (Averch, 1994). The use of key informants in a research process offers the researcher a great deal of flexibility in conceptualizing who is to be considered a key informant on the subject content being studied. The use of key informants, unlike the other qualitative methods covered in this chapter, is relatively low labor-intensive to implement, less costly, and easier to plan and implement.

Further, it provides youth with an immense degree of latitude in determining with whom they feel best matched in conducting interviews.

The use of key informants–focused research allows youth to develop a set of criteria of who is to be considered as knowledgeable, and accessible enough, to warrant inclusion in this type of study. This method also lends itself to youth researchers who consider themselves too shy to conduct focus groups or community forums. Key informants are very often individuals who are considered by their position and behavior to be exemplary within a community and therefore wield considerable influence in shaping opinions. These individuals are important to involve in a research study not only because of their perspectives on particular conditions or issues but also because of their influence in demanding change once results are obtained and disseminated within an organization or community.

However, it is critical that youth researchers establish a clear and uniformly accepted criterion of whom to include in a study. Failure to establish this criterion will ultimately mean that everyone, and no one, can qualify. The use of key informants also presents challenges to researchers when they pose very open-ended questions. The recording of responses, which sometimes means the use of recording devices and transcription, may make this method very labor-intensive, thus expensive. If recording devices are not used, then youth must be able to carry out an interview and write responses simultaneously, not an easy task for any researcher, let alone an inexperienced one.

Selection of youth key informants, particularly those who come by reputation rather than position within an organization or community, requires an active group process. The group should determine how to operationalize the selection criteria, the preferred method of contacting individuals, and the method of conducting interviews. The more the process of selection and interview is standardized, the less likely that bias will be introduced into this method. What can appear to be an easy method to plan and carry out can easily be converted into one that is labor intensive and controversial, although it is a method with good promise.

Focus Groups

The undertaking of research utilizing focus groups is one that appeals to many researchers, regardless of their abilities to actually conduct them properly. Focus groups have developed a reputation in the field of social research as an easy method to use. This is far from true, however. Focus groups bring tremendous value to a research undertaking, but if true to their principles, they are quite arduous to carry out.

Focus groups, according to the American Statistical Association (1997), can be considered in-depth, qualitative interviews with a small number of carefully selected participants. These types of groups can discuss a range of social topics. Data derived from focus groups provide a unique perspective on a particular issue (American Statistical Association, 1997):

> Unlike the one-way flow of information in a one-to-one interview, focus groups generate data through the give and take of group discussion. Listening as people share and compare their different points of view provides a wealth of information—not just about what they think, but why they think the way they do. (p. 1)

Focus groups provide researchers with an excellent method for obtaining qualitative data within a group context, unlike most qualitative methods, which emphasize a one-to-one relationship (Dean, 1994).

As already noted, focus groups have historically enjoyed a tremendous amount of appeal in community research and program evaluation. In fact, it is virtually impossible to find anyone in the human service or education field that has either not been a participant in a focus group or even led such a group. This popularity is both a blessing and a detriment to the use of focus groups in youth-led research efforts. It is my opinion that many, even the vast majority, of these efforts have not been true to focus group protocol and process (Krueger, 1988; D. L. Morgan, 1993). Consequently, one of the major challenges facing researchers in their use of focus groups is the wide range of interpretations of what constitutes a focus group.

Giri (1995) and Boyden and Ennew (1997), for example, advocate for the use of youth focus groups when the leaders are adults. Because youth outnumber adults, who are usually represented by one leader or co-leader, focus groups represent a viable way of minimizing or breaking down power differentials between the researcher and children and youth group members. Focus groups with youth, and led by youth, can generate perspectives often missed with a one-to-one method because of the synergistic effects of youth interacting and responding to each other. The degree of excitement pertaining to a particular perspective, for example, is much easier to judge in a focus group format than in a one-to-one format.

Youth in one youth-led project (VALIDITY) were involved in all facets of a series of focus groups of youth service providers, including analyzing the data and developing a conference to present their findings. This conference, in turn, provided a forum for generating new intervention initiatives. In addition, as will be noted in this book's Epilogue, youth-run conferences serve important sociopolitical purposes that advance the youth-led movement.

The Seattle Youth Involvement Network (2000) undertook a series of six focus groups of youth ages 14 to 17 to identify potential barriers to youth involvement. Time was set aside at the start of the groups to allow participants to socialize, eat, and fill out requisite demographic profile forms. This socializing was considered an important element for youth, because it provided them an opportunity to develop ease with the process, and each other, prior to the formal structure and process of a focus group.

Focus groups, however, bring with them a number of considerations and limitations, regardless of age focus and the ages of the facilitators. Group composition should be as homogeneous as possible, as the unit of analysis is the group. Mixing participants from different sociodemographic backgrounds effectively compromises the data. Group participant recruitment necessitates considerable attention, which means money and time, to group composition. The quality of the data, like that of any other qualitative method, is very much dependent on the skills of the group moderator. Analysis of data, particularly when content is transcribed, can prove very expensive. This can be extremely challenging when focus group members' codeswitch languages in cases where English may not be the primary language of participants. Finally, data are not generalizable, or subject to, statistical methods in the case of those researchers who are quantitatively oriented, although the data can augment other forms of data.

Although focus groups often are a viable way to elicit responses from children and youth, this method has limitations when used in youth-led research:

1. Youth, particularly those who are unaccustomed to being asked for their opinions, may provide socially appropriate answers.

2. Some cultures consider discussion of some topics outside of the home to be taboo and thus do not lend themselves to discussion in a group.

3. Group methods may not be politically acceptable within some countries because of fear that they may be revolutionary in nature, and members may not feel politically safe or may fear for their parents' safety.

4. Some children and youth may not feel comfortable speaking before a group.

5. Focus groups are the unit of analysis in a study and considerable time and effort are required to make the group members as homogeneous as possible; with youth, this may require considerable attention to sample.

6. Developing competencies to conduct focus groups requires considerable attention to selecting the right youth for the role and providing extensive training and support.

Group facilitation skills are much more demanding than one-to-one methods; at least that has been my experience. Consequently, screening youth for the right temperament and social skills represents an initial, and critical, step in designing youth-led focus groups.

It is important to note that although focus groups have historically been structured to transpire with participants in a circle, and to last approximately 90 minutes or so, youth participants may not feel comfortable sitting in a circle. Generally, my experience has been that youth move around, sit in different parts of a room, and eat while the focus group is meeting. It is not advisable to force youth to sit in circles or to disallow eating during the proceedings.

The model used in Sarasota, Florida, is an ambitious youth-led research project involving multiple methods and spanning an extended period of time. Eleven youth ages 14 to 17 participated (K. M. Brown et al., 2000; Bryant et al., 2000). This project utilized a qualitative, formative research model involving youth leading 22 focus groups and conducting 131 interviews for a total of 225 subjects. The research centered on ascertaining youth opinions of current interventions, interventions with a high probability of success, behavioral determinants, and the influence of parents in modeling alcohol and smoking behaviors. Not unexpectedly, youth received extensive training and support to conduct these focus groups.

Community Forums

The concept of town meeting, or forum, has a long and distin-guished history in New England, although it can be found throughout the United States. The meetings serve a variety of public functions. However, first and foremost, they bring together the citizenry of a com-munity to share and plan. Community forums, unfortunately, have not received the attention they deserve as a vehicle for undertaking community-centered research. This form of research can be imple-mented in a variety of ways, thus making it rather attractive for social research in general, and for youth-led research in particular. Forums can, for example, be utilized during the initial planning stages of a research project to inform the community about the upcoming research and to obtain information to help guide the development of research questions and methodologies.

The concept of the Youth Town Meeting has emerged as a way of having community forums specially tailored to tap youth input (Gloucester County Youth Council, 2002). These meetings can be simultaneously broadcast on local cable television stations to reach other youth and the greater community. Further, these types of town meetings can be held throughout all stages of a research project to provide opportunities for reactions.

Community forums provide researchers and the broader commu-nity with a chance to come together to discuss common concerns and plan interventions. Community forums provide an excellent method for obtaining data and for sharing findings with the community. Youth researchers in school-based studies, for example, can convene a student body in a school forum to share results and obtain feedback on priorities for action. The sharing of research findings in a public arena is highly unusual, but it is an effective way to involve residents in a process that generally eschews their participation and input. Community forums, in addition, are great venues for inviting the local media to record findings and recommendations for changes. These forums are also great opportunities to teach youth researchers how to engage in effective public speaking, a task with unlimited potential for leadership development.

Community Mapping

There are arguably few areas of research in the past decade that have captured the imagination and attention of youth-led researchers more than community asset mapping. This form of research, I believe, best epitomizes all of the fundamental values and principles undergirding youth-led research. Its emergence as a bona fide research method has gained widespread acceptance in this country (Annie E. Casey Foundation, 2001). This acceptance has, in large part, been fostered by the work of McKnight and Kretzmann (1990). Its use has encompassed needs, as well as asset assessment. It is the latter focus that has drawn the greatest attention because of the manner in which it has stressed community participation and decision making and community capacity enhancement.

According to O'Looney (1998), community mapping serves at least four major goals, all of which set the stage for community capacity enhancement:

Mapping describes a complex act that includes efforts to: (1) understand the human world as a landscape that includes physical, sociological, and cultural aspects and values; (2) identify areas that exhibit a degree of unity; (3) explain why things are where they are; and (4) identify points of strategic opportunity for positive social action and policy development. (pp. 201–202)

The Center for Youth Development and Policy Research (1995a) conceptualized the community youth mapping process as consisting of ten essential steps:

1. Identification of a converging organization
2. Formation of a public/private nonprofit community advisory board
3. Designation of a lead agency or organization
4. Definition of what "community" means
5. Recruitment of the mapping team
6. Development of the mapping protocol
7. Training of mapping team
8. Actual mapping field work
9. Analysis of mapping results
10. Reporting and using the findings

This community capacity enhancement method, depending on local circumstances (e.g., large census tracts) or weather (e.g., high heat and humidity or cold), can prove quite demanding. Nevertheless, mapping can also be fun, interesting, energizing, and offer a wealth of lessons and information for youth and their communities. Youth are thus provided with an opportunity to see their community through a different set of lenses—one that stresses assets rather than the customary deficits.

The reader can no doubt see a significant degree of similarity to other youth-led research methods. However, the premise on which community asset mapping is based is significantly different from those of other research methods: namely, the identification of community assets to be mobilized in collaboration with community-based organizations. These assets, in turn, can be conceptualized in a variety of ways to take into account age, gender, and other sociodemographic factors of the community being studied. The broadening of the concept of resources or assets, like the broadening of the concept of knowledge and expertise, has proved exciting in the field due to its shift in premise emphasizing that all communities have assets, formal as well as informal. The term *enhancement* versus *development* is deliberate as enhancement is premised on resources being present, whereas development is premised on having to put resources into place as there are no or limited resources there (Delgado, 1999).

The following description of a community mapping project typifies the nature of this type of research when undertaken by youth (Center for Youth Development and Policy Research, 1995a):

> Young people canvassing their neighborhoods in search of places to go and things to do. Young people called mappers canvass their neighborhoods, using a survey tool, to gather baseline information on the resources available to young people, children and their families in the communities. (p. 3)

This method can never be labeled as passive; it is a labor-intensive method that requires careful planning, coordination, and field support. Youth will be taxed not only intellectually but also physically.

Community asset mapping generally attempts to develop a greater understanding of four key community dimensions (O'Looney, 1998):

1. Develop a comprehensive awareness of a community's physical, sociological, cultural, and values parameters.

2. Identify commonalties and unity among residents.

3. Develop a greater understanding of a community's history.

4. Identify opportunities for positive social action and policy development.

Each of these areas, in turn, can be specifically tailored to youth. This form of mapping is a labor-intensive process, as it usually entails having youth go out and identify and assess informal resources. There are no resources directories that have this information. These informal resources may not be used to being interviewed, making the process of eliciting pertinent information arduous.

The outcomes of community mapping can take on various forms, depending on the goals established to guide it, such as generation of data specific to youth programs, generation of data on broader social questions that can be shared with participating agencies/organizations, establishment and strengthening of adult and youth collaborative relationships for other arenas and endeavors, and creation of partnerships between community and organizations (Autz, Dillon, & Quay, 2001; Center for Youth Development and Policy Research, 1995b; Delgado, 1998, 1999). There certainly is flexibility in developing concrete outcomes that can be used to achieve social change. In the case of youth-led research, these changes take on greater prominence when the community asset mapping has focused on the state of youth within the community (Schaafsma, 1998).

Delphi Technique

I imagine that most readers have never heard of the Delphi Technique as a research tool (Averch, 1994; Molnar & Kammerud, 1977). Because it is not a commonly used method, the reader may well ask, why is Delphi being brought into any discussion related to youth-led research? It stresses participation across a wide spectrum of people. It does not require face-to-face contact and, as a result, is not expensive. It lends itself to modifications to take into account a range of factors, such as funding, timing, age of participant, and communication abilities. Further, it is often an excellent initial step in helping to develop a more focused research agenda with very specific questions, which then lends itself to more conventional research methods. Data can be gathered on a community's most treasured asset or problem, depending on the goals of the research. Data, in addition, are also gathered on the public's perception of alterability of a problem or enhancement of an asset.

I have found the Delphi Technique to have much appeal for use in youth-led projects. Its appeal takes on added significance for youth researchers who have had limited experience in conducting research sponsored by an organization other than a school. The flexibility inherent in this method (e.g., number of panel members and respondents) lends itself to a wide range of goals ranging from less ambitious to extremely ambitious, based on the experiences of the researchers, their funding, and the time limit. Data derived from this method can be used to guide researchers in developing very specific research questions and methods.

Oral History

The slow but steady emergence of the use of oral history as a qualitative research technique has led to its use in youth-led research. Youth are often the focus of numerous news stories and reports, yet rarely are they encouraged to share their own stories in their own words. According to the Heritage Community Foundation (2002b):

> An oral history project attempts to preserve a small segment of a relatively recent historical period as viewed through the eyes, experiences, and memories of people who lived during that time. Capturing their experiences and memories is invaluable. Over a period of time, memories can fade and those feelings or emotions associated with the events can easily be lost or altered by time. (p. 1)

Oral histories provide respondents with a forum to share stories, personal information, and insights that because of their position, as in the case of those who are unvalued in this society, may well be considered insignificant and not worth seeking. These perspectives would be totally lost without a concerted effort to capture them and situate the material in places such as libraries, schools, and other community settings that open access to all interested in learning more about the respondent and the historical period being studied. The results of oral history projects have particular appeal because the respondents are real people who live in the community.

Oral history traditions within certain racial and ethnic groups facilitate the use of this method to capture knowledge that would otherwise go unreported in mainstream scholarly publications and research and the general media. Oral histories can be conducted in a variety of ways. Probably the most common is to have one interviewer with a respondent. However, it is possible to pair interviewers or to have a fishbowl format (Heritage Community Foundation, 2002a).

The fishbowl method is often used as a training tool. It can involve a classroom with a teacher modeling an interview process. After a predetermined period of time, the guest leaves, and the teacher gets reactions from the class on how the process transpired. Students, as a result, are provided with a chance to witness an oral history interview. Teachers can assign homework to reinforce lessons, such as responses to the content learned, development of questions that would have been appropriate to ask, and suggestions for how to improve the interview style.

Even though oral history projects can be initiated within and outside of classrooms, historically a strong case has been made for using this method in schools. This method is anything but tedious and lacking relevance for students. Youth are placed in the position of authority by asking questions and soliciting responses. In similar fashion to other methods, oral histories have advantages and disadvantages in youth-led research. This method relies on a respondent's recollection of events that may have occurred a long time ago, making recollection arduous. If the event was traumatic, the emotional content may be too great to discuss in a coherent and informative manner. This content, as a result, may be too stressful for both the respondent and the interviewer. Biases held by both parties are an integral part of the process (Heritage Community Foundation, 2002b).

The advantages of oral history projects are considerable and that is why they can play important roles within youth-led research. These projects can be sufficiently flexible in how they are constructed to allow for a range in the number of interviews that can be conducted. Interview sessions can be extensive, requiring multiple visits and extended hours, or one-shot sessions of limited duration. It is preferable for interviews to be conducted in person, but they do not have to be. Equipment such as video or tape recorders is optional.

The Mothers on the Move Oral History Project (New York City) is an excellent example of how youth can undertake community-based research using oral history methods and capture the insiders' perspectives on how this organization addressed achievement gaps in public education. In the process of addressing this goal, much is also learned about community and the external forces that shape outcomes.

The story of Jeunesse Jackson, age 14, reveals the multitude of benefits to be derived from undertaking an oral history project (Mothers on the Move, 2004):

> I found out about this project through my mother. Because she is a member of Mothers on the Move, she was able to get the information about it easily. She told me about it and I grew very interested. I wanted to understand why where I lived was so much poorer than where my friends lived. I wanted to know why the schools were so bad and what MOM was doing for them. I also participated in this project to learn about MOM from a different perspective. I wanted to understand what it was about from some of their members. Along with that, I also wanted to meet intelligent people just like me that had some sort of connection with me. Going into the project I had many questions and I figured the project would give me the answers. (p. 3)

The nature of oral histories allows this method to be a part of other methods, qualitative or quantitative in focus. Oral histories add the perspectives of depth and context to findings. Multifaceted youth-led research projects do not have to consist totally of expensive or labor-intensive methods. Oral history projects can be highly focused or broad in scope. There is no magical number of interviews that are required and no specific number of questions or time period for each interview. The goals of the project and local circumstances, such as funding, time constraints, and competencies of the interviewer, determine the nature and scope of oral history research.

The Canadian Heritage Community Foundation provides extensive background, practice guides, training curriculum, and an extensive listing of potential projects and questions to use in oral history research. Oral history projects require interviewers to conduct themselves in a professional and dignified manner and necessitate that they obtain signed release agreements at their first interview (Hicke, 2002). The flexibility of this method should not be interpreted as not having high standards of conduct, as there is a need for extensive training and support.

Review of Historical Archival Data

Historical archival data open up the research process to include nonrespondent-generated data. The use of archival data in youth-led research has generally been unexplored, even though this form of research can be inexpensive to implement and provides youth researchers with considerable flexibility in how to use the data.

Youth Justice Coalition/Free LA (McGillicuddy, 2003) provides an excellent example of the power of archival research from a social justice perspective. This organization developed a social change campaign focused on the high incarceration of youth in Los Angeles. They started the research process by developing a chronology of law enforcement policies and practices over 400 years. The historical context not only served to help youth of color better understand the historical significance of this problem, but it also helped them understand the immense challenge they faced. Archival research set the foundation from which youth could develop participatory research methods and instruments to gather data on the current problem of youth incarceration.

Another innovative project involving archival records is the one undertaken by MYTOWN (Boston). Youth undertook research on historical and contemporary events shaping the experiences of community residents over a 100-year period (1895–present). Youth used oral and written historical accounts and then led a tour of their community for outsiders. Youth effectively combined historical data with current accounts of life in the community (Horsch et al., 2002).

Probably one of the major obstacles to using archival data is the attitude youth may possess toward reviewing records of any kind. This form of research may be perceived as boring and not significant in bringing about major social change within a community. This is not true. Archival research, however, is not for every youth researcher, just as searching the Internet is not. Nevertheless, it has a rightful place within a menu of research methodologies that can be used in youth-led research.

The nature of archival research can be quite broad and inclusive of many different sources of data. Thus, it is necessary to this form of research. Archival research represents information gathered and stored for future retrieval. This information was gathered based on an assumption of its potential importance in helping to shape public opinions. This information, as a result, is based on the assumptions of what data are perceived to be of importance, and this will not, in all likelihood, reflect the same perspective in all sectors of a community. This is a bias, however. Information pertaining to undervalued communities gathered by elite authorities and institutions will, in all likelihood, be deficit oriented and represent prevailing views at the time the data were gathered. Photographs, newspaper articles, agency reports, agency data, and artifacts such as murals can be classified as archival data.

Hatry (1994) defines agency data as "data that are obtained from secondary sources" (p. 374). These data have already been collected and are available for analysis to better understand the issues of a particular population or geographical area. Marcantonio and Cook (1994), on the other hand, caution us about agency data and note that these sources of information may be limited, because record-keeping methods change over time, data may not have been collected with the creation of a social intervention as a goal, and data may not reflect the geographical area or population being targeted.

Participant Observations in Meetings and Community

Participant observation is a method that is within the grasp of any youth participant, although it is not without its share of challenges (Pass & Vasquez, 2004). This does not mean, however, that anyone can do it instinctually and that no formal training is required. On the contrary, those who practice this form of qualitative research would be quite vociferous in advocating an extensive training and support program to help ensure that the observations are not biased (Greiner, 1994). This method of research can be relatively inexpensive when compared to other methods, such as surveys, and it provides rich material for contextualizing social situations, an important aspect of any research findings.

The disadvantages of utilizing observational techniques can be quite formidable, as there is a heavy reliance on what can be observed or sensed by the researcher. Additionally, uncontrollable situations can hamper this method; safety in dangerous situations can compromise the process; the more subtle the phenomenon being studied, the more arduous it is to study; subjectivity is a constant concern; and the observer may become intrusive and compromise the phenomenon being studied (Greiner, 1994). Finally, the ability to observe and record at the same time can be quite demanding for the uninitiated as well as the initiated.

Spradley (1980) developed a framework for measuring how active a participant an observer can be: (a) nonparticipant (no involvement with the people or activities being studied); (b) passive participant (present at scene of action but does not participate or interact with other people to any great degree); (c) moderate participation (maintains a balance between being an insider and an outsider); (d) active participant (does what other people do when the situation dictates it); and (e) complete participant (involvement in all aspects even when they can take a less active part but elect not to do so). Each of these phases of the process requires special attention during training and ongoing field support.

❖ QUANTITATIVE RESEARCH METHODS

The use of quantitative methods for generating data has a very long history within the social science community, nationally and internationally. Although it has been the subject of intense debate within the past two decades, this form of data has a place within the social sciences and certainly within youth-led research. The availability of data in social agencies and governmental organizations, for example, represents a largely untapped source for youth-led research projects. Regardless of whether existing agency data are used in a youth-led research project, youth researchers should be exposed to the availability of these data to inform research questions and design. Some portion of their training curriculum should be set aside for this lesson. Youth must realize that undertaking research does not automatically mean that they have to generate primary data to consider it a research project. Use of existing data, particularly when funds and time are limited, can be a perfectly viable way of uncovering knowledge.

Quantitative research can be divided into two primary types: generation of new data and use of existing data. The preferred approach used in youth-led research will be dependent on the goals of the research, time considerations, and available resources, such as funding. It is possible, however, to develop a research design that effectively uses both approaches, although this can be quite challenging. The use of existing organizational data opens up an immense area for possible research, and not just research related to program evaluation. A wealth of data within agency and governmental offices can be used effectively in helping youth grasp the impact of social problems within their community and understand how social problems get recorded by educational and human service systems.

Use of Social Indicators

The use of social indicators available through governmental organizations and the use of existing agency data bring such advantages as
availability, cost-effectiveness, and organizational legitimacy. The use
of social indicators within youth-led research will no doubt raise a
few eyebrows. Social indicators can be simply defined as a statistical
measure of a phenomenon or condition gathered by a governmental
agency entrusted to do so. These measures or indicators provide a standardized definition of a condition in order to facilitate comparisons
across geographical boundaries such as communities, cities, states, and
regions of the country.

Social indicators are readily available and do not cost money to
access, particularly through the Internet. Countless reports are issued
by governmental agencies; the Federal Bureau of Investigation,
Department of Labor, Department of Education, and Department of
Health and Human Services are the four most prominent. Social indicators allow youth to ground a particular problem they wish to better
understand locally and across geographical boundaries. Nevertheless,
social indicators have faults in that they only record conditions brought
to the attention of authorities. If a rape, for example, is not reported to
the police, it simply did not occur, according to a social indicator on
rapes. Social indicators are generally problem focused and not asset
focused, so it is possible to develop a very distorted picture of a community by relying on these forms of data.

Youth can learn many lessons by being exposed to social indicators: (a) the advantages and disadvantages of using government-
generated data; (b) their easy accessibility, particularly via the Internet;
(c) how bias gets translated into data-gathering methods; (d) how
social indicators get translated into resource allocation by the government; (e) the importance of primary research as a means of rectifying
existing impressions and information based on social indicators; and
(f) learning problem-solving skills in accessing a wealth of free information. Like all other forms of data, social indicators have their advantages, disadvantages, and limitations.

Use of Existing Agency-Generated Data

Agency-generated data can be used in the evaluation of a service
or program and in community-based studies. These data already exist

so do not have to be created, making their use cost-efficient. Youth-led research can include agency data to help guide development of research questions. Youth can learn valuable lessons about how organizations gather data, in similar fashion to those lessons associated with social indicators.

Local agencies may not define a presenting problem in a similar manner because of funding factors and organizational mission. The same presenting behavior can be categorized in one fashion by one agency and in a totally different way by another. This makes comparisons across organizations and geographical spectrums hard, if not impossible, to accomplish. Data are always fraught with assumptions and biases. Data generated by youth-led research are no exception. Nevertheless, a wealth of information gathered by social agencies can be marshaled to inform research studies, or to validate findings, but the information must be viewed critically. Data obtained through the use of agency records, which I will address in my discussion of archival methods, are part of a broader category of archival research that has generally been viewed too narrowly in the field of social research and almost totally ignored within the youth-led research movement.

❖ QUALITATIVE RESEARCH METHODS

An abundance of qualitative research methods can be marshaled in support of youth-led research. Methods, after all, are the vehicles through which research questions are asked and answered. Some methods are less challenging to implement within youth-led research projects, whereas other methods bring with them a set of inherent challenges. The reader will be exposed to some of the more popular and not-so-popular methods, although countless methods may be used to broaden research options. Methods can be combined and implemented in varying degrees of significance and order. No one method is ideal; the goals of the research dictate the choice of methods, whether they are quantitative, qualitative, or a combination of both.

Surveys

The prominence of survey research is well established within the field of social research and has a long and distinguished history as a method for community research. Many different types of surveys can be categorized by the nature of their data collection methods; the most common types are door-to-door, telephone, key informant, mail, and e-mail. The expertise, time, money, and goals of the research dictate the selection of the survey method. Whitlock and Hamilton (2002) comment that establishing procedures for decision making, disseminating information, delegating tasks, and assessing progress are all critical to the survey research process, although the same can be said for any other method.

The Great Lakes Epicenter ("Designing Questionnaires," 2002) put forth a set of nine recommendations that have great applicability for anyone wishing to use surveys for youth-led research:

(1) Keep the questionnaire questions as simple to understand as possible as far as reading level, defining terms, and avoiding technical terms and abbreviations, (2) Make the questionnaire easy to code for the purposes of data entry and analysis, (3) Start out with a few lead questions to give the participant a chance to warm up and begin to feel comfortable, (4) Collect the needed information only and keep it as short as possible, (5) Don't expect the participant to recall information from a previous question, (6) Make the questions as clear and specific as possible to ensure you get the information you need, (7) Have the questions follow a logical flow, going from general to more specific and grouping like questions together, (8) If possible, derive the survey from other surveys that have already been tested, used, and validated saving yourself some work and also allowing later comparisons to other groups, (9) In multiple choice questions, always offer exhaustive responses including options for "no opinion" or "don't know." (p. 1)

I would add an additional recommendation that has particular relevance for youth. Namely, always be prepared to answer why a question is being asked. Being able to articulate a rationale goes a long way toward conveying a sense of mastery of the content being studied.

Survey methods offer the field of youth-led research a rich set of possibilities for tapping the voices of community residents, youth as well as adults, particularly when there is an advisory or survey steering committee to assist them (T. I. Miller, 1994). School-based surveys such as the one conducted by Jovenes Unidos and Padres Unidos (2004) in Denver, Colorado, can serve to energize youth in schools to achieve positive change in schools. Home surveys bring with them the added potential of eliciting the voices of those individuals who are not part of a service, educational, or recreational system. Thus, this method lends itself well to capturing the voices of a wide sector of a community.

Nevertheless, surveys, probably more than any other other research method, represent the greatest challenges to youth-led research undertakings. When surveys are applied to youth-led research, not surprisingly, they tend to be small-scale and invariably cross-sectional. Large-scale surveys, although case examples of youth-led research using this method are presented in Chapter 10, tend to be expensive and labor intensive, making their appeal limited. Longitudinal surveys, although very attractive for certain types of research, do not lend themselves to youth-led research projects. Turnover of research staff, for example, is not unusual in youth-led research endeavors.

Surveys bring with them a set of considerations or limitations. For example, if the population group being studied is economically marginal, they may also be illiterate in English or their other primary language. They might not possess a telephone or have e-mail accounts. Mailed surveys might be foreign to certain households and may simply be ignored altogether. If it is important for the survey to generate data as well as political momentum, anything other than an in-person interview will be unsuccessful. Data generated from surveys generally tend to lack depth, although they function quite well in setting the stage for follow-up, in-person methods such as key informants or focus groups.

The process of sampling is never for the faint of heart, particularly when involving sectors of a community that has had its share of fires. Maps obtained from city hall or other authorities may have very detailed listings of streets, buildings, and apartment numbers. However, these maps may be outdated. Fires, for example, may easily eliminate a building or set of buildings. A random numbers allocation involving these buildings may quickly result in a sampling process that is impossible to undertake because the buildings no longer exist.

Surveys also necessitate the development of elaborate interview schedules that systematically seek to minimize sampling bias. For example, survey interviews cannot be limited to 9 a.m. to 5 p.m. Monday through Friday. Interviews conducted during certain periods of the day systematically eliminate certain groups of people and over-include other groups. Youth who are school age tend to be in school during the weekday period, necessitating evening and weekend interviews. Parents of youth researchers may not allow them to conduct interviews during evening hours because of safety concerns or worries about when their homework will be completed. Youth researchers, in turn, may not want to undertake interviews during the weekend or other times that they consider important.

Safety concerns or cultural factors may require youth to be paired up (boy/girl) to minimize these considerations, making the research interviews that much more expensive and difficult to coordinate. I encountered one situation where two researchers were paired up, and they were more interested in having a romantic relationship than in performing their research tasks. The parents of the girl researcher met with me to express their concerns about the relationship, which necessitated numerous meetings with the pair and with the team to ensure that romantic relationships do not transpire during work time.

Although fraught with challenges, survey research methods are very attractive for youth-led research efforts. Surveys, by the nature of the task, bring with them a multitude of approaches for tapping a range of youth research competencies. This aspect can be very appealing to youth. Further, as already noted, survey data can serve as a foundation from which to launch more personal methods that emphasize open and less structured interactions. These methods can be more focused in their line of questioning because of the information derived from a survey.

❖ CONCLUSION

There certainly is no lack of methods for use in youth-led research. This chapter has, I hope, provided the reader with a broad range of methods that lend themselves to use in youth-led research. Some of these methods will not be new to the reader, and some will. Youth-led research does not limit the use of a wide variety of methods. Each of these methods can be implemented in conventional and nonconventional ways to take into account local circumstances, budgets, and goals.

Qualitative and quantitative methods can be used in this form of research. The nature of the research question(s) must be the ultimate determination as to which types of methods will be used in a project. Youth researchers need to actively consider, discard, and adapt methods only after they have made serious deliberations. The process of adapting or discarding methods is an educational lesson in itself, and it should never be shortchanged. No method or approach is perfect. The critical thinking that enters into the decision-making process is just as important as the outcome of the research.

7

Initiating and Sustaining Youth-Led Research

The preparation to assume the role as researcher represents the "heart and soul" of the youth-led research movement. There are numerous dimensions to taking youth and transforming them into researchers. No dimension can be considered of minimal importance, and no dimension can be easily substituted or shortcut. Each aspect will bring with it a set of demands, challenges, and rewards and can be operationalized along a long continuum based on local circumstances (Brase et al., 2004). In this chapter, I outline for the reader the multifaceted aspects of preparing and supporting youth in research roles. For our purposes, I highlight five aspects in this chapter.

What factors can be considered the most significant in ensuring that youth-led research succeeds? Horsch et al. (2002) identify five factors that wield considerable influence:

1. Organizational and community readiness to have youth fulfill researcher roles

2. Adequate training and support for involved youth throughout the research process

3. Adequate training and support for adult staff because of the uniqueness of the experience

4. Selecting the right team to take into account competencies, knowledge, and attitudes

5. Sustaining youth involvement over the duration of the research project

These factors address a variety of instrumental, expressive, and informational dimensions of a research project.

Each of the sections I address in this chapter, with the exception of Potential Products and Dissemination of Results, is further subdivided, highlighting dimensions of practice. Each category provides the reader with approaches, a delineation of activities, issues, a critique, and recommendations and considerations related to youth-involved research. Although these categories are treated as if they were separate from each other, clearly they are well interrelated from a practical standpoint.

❖ INITIATING YOUTH-LED RESEARCH PROJECTS

Youth preparation, defined as organizational and community support for youth to assume the role of researcher, is probably at the crux of this youth-led movement. Preparing youth to assume a research role is labor intensive and critical to any successful effort. Depending on the model of youth-led research adhered to, preparation can consist of the following facets: (a) training and preparation, (b) support, (c) data-related, and (d) work with the media. Extensive youth-led research models entail all four facets with a more limited research role involving just two facets (i.e., preparation and field support).

Recruitment and Screening

The process of recruitment represents a very important step in any research undertaking. Researchers with extensive experience in youth-led research are very often quick to note that it is essential to hire youth that have an inclination for this type of work. However, this often entails having to navigate around youth stereotypes of what is a researcher. The perceptions of Ashley Webb, age 14, prior to her involvement in an oral history project (Mothers on the Move, 2004) in

New York City, highlights the challenges faced in recruitment of youth for research roles:

> When I came to the first session of the research project I was asked questions: What is research? Who is a researcher? Research done was using the Internet, library or books at home to learn about the past. My answer to who is a researcher along with the others was a typical stereotype idea of a researcher. My idea was an old male who was extremely educated, with little or no family and dressed in a lab coat. I only thought being a researcher dealt with a "lab scientist." As time passed I managed to deconstruct that idea. Research is a systematic way of finding information. (pp. 3–4)

France (2000) believes that a critical element in youth-led research is how youth are recruited, particularly those from marginalized groups. An approach that uses youth to recruit other youth helps to increase the likelihood of maximum participation. Youth are ultimately the best recruiters of other youth, and participation in research is no exception. Recruitment of potential youth staff members can occur through a variety of means and sources. However, there is a general consensus in the field that it is best to have youth recruit other youth. Youth are in a propitious position to craft the most effective message and anticipate the kinds of questions and concerns other youth may have about participating in a research project. They are also in a better position, when compared with adults, to craft requisite application forms by asking questions in a manner that puts the project, and the organization sponsoring the research, in the best light.

An application form serves a concrete as well as a symbolic value by conveying to the applicant that participation in a youth-led research project is a "job," and like all other forms of employment, there is a formal screening process that invariably starts with an application. An application also provides invaluable information about an applicant that can serve as a basis for evaluating the project, in addition to providing relevant contact information.

Creating a youth-led research project that is inclusive rather than exclusive is challenging under the best of circumstances (Goggin et al., 2002):

> The field of positive youth development is an inclusive field, it is meant to be for all youth. But this position creates a dilemma. Youth who have had discouraging school, family, or peer experiences

may shy away from the image that an active youth voice presence conveys to organizations and communities. These, of course, are the young people who could benefit the most from involvement in program efforts that take them seriously. Specifying time and planning strategies that ensure social, economic, and cultural diversity will give your organization and community efforts a real sense of integrity. (p. 9)

Embracing a goal of inclusiveness brings with it a host of challenges in recruiting, training, and supporting youth in their research role.

In community-based studies, it also becomes very important to recruit local youth (Delgado, 1981):

The interviewer's knowledge of a community will be invaluable in a research undertaking. In addition to helping with questionnaire construction, it will be an aid in understanding community issues and needs, locating streets and buildings (particularly helpful during the sampling and assignment of interview phase), location of community institutions, formal and informal. (p. 611)

Local youth bring not only a grasp of local knowledge and contacts but also the incentive to make research "authentic" and a corresponding desire to see meaningful change as a result of the research. Employing local youth also increases community capacity enhancement because these youth can utilize their newly acquired knowledge and competencies in other arenas in community life.

The development of a creative set of strategies is always recommended for recruiting youth. A multifaceted strategy is needed to help ensure a diverse research team (Centre for Addiction and Mental Health, 2001). Fortunately, there are numerous national and local organizations that have had extensive experience in this aspect, although examples specific to youth-led research are not plentiful. These strategies generally fall into two categories: formal and informal. Informal strategies invariably entail posting notices in youth-focused places where youth congregate, such as schools, community-based organizations, and other local institutions. Involving local media, through newspaper advertisements and radio announcements, is also recommended. The advent of the Internet has brought with it the use of information technology, such as a listserve for recruitment purposes.

Youth can also design recruitment posters and public service announcements.

Informal recruitment strategies may prove to be more challenging and labor intensive than formal strategies, but they also may yield the greatest positive results. Attendance at community meetings and fairs, for example, allows youth to reach sectors that would not normally be reached. Leaflets may be distributed in places where youth congregate, such as theaters, dance halls, video and DVD rental establishments, playgrounds, and youth sporting events—places not typically thought of when disseminating research results.

However, after everything is said and done, word of mouth has proven to be the most effective, yet controllable, strategy for recruiting youth as social researchers. One youth researcher was quite eloquent in stating why engaging in decision making was instrumental in sustaining youth involvement and in recruiting other potential team members (Horsch et al., 2002):

> At first it's a little weird when you realize, "Hey, I'm making real major decisions." At first, our projects were little, and doing tiny stuff. And now they're getting like big, and we're getting out and doing more 'cause we're realizing it. A lot of my friends have come up to me, and said, "Oh, I want to do that kind of stuff, too. How do I get involved?" (p. 3)

The legitimacy that youth possess among each other is quite powerful. One of the main reasons for developing an advisory committee is that youth members are placed in an excellent position to aid in the recruitment through the use of word of mouth.

Not every adult can or should be expected to assume a research role. Consequently, youth, too, should not be held to a standard that adults are not willing to be judged by. Not being able to assume a research role does not mean that youth cannot fulfill other important roles in community service. Further, it is essential for projects to recruit youth who can fulfill different roles, leadership as well as support (Horsch et al., 2002). I recommend the use of an advisory committee to assist in screening youth researchers by providing criteria for senior staff to use in selecting interviewers with the appropriate characteristics for the study that will be undertaken (Delgado, 1981).

There are at least ten key qualities that youth researchers must possess to make them "good" at being researchers:

1. Knows community

2. Embraces the importance of service to community

3. Possesses confidence and high self-esteem

4. Is well regarded by other youth and adults

5. Has handled or has the potential to handle responsibility well

6. Has good problem-solving skills

7. Is willing to enter all sectors of a community

8. Is motivated

9. Can work independently and as a member of a team

10. Voices opinions

Clearly, it takes an exceptional youth to be a part of a youth-led under-taking, and this exceptionality must be acknowledged by senior staff throughout all phases of the research process.

Mullahey et al. (1999) advocate for an inclusive set of values to guide youth-led initiatives:

> Diversity and inclusiveness are key strategies in designing oppor-tunities for interaction and participation. Diversity has value and adds value as young people (or adults for that matter) with differ-ent competencies/experiences, beliefs, and knowledge brought together in constructive ways can bring them various perspectives to innovate solutions imaging a shared future and a commitment to the common good. (p. 7)

The long-range implications of creating a cadre of youth with progres-sive values on inclusion can be quite a significant accomplishment for any organization or community.

The concept of diversity should never be used exclusively as another way of referring to race and ethnicity. This perspective would be much too narrow in focus. The balance of the research team must also be taken into consideration. Gender, socioeconomic background, length of residence in the community, racial and ethnic composition of the community, sexual orientation, and educational levels are but a few of the key factors that must be taken into consideration in the develop-ment of youth-led research teams (Horsch et al., 2002).

A fundamental belief in inclusion, for example, must guide the selection of a research team. A balanced team helps to ensure that all members of a community will be represented. This not only will facilitate data gathering but will also play a critical role when analyzing data. Multiple perspectives only serve to increase the value of data. A balanced team, however, will necessitate that decisions related to racism, classism, sexism, homophobia, and ableism not manifest themselves in research-related decisions.

When research teams are composed of youth from a variety of backgrounds, the dialogue and experiences that transpire can bring with them important insights. Torre and Fine (2003) describe a dialogue that took place during a training session that captures this perspective:

> Sara, a white middle schooler, speaking to her peers Nicole and Tasha, both African-Americans, says, "The survey is fine, but I don't think we should ask about race or ethnicity—it just divides us." Nicole responds, "No, I think we have to ask, 'cause our experiences may be really different and we won't know that if we don't ask about it." Tasha adds, "Yeah, it might help black kids and Asian kids." Sara repeats her concerns, "That's the kind of thing that just separates us." (p. 1)

This example illustrates how training on research methods as an activity transcends this narrow domain and enters into social areas of critical importance in the lives of youth and in their interactions with peers.

Finally, attention must also be paid to the various research roles that must be fulfilled in the course of implementing a research study. A research project should never be thought of as monolithic in structure. There are numerous roles that must be carried out requiring many different types of expertise. Just as in any other endeavor, this will require putting together a team with complementary competencies.

Youth who possess outgoing personalities may do very well in conducting individual and group interviews; those who are shy but possess excellent organizational skills may do well in handling data; those who have computer skills, in turn, may input data and conduct analyses of results; youth with excellent writing skills may be involved in issuing press releases and writing reports.

Last, some youth may possess excellent written communication skills in more than one language, and this will prove very useful when reports, or at least summaries, must be written for dissemination among different constituencies, such as in the case of youth-led research undertaken on the border between Mexico and the United States.

Contracting and Payment

Contracting is widely considered to be at the heart of any successful youth-led initiative, and research is not an exception. An explicit and implicit understanding of expectations on the part of all participating parties will serve as a base from which to determine a course of action and redress should a party not perform according to contracted expectations. Although the information of monetary payment can complicate a youth-empowerment process, it does play a central role in the success of a project (Anyon & Naughton, 2003):

- It facilitates the creation of ground rules pertaining to participation.
- It establishes a mechanism for decision making.
- It clarifies who is responsible for carrying out the consequences of violating ground rules. (pp. 1–2)

This contract, like its adult counterpart, must at minimum outline ten elements:

1. Attendance and tardiness expectations

2. Payment amount, procedures, method, and timing

3. Role expectations

4. Chain of authority, along with immediate supervisor

5. Length of contracted period

6. Method for evaluation of performance, including a schedule of when this will occur

7. Redress procedures when a dispute cannot be resolved within a supervisory context

8. Procedures to be followed when a "situation" occurs in the field

9. Emergency contact information

10. Signature of parent or guardian (depending on the age of the researcher) and signature of youth researcher

In the Holyoke project described in Chapter 3, youth were paid an hourly wage for their participation in the research, with a fixed amount and a bonus set aside in individual savings accounts. These funds, in turn, were specifically earmarked for school-related expenses. The indirect goal was to have youth participants develop a history of saving funds and engaging in transactions with a banking system. This goal is not essential for participation in a youth-led research project.

Oakland's YELL youth-led research project (Anyon & Naughton, 2003) advocates payment as a means of achieving multiple goals beyond minimizing youth turnover:

> Given the high unemployment rate in Oakland it is essential that youth be given an opportunity to earn money through a job that builds their skills, provides career-oriented work experience and helps them get into college or work outside of the low-wage service industry. Offering stipends demonstrates that working for community change is a viable career, not just an extracurricular endeavor. Paying youth for their time is part of that message. (p. 5)

A very important message, too!

Youth will, nevertheless, have to open up savings accounts because they will be paid by check. This does present a project with an opportunity to engage youth in money management lessons.

Maintaining a 100 percent participation rate throughout the life of a project can be an unrealistic goal, and youth must be provided with a choice to make this decision; this can be a part of any form of contracting (France, 2000). It is advisable to build into a project scheduled time periods during which youth are allowed to leave a project without feeling that they have been a failure. These evaluation periods also provide structured feedback on youth progress in knowledge and skill set acquisition and the identification of goals for future growth. This is not dissimilar from what can be found in any professional job, except that the time period for review occurs more frequently than once a year.

Training

Burgess (2000) raises the need for adults to provide youth with the necessary tools for making a better and more equitable future, and advocates for community-based initiatives that encourage youth to recognize their own leadership potential and support them in developing this potential (Yeager, Floriani, & Green, 1998). Training, as a result, is widely considered an effective vehicle for youth-adult collaboration. Edgar Dale (1946) developed what is called the "cone of experience" as a way to conceptualize training and the importance of participants playing an active role. This framework emphasizes the importance of training and action and illustrates very well the need to conceptualize the transmission of knowledge in ways that increase the likelihood of it being translated into practice.

According to Dale (1946), people generally remember 10 percent of what they read, 20 percent of what they hear, 30 percent of what they see, 50 percent of what they see and hear, 70 percent of what they say and write, and 90 percent of what they say as they perform a task. Learner training activities, as a result, cluster on verbal receiving, visual receiving, and hearing, saying, seeing, and doing. This perspective plays a critical role in how training activities to help youth assume research roles are developed. Thus, the more hands-on opportunities that are integrated into a training curriculum, the higher the likelihood will be of achieving training objectives. The development of experiential activities, however, can prove time-consuming because of the need to structure "process time" into training sessions. Nevertheless, there is no substitute for experiential learning.

The potential problem of lack of information retention is often noted as a critical consideration in the use of youth in research projects. A number of strategies, however, have shown promise in addressing this concern, such as structuring group discussions throughout the life of the project and group teaching. Both of these strategies place youth in positions of teaching each other and also have the added benefit of creating team spirit. These approaches can be considered labor intensive, but they increase the likelihood of youth retaining information, and they allow youth to experience this knowledge in a variety of ways other than didactically.

There is no denying that youth, regardless of their aptitude and competencies, need training to become proficient researchers:

> Research is a skill and, like adults, children and young people need to be trained to gain experience to do it well. However, training young people as researchers is not a straightforward process. There are potential limits if children are left to do the research on their own rather than in partnership with adults. (Save the Children, 2000, p. 25)

The critical importance of proper training cannot be overly stressed in any form of research endeavor, regardless of whether it is adult- or youth-led (Delgado, 1981): "Careful training for interviewers is crucial in the process of a research project. Do not attempt to shortcut a project by not giving training the emphasis it needs. The study is only as good as its methodology and interviewers" (p. 613). Investment in quality training can always be counted on to pay excellent dividends, and the costs must be factored into a budget.

Training should be interactive and actively engage youth in their learning (France, 2000). Youth should be encouraged whenever possible to assume supportive, rather than competitive, roles during this phase of the research process that this support carries over into other facets and phases of the project, such as during field work (S. Howard et al., 2002). A supportive approach does not necessarily occur automatically. Thus, senior project staff must actively endeavor to model this value whenever possible.

Training youth in research methods provides an excellent opportunity for youth to engage in a process of exploration and decision making. This process should ideally address four dimensions (John W. Gardner Center, 2001): (1) methods, (2) types of information to be obtained, (3) concrete examples, and (4) a critique of the advantages and disadvantages. Youth are provided with a means of both critiquing research methods and identifying the method(s) they favor. This training is particularly recommended in situations where youth will play an influential role in designing the research study.

When training is well conceptualized, it not only provides a venue for further screening and enhancement of competencies, but it can also result in fostering team spirit. Team spirit goes a long way toward breaking down divisions between adults and youth and can serve as a support mechanism for youth within and outside of the project. Youth who have positive experiences with training may be better equipped to assume positions as trainers in this field in the future. If one of the primary goals of youth-led research is to eventually turn over all research activities to youth, their role as trainers takes on paramount importance.

On a final note, training can involve in-session formats and homework. Assigning homework provides trainers with greater flexibility and gives youth an opportunity to test instruments and obtain feedback from peers and other community residents; it also ultimately expands the amount of training that can transpire within a prescribed period of time. Homework assignments, in addition, allow youth to show off their work to other youth and community residents. In essence, homework is another form of engaging in public relations about a research project.

Verbal presentations of youth-led research findings are so critical to the research process that I strongly suggest structuring role-playing situations and providing formal training on the subject, including videotaping, to enhance the presentation skills of youth researchers. As to be expected, presentation competencies are easily transferable to other social arenas in the lives of youth.

Job Description or Prototypes of Research Coordinator and Researcher

Before providing a skeletal outline of two primary job descriptions often associated with youth-led research (research coordinator and researcher), it is necessary to ground these positions within a context that informs functions that are obvious and not so obvious. Although job descriptions tend to be contextualized to take into account local organizations and communities, there are still some basic elements that transcend locality. Two job descriptions will be provided to help the reader better conceptualize research roles and expectations. By their very nature, job descriptions tend to be sketchy and in outlined form. The reader, as a result, can tailor job descriptions to his or her particular circumstances, thus allowing conditions to be integrated accordingly.

Research Coordinator

The importance of a project coordinator is well acknowledged in the field of participatory research, including youth-led research. The expertise that is required of a research coordinator goes far beyond research methods and designs. Ideally, a research coordinator's knowledge should also extend to the community being targeted (Schensul, 1994):

> The first criterion for success is the selection of an experienced and knowledgeable facilitator. The chair of lead facilitator of the network [team] should be someone familiar with all sectors of the community and committed to supporting the involvement of community-based organizations in policy and planning. This person should be sufficiently experienced to ensure that all critical decision-makers to benefit in and/or be affected by the effort will be involved in the earliest planning steps. (p. 2)

The day-to-day management of youth-led research, like other forms of community-based research, places a tremendous amount of pressure on the project's coordinator, particularly in situations where youth researchers are novices to the field and engaged in their first "formal" research experience. Having a team with a range of research experiences obviously lessens reliance on a coordinator. A research coordinator's role goes far beyond what is typically found in a job description. France (2000) identifies the role of a coordinator as a motivator, supporter, and someone who can help the team focus. A coordinator, in turn, must be attuned to the emerging needs of youth researchers and arrange requisite training and deployment of resources to ensure that youth succeed in their assigned tasks (Hetzel, Watson, & Sampson, 1992; S. Howard et al., 2002).

Researcher

It is possible to develop a job description that addresses a core outline of responsibilities, with additional job descriptions targeting specific aspects of a research project such as data entry, report writing, and so forth. The following job description addresses the rudimentary elements necessary for the undertaking. However, job descriptions invariably have a very localized, or contextualized, nature to them. At minimum, the youth researcher job description must include the following:

1. A positive attitude and open mind toward involvement in social research

2. A strong willingness to receive positive as well as constructive feedback

3. Good written and verbal communication skills or a willingness to improve on these aspects

4. Strong interpersonal skills that will allow them to engage in one-to-one as well as group forms of research interviewing

5. Willingness to be an active member of all facets of a research process

6. Extensive knowledge of the community being studied

7. Bilingual language skills (highly recommended)

8. Ability to make the requisite time commitment for the duration of the project

9. Parent's or guardian's permission for youth to participate

The reader may well look at the above job description and note that it is not a conventional job description outlining work history, educational attainment, knowledge, and skill sets. An effective job description for youth researchers attempts to tap potential for contribution to the project, as well as potential for personal growth and community contributions. In essence, the newness of the field presupposes that most, if not all, youth applying for the position of researcher have not had formalized experiences in conducting research, yet show potential and willingness to do so.

The above two job descriptions help to illustrate the importance of the critical attitudes, knowledge, and skills covered in Chapter 4. The reader is, of course, free to modify these job descriptions to take into account local circumstances. Some aspects covered above may need to be highlighted or prioritized based on the resources available from the sponsoring organization. There can be other job descriptions for consultants, field supervisors, or advisors, but they are not as critical as the two addressed in this section.

❖ SUSTAINING YOUTH-LED RESEARCH PROJECTS

Any research undertaking, youth-led or otherwise, represents the culmination of innumerable decisions and considerations, some explicit and others implicit. The initiation of youth-led research requires the sponsoring institution to be explicit as much as possible to demystify the research process. There are numerous factors that need to be considered in youth-led research. The contextualization of this type of research takes on considerable importance when placing youth in decision-making roles in projects. For our purposes, only four factors will be addressed although the reader can no doubt add a considerable number to this list: (1) age focus (i.e., targeted age group) of research, (2) setting-specific research, (3) time structure, and (4) organization sponsoring research.

Age Focus of Research

Although much attention has been paid to youth conducting research involving other youth, it does not preclude youth undertaking research focused on adults. This age focus, however, brings with it a set of considerations that must be taken into account in designing a research project. Putnam (2000) and Van Til and Paarz (2001) put forth a conceptualization of social capital that has particular appeal for youth-led research–inspired questions. These authors distinguish between the concepts of "bridging social capital" and "bonding social capital." The former refers to an outward orientation and seeks to foster and involve interactions across social boundaries (i.e., race, ethnicity, socioeconomic class, gender, sexual orientation, place of residence). The latter is inward oriented and seeks to reinforce "exclusive identities" within homogeneous groups. Bonding capital can be visualized as transpiring within a broad unit such as community or neighborhood, or within a specific characteristic of these geographical entities.

A bonding social capital perspective within youth-led research can involve youth focusing their attention on just youth and their interactions within and between youth and adults in a neighborhood or community. Data would answer research questions pertaining to youth and also try to foster greater identity among this group. A bridging social capital perspective may involve youth undertaking projects that cross geographical lines and bring them into contact with groups and institutions outside of their neighborhoods, or it may entail their undertaking research that focuses almost exclusively on adult issues within and outside of their neighborhood or community.

Self-knowledge, like local knowledge, makes research that is age-specific much more relevant for youth. Checkoway et al. (2003) make an important observation pertaining to how efforts to connect this form of expertise within and between communities are sorely lacking. Lack of established mechanisms for communicating this information has prevented the field of youth-led research from more quickly reaching its potential, for example. Increased institutional interest by foundations, intermediary organizations, and natural networks has increased the likelihood that youth-led research projects will receive funding.

The reader might rightly question whether or not there is a particular age group that youth-led research does best in reaching, or an age group that is best not addressed through this type of research. I feel confident to say that there is no age group that cannot be the focus of youth-led research. Flexibility in all aspects of the research project allows for all youth age groups to be a part of this form of practice. As I already noted, each of the four categories related to age has been addressed in the professional literature on youth-led research. However, clearly the age group that stands out for benefiting from this

form of research is children and youth themselves. Youth IMPACT
(2001) notes, "Being youth ourselves, we found that in general, youth
were more open to talking to us about being 'real' with their feelings
about the programs" (p. 3). Nevertheless, it is important to pause and
examine how youth-led research involving adults and elders can have
a place in a research agenda.

Setting-Specific Research

The setting sponsoring youth-focused research wields a prodigious amount of influence over how the research gets designed and
carried out, just as it does in adult-focused research. Although a conventional view of research generally considers two possible types of
settings (institution or community), youth-led research should not be
limited by this conceptualization. Institutional settings are best thought
of as schools, community-based organizations, and nontraditional settings. The latter are places within a community where residents come
to purchase a product or a service, or to recreate, but in the process of
doing so, they also receive some form of social service or information
on where to obtain formal assistance (Delgado, 1999).

Schools

As evidenced throughout this book, schools represent an excellent
setting for generating youth-led research, be it at an individual or
group/team level. The amount of time youth spend in school and the
educational mission itself makes youth-led research a viable strategy
for carrying out service-learning projects. These projects, when integrated
within lesson plans, can be cost-effective because no one involved gets
paid for doing a service-learning project. There may be incidental costs
associated with a project, but they pale by comparison with those associated with community-based organizations.

School as a focus or vehicle for youth-led research, as I note in
Chapter 6, is quite viable. When youth-led research projects are conceptualized as involving youth and school personnel in multiple grades,
these projects also serve to connect youth with each other and foster a
positive school spirit in the process.

Community-Based Organizations

The role of community-based organizations in youth-led research
has received considerable attention as evidenced by the amount of

research generated using this setting. Community-based organizations in many ways represent a critical component in advancing the field of youth-led research. They can sponsor this type of research, or they can facilitate it when it is sponsored by schools, for example. They can also be viewed as the essential glue that helps tie youth-led research to the broader community. School-based youth-led research cannot assume a major effort without the support of community-based organizations serving as a bridge between schools and community residents.

Community-based organizations provide the field with much-needed flexibility to take into account a variety of project goals and resources. These settings, particularly when they enter into collaborative agreements with their community institutions such as schools and nontraditional settings such as houses of worship, expand the number of options for community-focused research. Not all community-based organizations are going to embrace a youth-led research model. Thus, it becomes particularly important to conduct an assessment of community-based organizations with an understanding that partnerships, to be successful, must ultimately engage like-minded partners. The point may seem obvious to the reader, but I have learned over the years that just because an organization has a youth mission and articulates youth-led principles does not necessarily mean it embraces a youth-led research model. Assessment must ultimately be based on a series of actions and initiatives, rather than what is verbally stated or written in the mission statement of the organization. Actions, in essence, speak louder than words.

Nontraditional Settings

I would be remiss if I did not mention the potential role nontraditional settings, such as houses of worship and other "informal" community establishments, can play in sponsoring youth-led research. Nontraditional settings can be defined as places where community residents purchase a product or service, congregate for recreational purposes, or both (Delgado, 1999). Residents, while engaging in these forms of transactions, also receive some social service, such as information referrals to agencies, translation of materials from English to another language, advice, and so on.

Nontraditional settings, like their community-based organizational counterparts, can undertake all of the types of research outlined in this book. Nontraditional settings can involve youth in youth-led research as part of their community service mission and share the results of the research with the broader community. These settings can also enter into collaborative partnerships with formal settings such as schools and community-based organizations.

Time Structure

All forms of research are subject to timing considerations. However, youth-led research is particularly sensitive to this topic. The age of the researcher, in most cases being a legal minor and in school, requires careful consideration of time from a variety of perspectives. As the saying goes, "Timing is everything," and key questions related to hours of the days, days of the week, season, and length all contribute to the optimal timing of research endeavors. Time-related considerations are best categorized into (a) hours and days of the week, (b) season(s) during which research will be conducted, and (c) length of the research project (e.g., in weeks or months). All of these categories are of equal importance in the planning and implementation of youth-led research.

After School

The after-school time period has received much attention in the field of youth services. If left unstructured, this period of time places youth in at-risk situations for engaging in antisocial acts (Carnegie Council on Adolescent Development, 1992a, 1992b, 1994). Efforts have been under way to introduce various forms of structured programming as a means for positively engaging youth in activities that promote youth development. Research, as an activity of youth development, is more and more being conducted during the after-school hours.

The after-school period is very often considered the second most propitious time period, after summer, for engaging youth in research endeavors. However, unlike the summer period, after-school time can be quite limiting from a scheduling perspective. Typically, a total of three to four hours immediately after school is devoted for research, with youth completing their assignment by 6 p.m. in order for them to get home for supper and complete the day's homework assignments when applicable. Although this time period brings with it a set of limitations, youth-led research can still transpire if the goals of the research are sensitive to the time availability of youth.

Depending on the extent of a research project, youth might be engaged in actual research three days or so out of the week, with the remaining days set aside for in-service training, consultation, support, and structured debriefing. Time may also be set aside for participation in "fun" activities such as trips, movies, and so forth. Youth IMPACT's research team, for example, worked three days per week, two and one-half hours per day (Tena, 2001). The remaining time was devoted to a range of constructive activities in support of the research project. A work week with the goal of having youth researchers engage in a variety of tasks that assist youth in growing as researchers and individuals can also serve to break the monotony that sometimes accompanies research. Youth-led research is not just about research; it is also about empowering and supporting youth during these critical years. Research, in many ways, is nothing more than a vehicle for providing youth a wide range of knowledge and competencies and, indirectly, also helping their families and communities.

During School Hours

When youth-led research is undertaken within a service-learning project and it is school-based, it provides youth with an opportune time to make an impression on their school as well as their community, other youth, and adults. Classroom-centered youth research projects allow students to work closely with teachers in constructing and implementing a project (Egan-Robertson & Bloome, 1998). These projects can consist of a wide variety of types involving one or more students working together. Teachers, in turn, are provided with an excellent opportunity to learn more about the communities that their students come from, further aiding curriculum development and teaching methods, and helping to break down barriers between schools and communities that are often present in socially and economically marginalized communities.

Unfortunately, the use of classroom time to carry out projects brings with it a potential set of limitations because of the length of a typical class period, which, based on my experience, limits the extent and ambition of a research project. When school settings have a rich and positive relationship with the community and its key institutions, these projects can be quite significant for all participants. However, if schools do not have this history, then projects can encounter numerous roadblocks within the community, seriously limiting their potential contributions to student researchers, the school, and the community. Nevertheless, when classroom research projects are well-conceptualized and supported, youth, as well as their teachers, can plan service-learning research that can be academically sound and serve the community as well.

Weekends and Holidays

Life, unfortunately, or fortunately, depending on one's perspective, does not unfold Monday through Friday, 9 a.m. to 5 p.m., a typical work week. This necessitates that research projects, too, unfold over the course of the entire week or within a circumscribed time period. This premise, however, brings with it a host of challenges in making research tie in within the ebbs and flows of community life. A broadening of the typical time parameters often requires tapping all sectors of a community and not just the ones that are easiest to access. Youthled research is, after all, about accessing all voices within a community.

A talk with any experienced researcher will quickly uncover many different stories about the importance of avoiding bias in a study. People's lives, youth not being an exception, are not restricted to a set number of days or hours of the week. The undertaking of research, as a result, should not be restricted to weekdays, as I already noted. Nevertheless, researchers, whether adults or youth, rarely embrace undertaking research on weekends and holidays. Nontraditional settings are very attractive for research involvement because of their operational time periods, which are not limited to certain days and times.

The use of bonuses has been one method that has met with success in getting volunteers to work during "unattractive" time periods. Another suggestion is to use flexibility as a criterion in choosing field researchers. Doing so will increase the odds that the team will be composed of at least some youth who are available and willing to work outside of prescribed time periods.

Season

Seasonal considerations are applicable to all sectors of the country. The season during which youth-led community studies are conducted may prove influential in research outcomes. I have found that the timing of youth-led community studies is very important in implementing this type of research. I found, for example, that research undertaken during the winter proved too arduous to implement because, at least in New England, snow and cold weather disrupted interviewing schedules (Delgado, 1998). Furthermore, in this research on the mapping of Latino community assets, interviewing storeowners during the holiday season proved challenging. Owners were generally unwilling to take time out from serving their customers during the busiest time of the year. I also found that summertime might not be conducive to community studies because the heat and humidity can curtail interviewing and lengthen the duration of the research project (Delgado, 1979, 1981).

Length of Project

Determining the optimum duration of a project depends on a large number of considerations such as research goals, financing, complexity of the project, the extent and nature of collaborative partnerships, and the degree to which the timing of the end of the project needs to coincide with the planning and start of a social change effort resulting from the findings, to maximize the momentum generated by the research. Is there such a thing as an optimal length of time for a project's duration? Making a project too long, possibly lasting multiple months, increases the likelihood of youth losing interest and increasing turnover; making it too short, such as several intensive days or a week, does not lend itself to engagement in a process of reflection, discussion, and consolidation of learning.

The actual duration, or length, of a project is a key factor in adult-led research and plays a critical role in the hiring of staff. A long-term project that can last three to five years will ideally hire staff who can make a commitment for the duration of the project. The longer the project, the more this consideration comes into play. Youth-led research is no different from adult-led research in this respect, with the exception that at present, youth-led projects rarely cover a multiple-year period. Nevertheless, youth commitment to engage in research is generally tied to the length of time the research is expected to take. There is probably very good reason for the popularity of summer-based youth-led research projects. This period is time-limited, youth are not occupied with school, and they are in need of earning some form of income. The weather, although possibly hot and humid depending on the part of the country being addressed, will not interfere with the project, unlike in winter, which brings with it excessive cold and snow in some locales.

❖ ORGANIZATION-SPONSORED RESEARCH

The influence that an organization can wield when sponsoring youth-led research is considerable and shapes every aspect of the research process, including the likelihood of achieving success in bringing about significant social change. In an assessment of four youth-led evaluation efforts, Sabo (2003b) identifies three key climate, or environmental, components that must be fostered by sponsoring organizations:

1. The presence of supportive adults who believe in youth's ability to grow in their role as researchers

2. Multiple opportunities for youth to assume research roles that facilitate their learning material formerly not available to them

3. Involvement of youth in research activities that alter their previous relationships with the broader community and allow them to make meaningful contributions

Organizations wishing to sponsor youth-led research as part of their overall mission would be wise to follow the recommendation of the Profiles of Youth Engagement and Voice in New York State study (Goggin et al., 2002) and designate one staff member to coordinate these efforts as their sole, or significant, part of their functions. As I noted earlier in this book, youth-led research initiatives cannot be started and stopped at will without serious consequences. These types of projects require considerable thought and resources to be conceptualized, planned, and implemented. Thus, start-up can be quite challenging.

Staff specifically assigned the job of initiating and overseeing youth-led research can assist in developing and integrating these projects into the fabric of the organization and community. They can be responsible for public relations efforts to publicize these efforts, or work closely with youth doing these tasks, and can also advocate for youth-led research in other settings. It takes a special type of expertise to initiate and coordinate youth-led research, and currently there are few formal sources from where to obtain this expertise. Experiential learning appears to be the primary source for this knowledge.

Lau et al. (2003) argue that organizational readiness to accept youth development does not customarily translate into readiness to accept youth-led research. This next step necessitates the presence of an organizational culture that embraces evaluation as a worthwhile pursuit, and that evaluation of youth development programs must ultimately rest in the hands of youth themselves. Program evaluation, much to the surprise of staff, can be perceived as fun and an activity attractive to youth. However, staff must believe in research before they can effectively convince youth of its worthiness and potential for fun, adventure, and learning.

Why would research led by youth be appealing to sponsoring organizations and other community-based settings? Besides a philosophical embrace of the mission and principles integral to this form of activity, youth-led research can generate "hard" data that can be used to substantiate programs and services targeting youth. Data can be easily integrated into funding proposals and grant applications. When hard data are effectively tied to capacity enhancement for all parties involved, research as an activity takes on greater significance.

❖ SUPPORT

Successful completion of a research project necessitates sensitivity to a host of issues (Nightingale & Rossman, 1994). Extensive support of research, both within and outside of the field, is very much a part of any research undertaking. Unfortunately, rarely are these factors discussed in scholarly articles and books. One generally gets the impression that research gets implemented exactly as planned. Nothing could be further from the truth.

Youth-led research support takes on prominence and needs to transpire in a manner that affirms youth competencies, but does so in a way that does not undermine their confidence. This support, like with adult-led research, must be anticipated and addressed as an integral part of a research project and not just because it is youth-led. It is necessary to conceptualize support for youth-led research in a multifaceted manner, with specific attention to instrumental (concrete), expressive (emotional), and informational needs. Although often thought of as separate entities, these three dimensions are interrelated. Five aspects of support, at minimum, must be firmly in place throughout all facets of the research project: (1) role of adults, (2) peer and adult field supervision and support, (3) advisory/steering committee participation, (4) incentives, and (5) use of journals.

Role of Adults

In this section, I outline a variety of adult roles and identify the potential facilitating and hindering aspects of those roles. By no means am I trying to give the impression that each of these roles entails having one adult fulfill the expectations. Because of cost considerations, it is not unusual for there to be only a few researchers wearing many different hats throughout the course of the project.

Youth-led research does not mean that adults are not in the picture (Matysik, 2000). Adults can, and should, be expected to play important roles as advisors, consultants, and community social brokers (Upshur & Barreto-Cortez, 1995). However, adult roles are very much dictated by local circumstances and goals for the research. Training and support for adult staff are necessary (Horsch et al., 2002). Adults face numerous challenges in facilitating youth-led research, and they, too, need training, consultation, and other forms of support.

Next, I identify, describe, and exemplify potential roles for adults, to help the reader better visualize adults' potential contributions to youth-led research. Adults can assume roles as teachers, collaborators, facilitators, and participants. Their role(s), in essence, is dictated by the expressed needs of youth participants.

Advisors

The role and importance of an advisor is well recognized in this society, whether it is carried out in a formal or informal manner. In many ways, an advisor role is one that youth are familiar with from their school experience. An advisor, as a result, can be nonthreatening and therefore quite effective in rendering assistance without imposing an authoritarian viewpoint. Advisors give advice, and if the advisor is trusted and respected, the chances of their advice being followed rise dramatically. This advice may be solicited or unsolicited, depending on the relationship between advisor and youth, and it can transpire during a structured time period or on demand.

An advisor role is generally flexible in both content provided and timing of advice. I have, for example, set aside time at the end of the work day and called this "open time" for youth who have specific questions or concerns but do not feel comfortable asking during established time periods. Other youth use this time to write in journals or sit around and just chat about events of the day. Interestingly, this time has also been used to provide advice for youth in addressing personal issues or answering questions about their future plans. In essence, open time is just that: a time that is open to any possible topics, with no obligations to participate.

Supervisors

A supervisory role is one that has an "official" role in a research enterprise and brings with it a host of expectations and even a detailed job description. Unlike any of the other roles that rely on adults providing advice or suggestions, this role brings an expectation of accountability. For example, supervisors may issue directives and expect them to be followed, and if they are not, sound reasons must be put forth as to why not. As part of their orientation to participation in a youth-led research project, youth should be informed how the role of supervisor is viewed by the sponsoring organization and the organizational chain of command. What may appear as a straightforward response to "What is a supervisor?" may not be the case with youth who have had little or no previous employment experience. These youth's perception of a supervisor will in all likelihood be informed by what they have heard from relatives, neighbors, or other peers. This perception can be of an authoritarian person whose primary goal is to monitor performance and who punishes those who fail to follow their dictates.

Supervisory roles can be classified along a variety of lines with titles such as senior supervisor, assistant supervisor, or even supervisor-in-training. This broad classification system facilitates the integration of youth into these roles, even when they are not seasoned enough to do so at the highest level. A career ladder that is clear about expectations and qualifications is one manner through which youth can stay involved with programs, particularly when provided with educational opportunities to obtain a college education and still work.

Consultants

Unfortunately, the role of consultant is one that is laden with all kinds of definitions or stereotypes. However, being an "expert" is usually a part of most definitions and perceptions of consultants, with expertise being generally associated with extensive formal education. The role of consultant brings with it a tremendous amount of flexibility in crafting the kind of assistance that is needed. Consultants are usually brought into a program or project when no one on the staff has the expertise required or when the service needed does not require a full-time staff member to provide it. This saves money and allows program staff the flexibility to hire staff with competencies that are needed over an extended period of time rather than just temporarily.

The costs associated with consultants can vary considerably. However, collaborative agreements can be developed to obtain consultation from other community-based organizations, institutes, and universities. Payment, in turn, can be in-kind services or access to institutional expertise of various kinds. Youth, in a reciprocal manner, can serve as consultants when they have a particular expertise in the area of the research focus or have had extensive experience participating in youth-led research projects. In fact, youth-led research must always endeavor to hire youth in all capacities, including as consultants.

Use of consultants, as already noted, brings a great deal of flexibility to a research project by allowing specific needs to determine the expertise that is needed. Thus, youth can be engaged with a project without making long-term commitments or having to spend considerable time at any time during a project's life, and they can develop their portfolio of competencies in areas that will make them attractive in areas that can eventually lead them on a research career path.

Peer/Adult Field Supervision and Support

The need for field supervision and support is an integral part of any research endeavor, and nowhere is this more appropriate than with youth-led research (Delgado, 1981): "Be prepared to provide extensive supervision and support. It is not realistic to assume that training will anticipate potential problems and provide the necessary skills and knowledge to successfully address field-related problems and crises" (p. 613). My experience has been that training serves as a basic foundation for a research undertaking, but it is never enough to sustain it through all of the twists and turns that are invariably a part of this endeavor. Supervision and support, as a result, play a role in helping to ensure that youth's contributions are meaningful and lasting.

It is rare for any research project to be planned and implemented without changes of various kinds due to unanticipated factors and circumstances. This often necessitates that support be an integral part of any research endeavor (Strand et al., 2003): "One of the valuable lessons from CBR [community-based research] is that real research seldom proceeds as neatly as textbooks would lead us to believe and that good researchers are flexible, resourceful, self-motivated, and willing to accept uncertainty and change" (p. 165). The youth-led research team must anticipate and learn from the experiences of engaging in "live" research. Much like the reality television shows that dominate the airwaves, research, too, can at times seem unscripted, causing anxiety when decisions are made on assumptions and faith rather than detailed information and systematic assessment.

In this section, I place particular attention on the emotional reactions youth may have to the material elicited in the interviews (Deatrick & Faux, 1991). The undertaking of social research, particularly that focused on developing a better and more sensitive understanding of social conditions, is always laden with the potential of eliciting a wide range of emotional responses from those undertaking the research. These responses are quite natural and must be systematically addressed in all forms of field-related support and supervision.

Closure at the end of the workday takes on greater prominence when youth are involved because of potentially emotionally distressing information they may have been exposed to during their work (S. Howard et al., 2002; P. Kirby, 1999). Some researchers would go on to argue, and I include myself in this group, that these emotional responses help to connect the researcher with the population group they are seeking to better understand. These emotions, in turn, must be tapped and allowed to play influential roles in the analysis and writing of final recommendations, which, in turn, must ultimately lead to a change in social circumstances for the better. I, for one, would rather be accused of over-identifying than underidentifying with research respondents.

Field support for youth can take on a variety of forms, from problem solving on the spot to assistance with conflict resolution between research team members, or between researchers and community, such as in situations where youth researchers have entered gang-controlled areas and there has been an "incident." The provision of this support can place a considerable amount of stress on field supervisors because they have to be readily available to intervene as necessary. It is not to say, however, that adult researchers do not require supervision and support while in the field. Based on my experiences and the experiences of others involved in this field, it is clear that adults' requests and needs are qualitatively different from those of youth.

Youth-led research, in similar fashion to other forms of consumer participation, will necessitate frequent meetings of a research team, making team members an integral part of the research process (Strand et al., 2003). Meetings provide youth with opportunities to set agenda items, lead or co-lead meetings, and contact and schedule guest speakers, for example. These meetings are also an excellent opportunity for the parents of youth researchers, community leaders, and stakeholders to attend and observe the workings of a research team in action. No opportunity should be overlooked to further engage the community that is the focus of the research. The more we demystify the research process, the more a community becomes empowered and an informed consumer of research results.

Advisory or Steering Committee Participation

There are a variety of ways that youth can participate in youth-led research in addition to actually performing research roles. The effective use of an advisory or steering committee can wield tremendous influence on a research project. An advisory role can be carried out in a one-to-one format, and this provides sufficient flexibility to encourage participation on an as-needed basis. Youth can play a significant role by their participation on committees, such as those that are advisory and policy making. In this section, I present examples of these types of committees, along with words of advice for practitioners wishing to use committees as one way of increasing youth involvement in research endeavors.

Goodyear (2003) argues that engaging youth in collaborative and equal partnerships with adults in the research undertaking helps to ensure the validity of the process. Having both youth and adults on youth-led research serves this purpose quite effectively. The North Carolina Youth Empowerment Study (NCYES), for example, was a three-year participatory research evaluation project of youth tobacco use prevention programs, which made extensive use of an adult-youth advisory committee (Ribisl et al., 2004). The NCYES Statewide Advisory Board assisted in the evaluation process, reviewed research protocols and data collection instruments, and helped in the analysis of data.

Youth-led research, as a result, can be conceptualized as seeking influence on one of three possible orientations: bridging, bonding, or a combination of bridging and bonding. The focus of the research will be influenced by its primary goals. The more research is focused, the easier it is to conceptualize and implement. Any youth-led research project attempting to better combine bridging and bonding capital will spread resources across a wide arena, making the project more challenging to carry out, although its impact can be much more enhanced by doing so. Advisory committees represent an established mechanism for bringing together key stakeholders not only to ensure the quality of the research but also to use as a vehicle for proposing and following up on initiatives resulting from these findings.

Unfortunately, an extensive review of the literature uncovered very few references to the use of advisory committees in youth-led research, although in practice it is not uncommon. Advisory committees can play an important function in helping youth-led research address potential barriers and assist with problem solving. Further, these committees can also provide important political support once the findings have been released to the general public. This support is very often necessary if positive social action is to result from the research.

Well over twenty-five years ago, I specifically recommended the use of an advisory committee involving youth: "Develop an advisory committee for the project and include adolescents. This committee can prove . . . invaluable throughout all the research phases" (Delgado, 1981, p. 613). Advisory committees provide expertise to a research undertaking without the research team having to pay for it. An orchestra is the metaphor that I like to use in discussing how an advisory committee needs to be composed. Each member brings a musical instrument. Too many of one instrument may not allow a musical score to be performed properly. In other words, only one tuba player or pianist is needed. A diversified advisory group has been proposed as one means of providing formal and informal support to youth researchers, but it is one that requires careful thought as to how it will be composed and what specific roles youth will play (France, 2000; S. Howard et al., 2002).

Conceptually, advisory committees need to have four forms of legitimacy: expertise (educational and experiential), institutional, ethical, and consumer. Ideally, all four types of legitimacy should be present for this committee to be effective in rendering instrumental, expressive, and informational maximum support to a project (Rein, 1977). Each of these types of legitimacy is needed to help ensure that the research being proposed and implemented has intellectual, social, and political support. This support has great importance in youth-led research because of the unusual nature of this type of research, its focus on social change, and the high probability of outside efforts to discredit the results. Advisory committees are thus thrust into a position to provide technical support where needed, as well as political support for recommended changes once the research is completed.

Advisory communities can consist of youth, as well as adults, and are excellent forums for intergenerational dialogues to occur. It is highly recommended that the chair of an advisory committee be a youth or, in situations where appropriate, youth and adult co-chairs, thus offering a chance for adults to be a part of the effort without substantially diminishing the influence and power of youth over the research project. However, participation must go beyond symbolism, with members bringing needed expertise and access possibilities for researchers. In other words, every member needs to be there for specific instrumental, expressive, and instrumental reasons. Advisory committees that are mere window dressing are of little use in youth-led research and, I would argue, in any form of serious intervention.

Incentives

The role and importance of incentives have not received the attention they deserve in the youth development and youth-led literature, although they are starting to receive attention within adult-led and -focused projects. Performance incentives ironically are a well-established form of practice in the private sector but have generally been ignored in the public sector. Thus, it is advisable to consider the subject of how incentives can be effectively utilized within youth-led research. Incentives can take on a variety of manifestations incorporating the goals, length of the research, and local circumstances, such as community norms.

Although adult supervisors may want youth to consider the experience of undertaking research to be a reward onto itself, and the payment of monetary funds to be an added reward, this is not case. It is necessary to develop a comprehensive system of rewards that can be given throughout all phases of a research endeavor. Typically, rewards can consist of pizza parties after each research phase or an elaborate dinner at a restaurant after completion. Attendance reinforcers for each phase might take the form of tickets to local movie theaters, DVD/CD certificates, and graduation at the end of the research where family and significant people within the community are invited to participate. The use of a lottery to award prizes for youth that have maintained attendance and performance expectations also has great potential for motivating youth.

Although the benefits far outweigh the financial costs, there are obvious budgetary considerations in implementing a project. Incentives can also involve nontraditional inducements such as school credits, scholarships, featuring team members in newspaper articles, interviews on local cable access channels, and weekend trips with all expenses paid for youth and their family. Incentives, as a result, must be considered throughout all phases of a research project in order to help ensure that performance goals are being met. Research projects with limited funds for purchasing these incentives can contact local businesses for donations. These donations have the added benefit of involving a broader sector of the community in the research process. This sector, unfortunately, is rarely asked to contribute in any form to a research undertaking.

Use of Journals

The use of journals with youth is well accepted in many fields, particularly in the field of education. It is a vehicle that can serve a variety of cognitive, emotional, and reflective goals, regardless of the setting. Journals can serve multiple goals and bring with them a high degree of flexibility in their use within youth-led research. Youth can use journals to (a) record observations, reactions, and unanticipated experiences; (b) reflect on observations and experiences; (c) plan next steps in the project and develop alternative scenarios for certain types of experiences; and (d) share experiences, reactions, and plans with supervisors or other team members (Riorden & Fulwiler, 1992).

A number of scholars already cited in this book are big advocates of the use of journals during the research process. It is a tool with many different purposes that can be carried out simultaneously. The use of a personal journal to help youth record their experiences and reflect on the research process offers the field a valuable method to better understand the transformation of youth throughout all phases of the research process and help identify content to be stressed during training and supervision. Journals also provide valuable qualitative data that can help explain research findings and serve as a daily form of support for youth by providing an outlet to record reactions, concerns, and surprises. In addition, journal writing can be an effective means of helping youth develop skills for note taking and writing, and as a means of facilitating communication between student and teacher.

Youth are usually required to spend time at the end of the workday to record in this journal. It is also possible to use the journal throughout the workday, however. Regardless of when entries are written, this time is structured as part of the research responsibilities, and researchers are paid to accomplish this task. Some projects require youth to make recordings anytime within or outside of the project. Logs are either collected at the end of the day or at the end of the week. A contract describing how they will be used and who has access to them is signed at the beginning of the project. The type of entry, it should be emphasized, can be narrative, quotes, drawings, scribbles, and so on. In essence, this flexibility allows youth participants to express themselves in a variety of ways.

I have had the experience of having youth at the end of the week share with the team one entry that they select because of its poignancy or significance to them. Teams, in turn, share their reactions by simply validating a key point, offering suggestions, or reflecting on the emotional response the journal entry elicited. These team meetings can be videotaped or tape-recorded, to be used in future training once requisite permission from youth researchers has been obtained. Journals, as a result, can play an integral part of the research process, just like they can with classroom-related assignments that require some form of reflection.

❖ POTENTIAL PRODUCTS AND DISSEMINATION OF RESULTS

In the beginning of a research endeavor, it is hard to imagine getting to the final stage of actually sharing the potential fruits of this labor. Youth-led research brings with it a host of conventional and innovative approaches to the sharing of findings and development of concrete projects for the general public. Practitioners have a wide range of options as to how best to translate findings into products and action. The sharing of the results is the first step in this process, with local circumstances and political considerations influencing the methods used.

Hendricks (1994) developed a set of six principles that should guide the dissemination of results:

1. It is the responsibility of the researcher for effectively conveying the results and not the audience's responsibility to easily make sense of the findings.

2. Take an active, if not aggressive, posture toward getting the results out to the broader community, rather than wait for requests for information to trickle in.

3. Findings must be presented in as simple a manner as possible with a specific focus on key points.

4. Bring examples to illustrate key findings so that the audience is better able to identify with and derive meaning from the results.

5. Be prepared to provide action steps, or recommendations, rather than rely simply on reporting conditions or problems.

6. Use a multitude of ways to get the message across, such as video, reports, press briefings, plays, television, and radio interviews. (pp. 549–550)

Dissemination

Unfortunately, one of the most frequent characteristics of conducted research is that the ultimate beneficiaries of the results generally have very limited or no access to the research findings. Funders of research get their report within a prescribed period of time; the scholarly audience may wait several years before publications finally find their way into journals. Youth-led research, however, lends itself to the sharing of results immediately through local channels, since participation from the community is a central tenet of participatory research and evaluation (Jobes, 1997).

A youth perspective on findings dissemination often brings the potential of a creative dimension to this important phase of the research process by identifying stakeholders, advancing innovative ways of presenting information, and suggesting new conceptualizations on practice emanating from the research (Goodyear, 2003). Youth's ability and legitimacy to unveil the issues and propose solutions to the public cannot be underestimated. One school-focused youth-led research project conducted by Generation Y (Chicago) consisted of a school discipline survey of 344 students and resulted in a release of both a written report (Suspended Education) and a video documentary that made the findings more accessible to students and their families (M. Weiss, 2003). Community youth researchers in Oakland, California, followed a somewhat similar path (Anyon & Naughton, 2003). Youth surveyed approximately 400 students, 50 staff members, and 100 community residents. In addition, they conducted two focus groups. This information was then used to develop a documentary movie about school safety and cleanliness, along with a written report on the major problems identified at the school.

One youth-led research project sponsored by the Institute for Community Research (Hartford, Connecticut) utilized poster boards placed in strategic places throughout the high schools in the city. These posters consisted of photographs of graffiti and drug-related items found in and around the high schools during the course of the research

(Becker, 2003). Youth felt that these photographs had far greater impact on exposing the problems of substance abuse than would a narrative summary of the findings.

The case of Kids First (2003) illustrates how youth can use forums as vehicles for creating change. The Oakland-based organization's results of a study of three area high schools were disseminated through school-based forums. Participants were asked to prioritize student recommendations based on survey results. This forum also served as a means of reconnecting youth to the research process and enlisting their support for recommended changes. In essence, school forums served scientific as well as sociopolitical purposes.

The Center for Youth Development (2000) stresses the immense importance of dissemination of findings: "The deeper question a community has to ask is: 'What are the most accessible means to share information on resources to ensure that it reaches youth, parents, non-connected adults, politicians, and policymakers?'" (p. 2). The significance of this phase of the research is too immense to be appreciated without a strategic plan in place that will reach key stakeholders within and outside of the community.

The dissemination of research findings has historically been limited to a set variety of outlets, such as a funding source, scholarly publication, presentations at learned conferences, and an occasional submission to a news report in the popular media. In fact, few projects, I believe, actively seek to disseminate their findings in all of the above ways. Usually, one or two seem to be the favored outlets. Youth-led research, too, can involve active dissemination to these same outlets. However, it can also involve letters to the editors of local and school newspapers, leaflet distribution in establishments frequented by youth, video creation, plays and exhibits of photography, presentations at youth gatherings, media interviews, and executive summaries to community-based organizations and schools (Kirby, 1999). The creation of a newspaper that publishes community research findings and recommendations for changes and is distributed within a school is another example of a creative way of informing other youth about their own community (Hart, 1992).

Youth-led workshops specifically established to disseminate findings represent a natural step in youth-led research. When findings are particularly sensitive or controversial, youth are often in the best position to frame and word the messages they wish to convey to other youth, for example, in the case of STD/HIV research. Potential youth barriers to reception of messages, such as a perceived sense of invincibility, can be minimized if youth rather than adults lead discussions (Youth and STD/HIV Prevention Project, 2002). Peer educational strategies offer much promise particularly in the social marketing of condoms, print resources, and other STD prevention–centered services, and tobacco and mind-altering drugs.

Products

There are numerous consequences that can result from youth-led research that can be considered both process- and product-related. The Centre for Youth and Society, University of Victoria, Canada, for example, lists thirteen changes that can be built into youth-led research (Centre for Youth and Society, 2003):

- Produce a 5- to 10-minute video on the research topic (interview researchers and community members) for educational purposes.
- Create a board game for children/youth/teachers/service providers to enhance education on research topic.
- Create a training manual for parents/teachers/service providers to enhance education on research topic.
- Assess youth and parent accessibility to information on the research topic.
- Deliver an educational seminar to the community or [school] on the research topic.
- Develop educational materials that promote child and adolescent successes for those affected by the research topic.
- Develop a training program for peer helpers or mentors to assist children or youth affected by the research topic.
- Assess community outreach services designed to assist youth affected by the research topic.
- Assess community involvement in reducing the prevalence of children or youth affected by the research topic.
- Write a literature review for educational or grant-writing purposes.
- Organize a meeting that brings together key policy makers in the area of the research topic.
- Facilitate youth-led forums or discussion groups on the research topic and include the youths' concerns and suggestions in the project report.

- Participate in a "practicum day" at the agency at the start of the project. (pp. 1–2)

The "products" listed by the Centre for Youth and Society (2003) can easily be supplemented by, for example, the creation of a Web site (Guishard et al., 2003) that can be a central point for community youth to obtain information of relevance to them. Libraries and schools can be used when households do not have access to the Internet. Another possible product can be the publication of a book, as in the case of GirlSource's (2000) *It's About Time!*, a book written by and for young women that addresses a range of health and well-being issues of this particular group. Ten young women (ages 14 to 18 years old) received requisite training as researchers, editors, writers, photographers, art directors, and advocates. The research entailed running focus groups, surveys, and key informant interviews. Development of a book, unlike a final report, has a higher likelihood of receiving a wider distribution, and it can also generate a source of income for the organization.

Role of Media

Finally, it is necessary to end this section with comments pertaining to the role of media on youth's youth-led research dissemination of findings and development of projects targeting the immediate and broader community. Media involvement cannot be relegated to the start and completion of a research process; its potential for helping researchers achieve their ultimate goals would be severely limited if conceptualized in this manner. True, the start of the research process benefits from publicity announcing the commencement of a research undertaking; nevertheless, the potential powerful role of media would be limited by relegating it to one or two phases of the research undertaking.

Dissemination of findings represents the final stage of a project, and youth researchers can benefit immensely from media support in helping to inform the general public about the key findings. However, media involvement throughout all stages of the research process enhances the potential of research to impact the efficacy of the research by maintaining a close public eye on the process, helping to ensure the validity of the results as they are promulgated to the community. Having youth play instrumental roles in the dissemination of research findings is a clever way of helping to ensure reaching disaffected, or disenfranchised, youth within the community (Goggin et al., 2002).

Youth know how best to reach their peers and know the most effective media for getting their messages across in a community dominated by adults.

❖ CONCLUSION

The initiation and sustenance of youth-led research require careful planning. Research projects of any kind are never easy to carry out. The same can be said for youth-led research. As I discussed in this chapter, there are myriad factors and considerations that must be addressed in order to successfully carry out a youth-led research project. It can be effectively argued that all of the facets addressed in this chapter are of equal importance. Some readers, however, may emphasize some aspects over others because of individual talents and experiences. Nevertheless, there is no aspect that can be totally overlooked.

The flexibility inherent in conducting youth-led research must never be confused with a sentiment of not being totally invested in the process. Flexibility in how projects get conceptualized and carried out allows for local circumstances to help shape what youth-led research will look like in a community. This flexibility, however, brings with it incredible challenges in shaping how youth-led research projects get planned and implemented. This chapter has hopefully provided the reader with a template of the different dimensions that must be considered regardless of the nature of the research project being implemented.

8

Ethical Conduct and
Decision Making

The subject of ethics has grown in importance within the past decade in response to public and governmental concerns about potential abuses perpetrated in the name of science. Consequently, ethics and ethical conduct is a subject that also applies to research undertaken by youth. Although everyone agrees it is an important topic, not all agree on how best to protect the rights of those being researched.

Probably one of the most significant ethical dilemmas rests in adults not valuing the views and opinions of youth (Morrow & Richards, 1996; S. Howard et al., 2002). Children and youth are often considered the property of their parents (usually adults) and do not have rights and cannot refuse or accept participation in research without parental consent (Morrow & Richards, 1996). The abuses inherent in viewing youth from this perspective very often get overlooked in safeguarding the rights of parents.

The rapid expansion of the field of youth-led research, however, has made it arduous to stay abreast of advances in the area of ethical conduct and decision making, with specific reference to youth as target groups and as researchers (Pritchard, 2002). For example, in an Internet search, I could not locate even one article or document specifically devoted to this important subject, unlike the experience one would have in researching the literature on adult-led research. As a result, I have the ambitious goal in this chapter of identifying the key issues and considerations and setting forth recommendations pertaining to the role of ethics in youth-led research.

❖ IMPORTANCE OF ETHICAL DECISION MAKING

Save the Children (2000) specifically emphasizes the importance of ethical decision making when involving youth as researchers:

> Every piece of research is context specific, and ethical considerations must bear this in mind. There are some underlying principles that should inform all work with young people. Ethical decisions occur at all levels of research—in the selection of the topic, area or population, source of funding, negotiating access to young people, and in actually conducting the research and publishing the findings. The expectations of the researchers and the support available to the young people must also be considered. Any researcher who does not give due considerations to ethics is potentially damaging the people researched and those carrying out the research. (p. 8)

Thus, the ethical decision-making process covers the entire life span of the research and seeks to address a wide variety of factors.

❖ CONTEXT FOR ETHICAL DECISION MAKING

It would be impossible to speak about youth-led research without serious discussion of ethical dilemmas and decision making without taking into account the context and age of the researchers. Tempting as it may be to develop a set of prescriptive ethical codes of conduct for youth-led research, I believe it is in the best interest of the field to advance an approach that is descriptive and informative, rather than one that is authoritarian or prescriptive. Diener and Crandall (1978) state that research ethics must never be considered as a set of repressive moral dictates but as "dynamic personal principles that appeal to vigorous and active scientists who face difficult real-world decisions" (p. 2). Thus, a user-friendly code of conduct related to youth-led research must ultimately encompass dilemmas that can occur at all stages of research, and must help the researcher in recognizing competing obligations and choices between principles.

In their review of ethics and participatory research, Macaulay et al. (1999) conclude that there are nine specific areas of decision making that must be negotiated between the researcher and participating community, and they have relevance for youth-led research:

- Research goals and objectives
- Methods and duration of the project
- Terms of the community-researcher partnership
- Degrees and types of confidentiality
- Strategy and content of the evaluation
- Where the data are filed, current interpretation of data, and future control and use of data and human biographical material
- Methods of resolving disagreements with the collaborators
- Incorporation of new collaborators into the research team
- Joint dissemination of results in lay and scientific terms to communities, clinicians, administrators, scientists, and funding agencies (p. 775)

Macaulay et al. (1999) articulate a point of view on ethics that disagreements and conflicts should be anticipated as integral parts of any form of participatory research project and that these instances provide participating parties with an opportunity to engage in meaningful discourse. In the case of youth-led research, the age of the researcher further increases the likelihood of conflicts with ethical implications. Participatory research places an incredible set of demands on the training and support of youth researchers, and this needs to be factored into the job responsibilities of specified research team members.

Save the Children (2000) identifies seven general areas related to youth-led research that must be seriously addressed from an ethical standpoint: (1) participation and protection, (2) conflicting agendas between adults and youth, (3) informed consent of interviews and youth researchers, (4) research purposes, (5) confidentiality and trust, (6) clarity pertaining to benefits of the research and the time commitment of both subjects and researchers, and (7) payment, which necessitates the development of a clear and equitable reward system involving both subjects and researchers. Each of these seven areas brings with it inherent challenges for youth researchers, but also critical opportunities to learn and grow as a researcher embracing a community capacity enhancement paradigm. This paradigm serves to guide decision making throughout the research process.

❖ AREAS OF POTENTIAL MISCONDUCT

Regardless of the age of the researcher and the focus of the research, researchers will most likely encounter ethical challenges at critical junctures in the research process. Richards and Schwartz (2002) point out the paucity of articles on ethical issues in qualitative research in medical journals. They identify four major potential risks associated with qualitative research: anxiety and distress, exploitation, misrepresentation, and identification of the identities of the participants in published articles. Each of these potential areas of ethical conflict requires careful decision making and the establishment of agreed-on standards of what constitutes ethical responsible behavior. The field of youth-led research, in turn, relies quite heavily on qualitative and participatory research, making the points raised by Richards and Schwartz particularly meaningful.

Ivan-Smith (1999) identifies seven general areas for potential misconduct in youth-led research and does an excellent job of giving shape to a subject that can easily be expansive and amorphous, but still very important:

1. **Participation and Protection:** No harm must come as a result of participation. The duty to protect takes on added significance and is a fundamental consideration. Awareness and ultimate elimination of the adult-youth power imbalance must be a guiding principle.

2. **Conflicting Agendas:** Soliciting youth voices when they coincide with adult interests, and neglecting them when they do not, is a serious violation of the premises youth-led research is based on. Differences must be negotiated in an open and fair process that does not undermine youth.

3. **Informed Consent:** Both youth researchers and respondents must be well aware of the purpose of the research and what is

expected of them. Consent for participation must be obtained from both youth and guardian in a language that is understood. This means avoiding "legalese" in the primary language, in cases where it is not English.

4. **Purposes of Research:** All parties must be cognizant of the reasons for undertaking and participating in the research, and how the findings will bring about positive change. These reasons must not be abstract and need to be conceptualized with clear examples of the possible changes that can result from the findings of the research.

5. **Confidentiality and Trust:** Confidentiality of responses must be ensured. When it can be breached—how and under what circumstances can this occur? Trust cannot be demanded; it must be earned.

6. **Clarity in Process:** Although it appears to be self-evident, the research must stress clarity throughout all phases as a means of minimizing misunderstandings and feelings of betrayal. This clarity is not restricted to purpose and also applies to methods, process of analysis, and strategies for dissemination of results.

7. **Payment:** Whenever possible, compensation to both researcher and participant must be addressed and maximum remuneration, rather than minimal remuneration, must be the goal. Exploitation results when the maxim of "How cheaply can we pull this off?" is stressed.

An area in Ivan-Smith's list that is implicit, but needs to be explicit, is when and how can youth be terminated from a research project. In addition, an exit interview is in order to help the youth learn from this process. A successful termination can be a positive life-altering experience.

The seven areas identified by Ivan-Smith (1999) inform the research process and can be used to structure researcher training. This content can easily be woven into training sessions or addressed separately, in sessions specifically devoted to ethics and research. Further, this material cannot be relegated to a training module and should be addressed throughout all phases of an ongoing research project.

❖ UNIVERSITY-SPONSORED RESEARCH

University-initiated research presents considerable challenges or barriers to youth-led research. One colleague of mine attempted to involve youth in a Delphi Technique research project but eventually had to abandon this effort at youth involvement because of considerable resistance from the university's institutional review board. Colleagues in other universities across the nation have reported similar experiences. Thus, community-based organizations hold the most promise for initiating and supporting youth-led research endeavors. This does not mean that universities cannot play an important supportive role, however.

❖ CONCLUSION

The subject of ethical conduct and decision making will receive increased recognition as a topic worthy of in-depth attention in the not-too-distant future. This field will continue to evolve and address many of the issues I identified in this chapter and will encounter many more that we cannot even guess at this point in time. Controversy, fortunately or unfortunately, is to be expected and should be viewed as progress in establishing this field as a legitimate field of practice.

The undertaking of a research project is never for the faint of heart, regardless of the age and background of the individual responsible for the project. Youth-led research brings with it the challenges inherent in advocating an innovative approach with a marginal group such as youth. A clear understanding of the goals of a research project will assist sponsoring organizations in bringing youth-led research to life within a community and will do so in a manner that resonates for both youth researchers and community.

9

Funding of Community Research and Program Evaluation

There is little doubt that the question "How much does it cost?" will be an integral part of any serious considerations of youth-led research, now and in the future. The course these discussions take will ultimately dictate how youth will view this form of intervention. The initiation of a research project is never undertaken without a keen appreciation of its costs. All too often, however, when the subject of cost enters into any discussion, it invariably focuses on a rather narrow spectrum, such as the financial costs in dollars and cents.

Although the subject of finances is never to be minimized, such a perspective is much too narrow in scope under most circumstances, and no more so than when it is addressing youth-led research projects. Youth-led research, as a result, must take into account the benefits and consequences (expressive, instrumental, informational) to youth, the organization sponsoring the research, the community at large, and finally, the broader community of youth. Such a multifaceted perspective on costs necessitates the use of multiple measures or considerations of what constitutes costs and what defines "the bottom line." It does not mean, however, that an accountant needs to be an integral part of these deliberations. It does mean that serious discussions on this subject must be a part of any initial discussion of a youth-led research project.

The discussion of funding of social interventions always seems to end in some form of heated discussion on what are the "real" versus "paper" costs. Youth-led research, I am afraid, is not exempt from this debate. This does not mean that an honest, detailed understanding of its financial and social costs cannot take place. It would be unfair, nevertheless, to place youth-led research on a pedestal when we could not do so with adult-led research.

Financial costs, real or perceived, are influenced by who is asking the question and by a number of explicit and implicit factors that are operating during this deliberation. A narrow accounting perspective would be too limited a perspective. A broad and all-encompassing view would be too broad. Nevertheless, our ability to launch and sustain youth-led research projects will ultimately rest in our ability to undertake these efforts at low cost, to minimize possible budget cuts and the disruption they cause in programming (Hatry, Newcomer, & Wholey, 1994). For many of us with extensive histories in the field, this should not come as any great surprise or challenge, for that matter.

In this chapter, I outline a variety of ways to approach financial considerations and offer strategies for obtaining financial underwriting of youth-led research. The reader will undoubtedly have much to add to this important topic. At the very least, I will set a foundation from which to build on and incorporate local circumstances, and I will not attempt to provide actual dollar figures. There are just too many factors to consider in arriving at a final dollar figure pertaining to costs. Thus, my goal is to simply raise a series of considerations that must enter into any serious discussion on costing out (financially and socially) youth-led research.

❖ FINANCIAL CONSIDERATIONS

The jury is still out on whether or not youth-led research can be considered cost-effective. Like any effort at determining cost-effectiveness, the answer is very much predicated on who is asking the question and what is considered to be the ultimate outcome. In this section, I explore how these youth-led research projects have been funded, the extent of funding, and possible sources for funding future projects. In addition, I raise challenges, concerns, and recommendations to assist organizations in better ascertaining the nature and type of funding that should be sought.

Consumer involvement has a dynamic impact on the design and implementation of research and increases the time needed to carry out a study, as well as the financial costs of doing so (Trivedi & Wykes, 2002). Youth-led research costs will no doubt increase as the degree of youth participation in a project increases. Estimating actual costs of youth-led efforts may seem like a rather straightforward process, and if done often enough across the country, we can develop clear guidelines as to what we can expect once we seek to initiate these types of projects. Youth-led research, like its youth development counterpart, brings a tremendous amount of variability (in-kind and other intangibles) that make generalizations difficult to achieve with any high degree of reliability (Whitlock & Hamilton, 2002). Youth as researchers bring with them a set of considerations unique to their age group, such as transportation, scheduling, finances, and support.

Broad and Saunders (1998) take a broad perspective on the costs of conducting peer research and identify five factors that look at social, psychological, and financial dimensions:

1. The emotional costs to the researcher (what do I do with the information/the feelings?) can be quite considerable as young people's troubled stories are told again and again.

2. The emotional costs to the young people arising from the disclosure of private or personal information (the experience might be cathartic or, more usually, bring up painful memories).

3. The financial costs of conducting peer research. A research budget which includes the additional costs of conducting peer research (training, etc.) needs to be drawn up.

4. It takes longer to train, recruit, and supervise young peer researchers, to maintain integrity, standards, and consistency.

5. Peer-led recommendations, however discreetly put, for "more improvements now" from service providers, may make the agencies concerned defensive, possibly fueling fears that research findings will be used against the project(s) involved in some way. (pp. 7–8)

Newman, Smith, and Murphy (2001) broaden the discussion of research costs by noting that carrying out any youth development program true to its philosophical roots and values always costs more than current funds will cover. Hiring, training, and supporting staff to carry out their functions necessitates greater funding than is currently available. Maintaining optimal staff-youth ratios, too, is impossible without expanded funding. Thus, youth-led research is no different than any other youth development–inspired initiative. Compromises are integral to this form of intervention, and the reader and practitioner must come to terms with what is the minimum (rather than what is the optimum) funding necessary to carry out youth-led research projects.

Answers to some of the following questions pertaining to costs will be required prior to the commencement of any research project: What are the short- and long-range benefits for youth researchers? How will their immediate families benefit from their participation? Will the organization sponsoring the research become stronger through a youth-led initiative? How will the community benefit in the immediate and distant future? Finally, how will the youth in the community benefit? The answers to these and other questions are not easily found, particularly if the benefits of engaging in the process are as important as the ultimate product, which is usually a research report addressing very specific program-related questions. Arriving at answers is also compounded by the paucity of research on the effects that youth-adult partnerships may have on youth, adults, and organizations or the conflicts and misunderstandings that these partnerships cause (Norman, 2001).

London (2002), for example, contends that youth-led research is not inexpensive because of stipends and the extensive support that they require throughout the research process. The ultimate answer to whether or not youth research is cost-effective, however, again lies in who is asking the question and what they consider to be the ultimate outcome of their research. If the process of undertaking the research is of equal or more importance than the outcome, then the answers to cost-effectiveness questions are easily found. However, if the outcome or product of the research is the primary goal, then the costs associated with this type of endeavor may be too high to warrant youth-led initiatives. Youth-led initiatives, however, emphasize the importance of the process, or journey, for participants. Thus, the premise behind youth-led interventions leads one to consider this approach only when the gains attributed to process and/or participation have great importance.

In a rare effort to quantify the amount of time needed to support a youth-led research or evaluation project, Youth in Focus (2002) notes:

> By far, the most critical and underestimated resource for a successful youth-led project is time. Staff, youth evaluators, and leadership all emphasized that it took longer to do a youth-led research and evaluation project than they expected. On average, they recommend a commitment of ten to twenty hours per week for the staff coordinator of a basic, single-organization project, and for youth evaluators, a minimum of six to ten hours per week. (p. 19)

Fetterman (2001) raises a potential area of concern, which is the possible exploitation of youth. It may be tempting to cut costs associated with hiring youth because of the amount of time, energy, and resources needed to help develop their research competencies. Consequently, reluctance to pay a wage commensurate with the tasks may be one way of recuperating hidden and not-so-hidden costs associated with this type of research. This tendency must be avoided because it will ultimately undermine the spirit of any research endeavor that is so community capacity enhancement–centered. The democratization of knowledge must never come at the expense of youth and their sense of self-worth.

Thus, sponsoring organizations need to explore multiple answers to this question. Although adults can well argue that the experience should be a reward unto itself, few adults engage in prolonged activities simply based on the inherent rewards associated with participation. Invariably, monetary compensation, or reward, if you wish, enters into a decision about whether or not to participate. Youth should not be an exception to this consideration of both experiential and monetary rewards.

❖ TYPICAL BUDGET ITEMS AND CONSIDERATIONS

Food

The reader may be puzzled by this budget item. However, anyone who has spent time working with youth will undoubtedly understand why an item such as food needs to be included in youth-led initiative budgets, and research is no exception. Mind you, I am not talking about funds to pay for restaurant tabs where meetings are held over a meal, although that is always recommended as a means of encouraging youth to participate and stay with a project. Instead, I am making reference to food bills associated with weekly meetings with youth researchers, where pizza, sodas, and desserts are an integral part. Depending on the number of researchers, this budget category can easily run into several hundred dollars per week.

One project director stressed the importance of providing food and transportation (Horsch et al., 2002): "Very simply, if youth are hungry, they will not be able to concentrate; if youth can't get there, they can't participate. Sharing meals also creates a congenial atmosphere conducive to work and relationship building" (p. 4). Sharing meals and snacks between team members and adults also serves to break down barriers between youth and adults, facilitating communication and sharing.

Providing food, however, should not be done without its serious prior deliberations and considerations. It is tempting to limit the decision to what types of junk food will be provided. Nutrition is something that is often lacking in many youth's lives, both in and out of school. Thus, it is necessary for senior project staff and youth researchers to talk about what kind of food is to be provided, and how to arrive at a compromise should youth researchers just want snack food that is less than nutritious.

Rent for Space

Rent may be relevant when the organization sponsoring the research is located within the boundaries of the community being studied. However, in situations where this is not the case, it may be necessary to consider having an outpost located within the community as a means of facilitating the implementation of the study. This base serves multiple functions, such as cutting down on the time and effort of traveling back and forth to the sponsoring organization for meetings.

It also serves an important sociopolitical purpose: that of providing the community with a chance to have access to project staff should questions arise about the research. If the sponsoring organization is able to establish a base in an organization with a positive reputation within the community, then it benefits from the institutional legitimacy of that organization. This can easily translate into positive reactions to the study and thus facilitate its implementation and acceptance of the findings when they are disseminated. However, paying rent may take away from funds that might be better spent elsewhere.

Incentives

The use of incentives to help motivate and sustain youth in carrying out research is one category that deserves serious discussion. Incentives with youth-led research, for example, must be examined within the total constellation of other youth-run services within the organization. To grant incentives to youth researchers, for example, may cause adverse negative reactions from youth involved in other youth-led projects that do not employ incentives, and thus set apart the work youth researchers do as "more important" than the work other youth engage in. Incentives as a mechanism cannot and should not be relegated to one program at the expense of other programs.

Stipends

A number of scholars have addressed the issues associated with paying child and youth researchers (S. Howard et al., 2002; P. Kirby, 1999; Wilkins & Bryans, 1993). Payment of salary or wages symbolizes recognition of knowledge and skills, conveys worth, serves as a powerful motivator, and increases youth participation in decision making. However, payment can also compromise youth participation by creating a division between manager and workers. In certain situations, it can be a means of social control, and there may be a host of legal considerations in cases where youth are under the age of 16 (P. Kirby, 1999). The reader may well argue, as I do, that similar limitations are also applicable in adult-led research. However, adults, unlike youth, have far more options to leave one research project and move on to another.

The question of whether or not to pay youth to engage in research may appear to be a straightforward question with an equally straightforward response: Of course you pay youth. Nevertheless, do you pay youth when their participation is part of a school project and therefore couched under a curriculum-focused umbrella? Research is, in fact, a multibillion-dollar industry that employs thousands of individuals and is increasingly supporting a bigger share of organizational budgets, particularly in the case of major research-focused universities. A high percentage of social research, however, targets youth and adults from marginal communities. Yet these communities play a minimal role, at best, in setting the agenda and benefiting financially in the short or long term from this form of activity.

Stipends for work performed are undoubtedly the most costly of all the expenses associated with youth-led research. This category includes time spent in training, as well as actually doing field research and other tasks associated with a research project. Further, time spent in activities that are not considered directly relevant to the research project and that can be categorized as fun must also be factored into this category. The importance of paying youth to work as researchers cannot be overly stressed (Youth in Focus, 2002):

> Paying youth [evaluators] helps show them respect, it's actually treating them more like adults. In an area with high poverty like ours, paying youth can focus their attention on the importance of the skills they are learning and help them develop career potential. (p. 23)

It may be tempting to figure out ways of cutting down on this cost. However, as I already noted in the principles covered in Chapter 3, the expertise that youth bring must not be undervalued to make it easier to pay them minimum or near-minimum wages. An organization's ability to pay a respectable stipend or wage brings with it a higher likelihood of youth staying with a project until it is over rather than leaving midway. Early or premature departures increase the organizational costs of recruitment, training, and support and may also result in negative publicity.

In situations where minimum wage is dictated by the funding organization, then it becomes incumbent on the host organization to find ways to supplement stipends, for example, by providing perks such as tickets to local theaters or coupons for local restaurants and food establishments. These perks serve to symbolize the importance of the work that youth do and show them that they are valued by the organization. It is rare for youth, particularly those from undervalued backgrounds, to experience perks of any kind from their involvement in activities.

Data Entry and Analysis

Costs associated with data management can be quite difficult to determine ahead of time because of the wide variation in youth's computer software skills and other competencies. Fortunately, user-friendly programs and youth familiarity with, and comfort level with, computers make the important task of data entry and analysis easier to accomplish. Nevertheless, the final costs associated with this phase are largely determined by the goals of the research and the competencies of the youth. Having to factor in training, supervision, and consultation activities greatly increases these costs. However, if these costs are viewed from a capacity enhancement perspective, namely, building on the capacity of youth, then these costs have long-term benefits for a community, beyond the immediate research project.

Transportation

The topic of transportation may not be a budgetary factor when youth undertake research within their immediate home environment. There are tremendous advantages to having youth research their own communities, since their familiarity with their surroundings is a key factor in increasing their comfort level. In addition, this type of experience helps ground them in the importance of the research. However, transportation takes on added significance when youth are expected to travel to other sections of their city or when adverse weather conditions make walking difficult, as in the case of door-to-door surveys. Weather conditions combined with geographical distance may necessitate that transportation be provided during different periods of the workday.

If an organization does not normally provide this form of transportation, it brings with it a set of challenges concerning costs and insurance. Although it may be tempting to have program staff provide transportation to researchers on an as-needed basis, it is disruptive to these staff and makes youth dependent on the good wishes of staff when transportation should be considered a right and an integral part of conducting research. Consequently, any serious planning of a research project must take into account the transportation factor.

Administration

It would be foolish to think of this category as strictly consisting of senior project personnel who are responsible for the entire operation of a research project. The time and organizational effort on the part of organizational senior management must also be taken into account in factoring costs. Personnel costs represent one administrative dimension. However, communication costs such as cell phones, photocopying, report writing, and press releases, for example, can prove to be very expensive, yet they are an integral part of any research endeavor. Reports and press releases may have to be provided in multiple languages if the results are to be shared with an audience that does not speak English as their primary language. Costs related to electronic recording devices such as videos and tape recorders, if applicable, are included in this category.

Overhead

Often, some percentage of the grant proposal budget is relegated to the factor of overhead. Overhead costs are needed in cases where research activities do not conform to the usual set of activities and tasks undertaken by the sponsoring organization. For example, research project goals may necessitate additional research hours, requiring the organization to be open during times when it is usually closed, such as holidays, evenings, and weekends.

This flexibility in hours and days of operation necessitates administrative coverage and requisite cleanup activities. Further, this funding category may necessitate having a field-based office or renting space in a community-based organization, either of which adds significantly to the costs of conducting youth-led research.

Miscellaneous

Finally, financial considerations of youth-led research would be incomplete without mention of the all-famous miscellaneous category. It is easy to think of this category as a "catchall" for expenses that were unanticipated. It is advisable, however, to seriously consider what expenses should go into this grouping, since this category very often gets close scrutiny from funding sources. My preference has always been not to have this category, and instead, find a home for these types of expenses in other funding categories. The time and effort devoted to what items should be assigned to other categories also enhance clarity of the research project, particularly when this is an activity that is new to an organization.

❖ PAYING INTERVIEWEES

The role of payment within a research project has received some degree of attention and is of sufficient importance to warrant a category unto itself. This perspective, however, has focused on paying participants with payment being viewed as an incentive to participation (Guyll, Spoth, & Redmond, 2003). Payment to participants, as already noted, takes on added significance in the case of low-income potential participants because the additional income, small as it may be, can spell the difference between participation and nonparticipation in a study.

The costs of the research will undoubtedly be influenced by the decision to pay interviewees. The philosophical stance of paying interviewees particularly when they are low-income is not without its advocates and critics, and I include myself in the former. The costs associated with the category are further compounded by the need to maintain detailed records of these financial transactions. Further, youth are thus thrust into positions of having to carry cash around with them as they conduct interviews, causing, in some situations, concerns about their safety. Nevertheless, the exchange of cash for information places youth and their respondents in positions of engaging in a professional relationship that signifies the importance of the act of asking and responding to questions.

In an early work, I specifically address the financial costs of a door-to-door survey involving youth, in this case, Latinos (Delgado, 1981):

> The expense of undertaking a door-to-door survey has often been prohibitive for organizations, particularly grass-roots agencies with limited operating funds. The use of adolescents is economical because they often qualify for summer youth programs and the local government may pay their salaries. If this is not feasible, adolescents are often willing to work for minimum wage or far lower than what would be required to hire adult Hispanics with either extensive education or "experience." (p. 611)

This flexibility in payment, however, does not preclude incentive clauses that effectively increase the salary of youth researchers. Incentives can be obtained through donations from local businesses (e.g., movie tickets, coupons for CDs and DVDs, food vouchers to local restaurants, etc.).

❖ STRATEGIES FOR FINANCING YOUTH-LED RESEARCH

As an activity, youth-led research lends itself to the use of a variety of strategies for obtaining financial support. The "best" strategy is dependent on the organizational capacity of the sponsoring organization and local circumstances. Nevertheless, there are at least four primary strategies that can be used to support youth-led research: (1) grassroots efforts, (2) collaborative partnerships, (3) foundation and corporate grants, and (4) governmental investigator–driven grants. These four strategies can be used singularly or in combination with each other to take advantage of local circumstances.

Grassroots Efforts

Youth-led research, particularly program evaluation, can be funded through grassroots efforts when the research is closely integrated with program development (Gildin, 2003). Grassroots efforts are labor intensive but can do much to build the reputation of programs within communities because of the public relations aspects of identification of potential participants and adult volunteers. Fund-raising activities, such as fairs, raffles, car washes, and solicitations of donations from local businesses, not only generate funds but also serve to ground initiatives within the basic fabric of the community. Consequently, although fund-raising requires considerable time and effort, it is recommended that this effort be broadened. Ultimately, research efforts funded through grassroots initiatives enjoy the greatest amount of community support and political buy-in. This takes on added significance when a program results from the research.

Collaborative Partnerships

Organizations that wish to sponsor youth-led research can use a variety of strategies when initiating these projects. Grants that are specifically obtained to fund a research project are probably the most common strategy. It allows sponsors to conceptualize and develop budgets specific to a funder's request. However, youth-led research projects lend themselves very well to creative approaches that stress collaborations and partnerships between community-based organizations, including schools (Schensul, LoBianco, & Lombardo, 2004).

There is a very compelling case to be made for development of collaborative youth-led research projects by allowing the pooling of resources/expertise that can be complementary in nature. One organization can provide space, with others possibly providing administrative support, advertisement, computers and software, or transportation.

These collaborative efforts help to ensure that a project is well grounded within the community and increases the likelihood that the results of the research are not only accepted but also acted on.

Nevertheless, collaboration means setting aside time for meetings and the instituting of a mutually agreed-on process that allows for differences and conflicts to be addressed. It also means finding organizations that share the philosophy supporting youth-led research, which is not easy or automatic. My experiences speak to the advantages of collaborative youth-led research, but with a keen understanding and appreciation of the limitations inherent in collaborative strategies.

Foundations and Corporations

Youth-led research brings with it a certain "cache" that makes it very appealing to foundations and corporations (Hein, 2000; Walker, 1998; H. B. Weiss & Lopez, 2000). Many in the field will argue that youth-led research owes much of its appeal and history to visionary foundation and corporate funding officers, and that government (national, state, and local) funding is relatively new. The foundation and corporate worlds have essentially helped place youth-led initiatives on the funding map, so to speak. Probably more than any other type of youth-led initiative, youth-led research, in turn, owes much to these sources of funding.

Foundations and corporations, but particularly foundations, have developed a well-acknowledged role in helping to support innovative programming in the United States. Their willingness to take chances is one of the major contributions they have made to the field of youth-led research, as well as in other youth development and youth-led arenas. Nevertheless, it becomes particularly important for organizations to realize that foundations do not like to continue to fund organizations over an extended period of time. This necessitates an active search agenda that explores foundations and corporations, with an understanding that funding may be limited to a one- to three-year period.

Governmental Investigator–Driven Grants

A strategy focused on obtaining governmental and, more specifically, federal government grants to support youth-led research is one that requires serious deliberations because of potential shifting federal priorities, and the lengthy process usually associated with writing, reviewing, and funding these grants requires a tremendous investment of time and effort and should be done after careful considerations of the consequences if funding is not obtained. The availability of funds to sustain such efforts makes youth involvement or youth-led research a highly attractive concept for obtaining government grants.

The potential of government investigator–driven grants as a viable source for youth-led research is very much dependent on the philosophical embrace of key principles by the principal investigator and the applicant organization. Federal demonstration projects can have built-in evaluation efforts that use youth-led community assessment researchers and program evaluators, and thereby bring a much-overlooked dimension to youth programming and initiatives. However, as the reader no doubt realizes, this attempt to include youth in key decision-making roles can succeed only if this approach is part of the philosophical embrace of the lead investigator, the sponsoring organization, and the funder. To conceptualize such an initiative strictly for the sole purposes of obtaining needed funds for an organization severely undermines what youth-led research is capable of achieving.

❖ CONCLUSION

If readers were expecting a clearly outlined budget and guidelines for youth-led research in this chapter, they must surely be disappointed. Costs can easily be manipulated to project a picture that can reflect extreme situations such as excessive costs or very low costs by strictly focusing on the monetary aspect. However, such a narrow approach does not do justice to the potential of youth-led research and intervention. Costs, whether anticipated or not, are part of any social intervention, youth- or adult-led. Consequently, I have sought to widen the discussion of the costs of youth-led research in the hopes of making this type of youth-led intervention more appealing in the field. I also wanted to stress the complexity of the issue of costs within youth-led research, especially how difficult it is to measure and predict costs. Although significant, demystifying the costs is but one step in making youth-led research easier to embrace.

By framing the question of costs in a broader arena or light, the question then becomes "How much should society be willing to pay to invest in capital for a future that has the potential to be unbounded?" If the form of capital were related to minerals, land, equipment, or computers, the question would be easily answered. If, in turn, the form of capital is related to youth, I do not believe that the answer would be so easily forthcoming. Why? This and other societies always seem better able to invest in tangible goods. Youth, unfortunately, are rarely considered in this category. My position, as the reader has no doubt concluded, falls into the category of broadening the question of costs to include the benefits of youth participation in youth-led research.

PART III

Field Examples

I t would be relatively simple to write a book on youth-led research and avoid any attention to case studies. Such a book would lack in-depth description and analysis and therefore would not do justice to the topic. Case studies provide the reader with a multidimensional picture of how youth-led research is operationalized in the field. Case studies, I believe, have the wonderful capacity to bring subject matter to life in a way that no other approach can approximate. In short, case studies are not just theoretical, but represent "real life" in a movement, and thus serve to both inform and excite practitioners and would-be practitioners.

As noted by Calvert et al. (2002), the field is in desperate need of case studies highlighting the implementation of youth-led initiatives:

> Case studies of organizations and communities that have success-fully infused young people in authentic leadership roles are needed. Such studies provide examples for other organizations and policy-makers. Case studies can examine the critical degree of youth involvement and the kind of roles and daily practices that lead to the strongest outcomes. (p. 10)

These authors challenge the field to initiate longitudinal studies that track individuals as they change roles and move on to new settings and roles, with particular attention to social justice themes and diversity.

Part III is specifically written to highlight field-based examples of youth-led research, to provide the reader with concrete examples of what is possible when there is a commitment to this form of research. In an effort to provide a wide assortment of case illustrations, I have sacrificed depth and level of detail. The intent of these cases is not to provide the reader with all the information necessary to successfully replicate the example. Rather, the intent is to spark or stimulate new ways of bringing about youth-led research (e.g., through use of oral histories within a classroom setting or community-based groups), rather than continuing with established approaches. Oral histories are important and viable research options. However, the field of youth-led research is much more encompassing and can easily utilize oral histories to buttress other forms of research.

I chose the four case illustrations in Chapter 10 for their diverse research approaches and their diverse elements; they differ in focus, setting, participant age, and duration. The case illustrations in no way represent the totality of the field of youth-led research. Each of these case illustrations, however, provides the reader with a brief glimpse as to the potential of the field to include innovative approaches. These cases utilize a variety of research approaches for gathering data on community assets, needs, and evaluation of program effectiveness. Generally, these approaches emphasize small-scale activities that are specifically focused on developing an in-depth understanding of a particular issue or need.

10

Field Examples of Youth-Led Community Research

I n this chapter, I provide the reader with a range of case examples rather than a single case study. This decision was reached after much deliberation. Books focused on practice, even those focused on the practice of research, must contend with the tension of breadth versus depth in presenting case material. Each of these approaches brings with it numerous advantages and disadvantages. I believe that by providing a range of case illustrations on the topic of youth-led research, the reader is best served since this form of practice can take on numerous manifestations, based on the setting of the study, focus, methods, and goals.

Ideally, each type of youth-led research study should have a detailed case study devoted to it, highlighting what makes the approach special. However, space does not permit this approach. Thus, I have chosen a total of four case examples to further enhance the reader's appreciation for youth-led research. These case illustrations consist of greater detail than those case examples used throughout earlier parts of this book. However, they will not possess the level of detail or specificity customarily found when one chapter is exclusively devoted to a case study.

❖ RATIONALE FOR SELECTION

Each of the case illustrations was selected with the following considerations in mind: (a) setting (school and community); (b) geographical region: New England (Boston and Hartford) and West Coast (Oakland and San Francisco); (c) primary research methods (surveys, focus groups, key informants); (d) source of funding (foundation, local and state government, subcontracts); (e) focus of the research (school climate, biased media, substance abuse, communicable diseases); (f) length and timing of research (summer and academic year); and (g) single and multisite focus. The final case illustration—the Institute for Community Research—is different than the others in this chapter because it presents a series of youth-led studies, rather than emphasizing one study, and highlights an organization exclusively devoted to community participatory research.

❖ CASE ILLUSTRATIONS

Youth Media Project, Oakland, California

The influence of media in the lives of youth, particularly the role of music and radio stations, is well appreciated in this society. Interestingly, this arena lends itself to youth-led initiatives, including research. Radio stations targeting youth audiences have an obligation to make their programming responsive to their needs, opinions, and perspectives. I chose to discuss the following case illustration because of its focus on radio programming and how youth activism, based on a community assessment, led to a concerted effort to change one radio station's biased programming.

The research undertaken by the Youth Media Council, Oakland, California, represents a rather novel approach to community assessment; in this case, it is an assessment of a radio station. Between September 10 and September 30, 2002, the Youth Media Council undertook a content analysis of Bay Area radio station 106.1 KMEL. This station was widely considered to be the primary station for youth, particularly those of color, in the area. This assessment involved a team of ten youth and young adult researchers who did a content analysis of twenty-four prime-time broadcasts (6 a.m. to 10 a.m. and 3 p.m. to 6 p.m.). In addition, four broadcasts of KMEL's nationally syndicated weekly talk show, "Street Soldiers," were monitored between September 15 and October 6, 2002.

The Youth Media Council undertook the assessment because of concerns about how the media generally portrays youth, especially youth of color, effectively criminalizing and silencing youth voices. Four research questions guided the content analysis (Youth Media Council, 2002):

- Whose voices are heard and whose are excluded?
- What are the primary themes raised?
- Who is held responsible for problems raised?
- Are policies, root causes, or solutions mentioned? (p. 6)

The content analysis of 106.1 KMEL uncovered four themes that effectively biased the public's perception of youth: (1) exclusion of the voices and perspectives of youth organizers and local artists, (2) neglect of discussion pertaining to policy debates affecting youth and people of color, (3) disproportionate emphasis on crime and violence, and (4) no clear, distinct avenue for listeners to hold the station accountable for its actions. Each of these biases is significant in and of itself; however, when in combination, they wield a tremendous amount of influence on public perceptions of marginalized communities (Wilson & Gutierrez, 1985).

The Youth Media Council (2002) created a report with a goal that is typically associated with most forms of youth-led research: *"We hope this unique report will serve as a springboard for young people to continue raising their voices and to reclaim the media as a tool for social change* [italics per original source]" (p. 6). The central goal of achieving social change as the result of research is well encapsulated within the previous statement and highlights the potential of youth-led research to stimulate youth-led community organizing (Delgado & Staples, 2005).

The Youth Media Council (2002) developed a set of five recommendations for 106.1 KMEL to redress biased coverage:

- Provide a policy context for problems raised in content.
- Highlight root causes like racism and lack of access to services.
- Let youth speak for themselves about youth and youth policy.

- Balance coverage of youth by giving airtime to youth organizers and advocates.
- Link social problems to public policy solutions and examine the impact of ineffective policies that are hurting local communities. (p. 12)

These recommendations go far beyond benefiting youth, to benefiting their entire community, a true hallmark of youth-led research endeavors. Connectedness between youth researchers and their peers within the broader community increases the number of potential beneficial outcomes of research by informing the greater community and possibly serving as a recruiting mechanism for future studies by youth.

Boston Student Researchers for High School Renewal, Boston, Massachusetts

This chapter would not be complete without case studies based within school settings. The importance of schools in the lives of youth is well recognized, and so is the schools' role in helping youth assume roles as researchers within and outside of these settings. The most frequent type of school-based, service-learning project takes a unidimensional perspective involving one school and its community. It is rare to find a service-learning project that involves multiple schools and even rarer to find such a project taking a research focus (Boston Plan for Excellence, 2004a, 2004b).

The Boston Student Researchers for High School Renewal not only involves multiple schools but also is a collaborative effort between multiple organizations, in this case, a collaboration between the Boston Public Schools, the Boston Plan for Excellence in the Public Schools, the Boston Private Industry Council, and Jobs for the Future. Collaboration brings the potential for combining resources and increasing the impact of the findings beyond one institution. Youth researchers made a PowerPoint presentation to the superintendent of schools, administrators, and community members and shared preliminary results of their study.

The Boston Student Researchers for High School Renewal (SRHSR) project is part of an overall initiative called High School Renewal (HSR), funded by the Carnegie Corporation, New York. SRHSR represents one strategy to help reduce student alienation within schools and more effectively connect adults with students. The undertaking of the research on "school climate" is an attempt to give voices to students about their experiences in school. Data were obtained on peer relations, school physical structure, and student-teacher relationships.

The process used to select a research topic was not easy, although unusual. After much deliberation, the researchers selected the broad topic of school climate and decided to gather data on a variety of issues, concerns, and problems. This case illustration involved eleven youth researchers of mixed gender and racial-ethnic backgrounds, from eight different Boston public high schools. A survey was developed and mailed to eight high schools, and over 1,500 surveys were returned.

The importance of the research experience is well attested to by two of the student researchers ("Boston's Student Researchers," 2003, p. 65):

When I got involved with Student Researchers, I was really wondering how to make the community to think, to achieve, to make change. . . . I learned that it really just takes the action of one person to motivate others. It's starting with yourself and making sure that your actions reflect what you want to see changed. (Gervase Jones)

You can make change happen. You gotta have a positive attitude. You want to make it better, then make it better. It starts with you. (Christian Stallworth)

These comments place youth in a central position regarding change within their lives, institutions, and community. I cannot help being impressed with the degree of empowerment that resulted from participation in this research undertaking. Youth can contribute in a meaningful manner and be empowered to do so by adults and other youth.

The following were the key overarching findings from the survey (Student Researchers for High School Renewal, 2003):

1. **Student-Teacher Relationships**—A majority of the students feel respected by "all/most" of their teachers; a majority report "all/most" of their teachers believe all students can learn if they try, answer their questions in class, encourage them to participate in classroom lessons. Students in bilingual programs report particularly positive student-teacher relationships; 25 percent of the student respondents consider themselves alienated.

2. **Peer Relationships**—There are negative interactions among students, particularly along racial and ethnic lines; students report little respect for each other; lack of respect increased with grade level; small schools yielded slightly more positive responses about peer relationships than did large schools.

3. **School Environment**—There is a range of feelings about the culture of academic achievement; school pride is lagging in most schools; students expressed concern about school cleanliness; rules about respecting school property are not enforced consistently; issues of safety are problematic in all schools; disruptive behavior is prevalent at most schools. (pp. 3–5)

The findings served as a basis for development of a series of recommendations and suggestions for future study. Student Researchers developed a set of three major recommendations for practice (Student Researchers for High School Renewal, 2003):

(1) *Students must be provided with more opportunities to talk and work with adults and each other* [italics per original source]—student involvement in re-evaluation of events that promote cultural awareness; increased decision-making power; undertake more focus groups between and among students and teachers; bring student voices to the district school level; (2) *Involve key members of the community in development of strategies addressing school issues*—parents, community leaders, city officials, Boston Police Department, Massachusetts Bay Transit Authority; and (3) *Create and sustain school structures to build a sense of community*—institute forums to discuss race and culture, create activities that actively promote school pride and student respect for school property. (pp. 5–6)

The emphasis on bringing about change as the result of the research findings is an unmistakable marker in youth-led research projects, and this endeavor was no exception.

Not surprisingly, Student Researchers recommended that future research should consider addressing two key questions:

- Why are bilingual students reporting more favorable relationships with teachers than are students overall?
- Why are small schools not showing significantly better relationships with teachers than larger schools?

These questions were raised by youth, who attempted to develop a more in-depth understanding of why results did not meet expectations. The first question relates to a positive finding, which needed to be understood further in order to improve the school climate for all students. The second question focused on developing a better understanding of how small schools foster better relationships between students and teachers.

This case example shows that it is possible to undertake large-scale surveys within youth-led research and to do so within an academic year schedule. Having appropriate external support, however, makes this possible. It does not mean that youth cannot undertake surveys focused on their particular school or community. Surveys that cross school and community boundaries necessitate adequate funding and support, but they bring richer meaning to the ultimate results, and may also result in efforts to build coalitions across schools and communities within a city.

McClymunds High School, West Oakland, California

The second school-based example brings an added, and often overlooked, perspective to students undertaking research. The case study of McClymunds High School, West Oakland, California, provides a West Coast example of the use of surveys, and in this case, the extensive use of focus groups, too, to complement the Boston case example. Unlike the Boston case, the McClymunds High School research focused on just one school. The following case illustrates how school-based research surveys can seek to answer a wide variety of questions pertinent to adolescent youth.

The West Oakland YELL (Youth Engaged in Learning and Leadership) Project, sponsored by the John W. Gardner Center for Youth, was a school-based project at McClymunds High School that utilized a survey and focus groups to assess the school's strengths and needs, with a specific focus on school funding, teaching, and learning. "The project aimed to generate information from a youth's perspective that can inform other youth development efforts and local policy decisions that impact young people" (YELL, 2002, p. 3). A team of adolescents from mixed gender and racial-ethnic backgrounds received training on a variety of research methods at the Stanford University School of Education.

YELL produced critical information pertaining to community resources from a youth's perspective. However, it also provided youth with skills in research, leadership, teamwork, interpersonal relations, and communication. YELL's dissemination of school-focused research findings included not only a written report but also a radio program. An emphasis on multiple sources of information typifies this and other youth-led research projects, with particular value being placed on non-conventional reports as a means of disseminating the research findings to a variety of constituencies.

Institute for Community Research, Hartford, Connecticut

The final case illustration involving the Institute for Community Research (ICR), as noted earlier in this chapter, highlights how one organization devoted to participatory research can initiate a number of youth-led research projects and create a cadre of youth researchers involving a wide range of areas and population groups (Owens & Jones, 2004; Schensul & Berg, 2004; Schensul, Berg, et al., 2004).

ICR (2004a) seeks to accomplish six goals through its research projects:

- Establish partnerships that make research accessible to broad audiences.
- Train youth, adolescents, and adults to conduct and use research for community change.
- Develop new models of public health prevention, and test new ideas for effectiveness.
- Promote cultural expression and community cultural resources.
- Use research to advocate for positive change.
- Share results, models, and information through conferences, workshops, publications, and other public forums. (p. 1)

ICR, as a result, has initiated and implemented a series of youth-led research projects. The Youth Action Research Institute within ICR is the primary mechanism for youth-led research initiatives (ICR, 2004d). This institute recruits and trains preadolescents and adolescents to undertake ethnographic-focused research. Youth researchers play a vital role in training other youth to assume the role of researcher. In addition, ICR is also responsible for the development and dissemination of action research curricula and other products, such as research instruments, with the expressed purpose of empowering youth (Berg, 2004; Schensul, LoBianco, et al., 2004).

A number of other research projects are carried out through the institute. The Sexual Minority Youth Action Research Project (state grant) recruits and trains lesbian, gay, bisexual, transgender, and questioning (LGBTQ) youth of color and their allies, to "use research as a tool for addressing issues of concern and importance to them, their communities and schools" (ICR, 2004b, p. 1). Participatory research involving LGBTQ youth of color is not only possible but highly encouraged (Owens & Jones, 2004). Research teams investigated the availability and access to support systems for LGBTQ youth in two urban areas of Connecticut. The Diffusing Youth-Based Participatory Action Research for Prevention Model (ICR, 2004b) is a substance abuse prevention initiative that relies on a participatory action research training process. This model seeks to recruit and train youth to undertake research in different types of settings and with different urban-based population groups (Brase et al., 2004).

The scope and types of projects initiated by the ICR makes this organization unique in the world of youth-led research and highlights the potential of using research as a vehicle for engaging and empowering marginalized youth in urban communities. The organization's emphasis on publishing reports and scholarly articles, in addition to sponsoring conferences and workshops to outline the process of youth-led research, serves to unite the worlds of practice and academia in a manner that best captures and builds on each arena's strengths.

❖ CONCLUSION

The case examples presented in this chapter represent only a small fraction of the important work that is currently being undertaken in the field of youth-led research. Due to lack of space, I could not do justice to the impressive work each of these organizations undertook in carrying out their projects; neither have I done justice to how the experiences transformed the lives of many of the youth researchers. It seems like every community in the United States has examples of youth-led research within schools and community-based settings. The professional literature on the subject has only managed to touch the tip of this iceberg, so to speak, and as the field continues to mature, there will no doubt be systematic efforts to consolidate the lessons learned. The emergence of a meta-analysis will serve as a signal of how far the field has evolved over the years and will provide us with a compass to help us choose where we want to go in the future.

The reader has no doubt developed an informed opinion on how and when youth-led research can transpire within his or her respective community. The field has an abundance of approaches that take into consideration local issues, resources, and goals. The broadness and reach of the field, in many ways, are limited only by our imagination and willingness to push the boundaries associated with social research. Thus, this can be considered a field that has the potential to match the energy, hopes, dreams, and commitment that youth possess; there are not many fields that fit this description.

PART IV

Future Challenges

11

Challenges and Implications for Practice

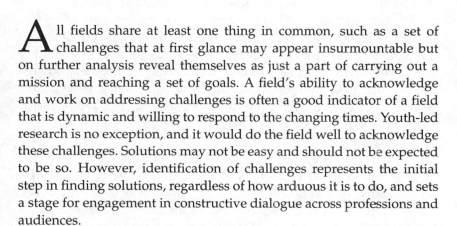

All fields share at least one thing in common, such as a set of challenges that at first glance may appear insurmountable but on further analysis reveal themselves as just a part of carrying out a mission and reaching a set of goals. A field's ability to acknowledge and work on addressing challenges is often a good indicator of a field that is dynamic and willing to respond to the changing times. Youth-led research is no exception, and it would do the field well to acknowledge these challenges. Solutions may not be easy and should not be expected to be so. However, identification of challenges represents the initial step in finding solutions, regardless of how arduous it is to do, and sets a stage for engagement in constructive dialogue across professions and audiences.

This chapter identifies seven challenges that, I believe, are at the central core of the field and will play critical roles in its efforts to evolve within the next decade. The reader will undoubtedly identify a different set of challenges or bring a different conceptualization to the challenges addressed in this chapter. I embrace the belief that a field of practice without challenges is a field of practice not worth practicing.

Challenges serve to engage and mobilize rather than dissuade, divide, and immobilize. The field of youth-led research, like its more encompassing youth development or youth-led movement umbrellas, brings with it a unique, core set of challenges. The following sections focus on these unique challenges.

❖ HOW CAN WE CREATE AND MAINTAIN A CADRE OF YOUTH RESEARCHERS?

Any organization involved in carrying out an active and ongoing research agenda will quickly attest to the importance of creating and maintaining a cadre of well-qualified researchers on staff. As this book has no doubt reinforced, research is an activity that requires considerable time, effort, and preparation to accomplish its tasks in a manner acceptable to a wide community, including the scientific world. Thus, recruiting and maintaining a cadre of researchers cannot be left to chance. I (and many others in the field) would argue that recruiting and maintaining researchers is especially challenging to organizations involved in youth-led projects because of the paucity of youth-trained researchers in most communities across the United States.

Institutions that carry out research projects, particularly those that are very successful at doing so, are able to recruit and maintain a team of researchers with a wide range of competencies. In addition, they are in a position to have access to staff with certain competencies when internal staff does not possess them. These institutions are not only better able to compete for grants, but they are also in the position to carry out the requisite activities associated with social research in a timely manner.

Similar expectations of youth-led research are required. Organizations such as the ones highlighted in Chapter 10 of this book (Community Research Institute, Hartford; Student Researchers, Boston; Youth in Focus, Oakland; and Youth IMPACT, San Francisco) best approximate this goal and show both the rewards and challenges associated with maintaining an active youth-led research agenda. These organizations were able to carry out their research missions because of their foresight and strategic planning in building organizational capacity.

The ability of youth-serving organizations to develop partnerships in the world of service and education holds great promise for the field of youth-led research (Institute for Community Research, 2004a, 2004c). Development of collaborative projects that complement each sponsoring organization's competencies is quite appealing. Some organizations may have a strong base in developing surveys, whereas another may be particularly competent in conducting focus groups. Joint research undertakings lead to potential joint programming, representing a natural starting point in the evolution of a service or program. Combining of resources, as addressed in Chapter 7, opens up a wide range of possible research projects that cannot otherwise be carried out. Partnerships, as a result, also offer the potential for institutions to carry out ambitious projects with minimal outlay of financial funds, although interagency collaboration is never for the faint of heart, because of the difficulties inherent in getting two or more institutions to put aside their own agendas in search of an agenda that stresses cooperation.

❖ HOW CAN WE DOCUMENT THE LONG-TERM CONSEQUENCES OF PARTICIPATION IN YOUTH-LED RESEARCH FOR ALL PARTIES INVOLVED, INCLUDING ADULT COLLABORATORS AND THE COMMUNITY?

Blyth and Burden (2003) rightly note that the importance of documenting the outcomes of youth-led initiatives cannot be overstated, particularly when universities are involved: "While research cannot and should not control . . . family, organizational, community, and national policy processes of how we invest in our youth, research provides a critically important set of tools and approaches that must become more fully and effectively engaged" (p. 14).

Although understandable, the never-ending quest for "evidence-based" research findings proving that youth-led research "works" can be quite frustrating and annoying. The cry for proof is not unreasonable if this quest does not expect more from youth-led research than any other social movement. A long-term versus short-term perspective on benefits necessitates that adequate time and resources be allocated to finding the answers, and that evaluators be familiar with all of the challenges inherent in both immediate and longitudinal research involving youth, particularly those from marginalized backgrounds. Very often the lives that these youth live can be classified as tumultuous.

Nevertheless, this country has generally eschewed investing sufficient funding to help determine the long-term changes resulting from social interventions, and it would be foolhardy to ignore this trend. Thus, those advocating for long-term evaluation of the impact of intervention on communities face an uphill battle for funding. Given this situation, it is within this backdrop that any dialogue on long-range effects needs to be addressed. Further, there is little question that success in this arena is contingent on the practice and academic fields coming together (Blyth & Burden, 2003):

> Much of the momentum behind the youth development field to this point has been driven by lessons from the practice tower. The research tower has been built, to a large degree, in isolation. There is a value in both places and in their connection. (p. 19)

It is important to pause and note that long-term evaluation efforts must actively involve youth in all facets. It would be shameful to utilize an adult-led effort to evaluate youth-led research, since this counters everything that youth-led research stands for and embraces. Youth-led research has emerged as a field precisely because of the failures of established research practice, which has almost totally excluded youth from positions other than research subjects. Long-range studies must be based on a political will to follow through over the course of years and must have legitimacy so that when the results are shared with the general public and scientific community, they have meaning. These results can be expected to consist of both positive as well as negative outcomes, and effort must be made to allow both sides of the equation, so to speak, to be heard and acted on.

❖ TO WHAT EXTENT SHOULD GROUP-SPECIFIC RESEARCH FOCUS ON GENDER AND ETHNIC GROUPS?

Youth-led research can take a very broad or very narrow perspective on inclusion. Thus, it has the potential to divide or unite youth depending on the goals of the research. VALIDITY (Toronto, Canada) is an excellent example of an approach that is centered exclusively on gender and sexual orientation. VALIDITY's focus groups, for example, were arranged by age and for girls and young women with similar backgrounds and experiences. These groups included women of color, young lesbian and bisexual women, Native young women, rural Francophone young women, pregnant teens, single moms, and street-involved young women (Centre for Addiction and Mental Health, 2001).

The subject of diversity is one that has historically faced conflicting perspectives within the United States. On one hand, we wish to believe that everyone deserves an equal chance or even playing field in this society. However, a quick perusal of any set of social statistics will bring up discussions as to why disparities exist within groups, racial, ethnic, or otherwise. The answers to these questions are influenced by deep-seated values and perceptions prevalent in all social institutions within this society.

Youth are not exempt from these factors and considerations. Consequently, senior staff involved with youth-led research projects must welcome the opportunity to openly discuss issues associated with oppression of various kinds. Unfortunately, adult-led research rarely addresses this topic, even in situations where the researchers are dramatically different from those being researched. Youth, unless they are very fortunate, rarely have settings where this subject can be openly and safely discussed. I believe that youth-led research projects can perform a critical public service by creating a climate within which these issues can be openly raised and discussed within the context of research (Rubin & Rubin, 1995; M. Williams & Roche, 1999). We can choose to ignore this opportunity, but that does not mean that these issues will not surface and possibly seriously compromise the integrity of the research.

❖ HOW MUCH EFFORT SHOULD BE
   PLACED ON ESTABLISHING COLLABORATIONS
   BETWEEN UNIVERSITIES AND COMMUNITY-BASED
   ORGANIZATIONS IN SPONSORING
   YOUTH-LED RESEARCH?

It may be sacrilegious for someone based in a university setting to raise this question, but it still needs to be raised, seriously discussed, and addressed with appropriate actions. The elite govern universities, and, when discussing research, these institutions overwhelmingly subscribe to a model that is adult-centered, and they control the right to determine who is a "researcher." This determination is predictably based on a "formal" assessment of credentials and expertise legitimacy and is invariably tied to higher-education degrees. A number of university-based scholars who conduct community-based research, most notably those utilizing participatory principles, show that it is possible to involve communities in research, although this involvement is not without its set of challenges (Strand et al., 2003).

Nevertheless, community-based organizations engaging in collaborative partnerships with universities must seriously consider the potential trade-offs these relationships will engender. Funders of social research have started to slowly move away from a model that is heavily dependent on universities initiating and controlling the research process to one that has vested more power in community settings dictating the research process and outcomes. The Centers for Disease Control and Prevention exemplifies this shift in one federal agency. However, it would be foolish for me to say that this shift has been accomplished to the satisfaction of all interested parties.

Evaluation, whether focused on process or output, must always be an integral part of any youth-led research project. I recommend that evaluation be tailored to the scope of the project and the availability of resources for successfully undertaking this task. The reader may argue that this recommendation is not new. However, I never cease to be amazed by how rarely this suggestion is followed. Those involved in youth-led research should never accept the notion that evaluation is only possible when "appropriate" resources are made available. If not available, then evaluation is impossible.

The either-or proposition will never advance the field forward since it is rare to find the appropriate resources being allocated to this task. Designing limited scope evaluation allows for meaningful results to emerge. Using existing data and relying on ethnographic data that can be more easily obtained can provide important proof of how a project altered the lives of youth participants.

Full-scale evaluations with requisite funding, time, institutional and community support, and youth staff expertise are wonderful, and when they transpire, it is considered a "magic moment." The typical evaluation of a youth-led research project, however, has minimal funding. Thus, the more the field can integrate evaluation as part of the ongoing research process, the more likely it will be that the field generates data, qualitative and quantitative, that can help shape future youth-led research projects.

❖ WHAT ARE THE CHARACTERISTICS AND CONDITIONS THAT FOSTER YOUTH-LED RESEARCH?

This very question can be asked of any significant social intervention regardless of its focus and regardless of the age of the ultimate beneficiaries of the intervention. Youth-led-research requires careful evaluation, both short- and long-term, of how this form of intervention effectively alters the lives of youth who participate, the organizations that serve them, and the communities in which they live. The role of case studies of successful organizations can go a long way toward helping to shape research questions directed at better understanding what makes these organizations successful. The answer to this question will necessitate a positive working relationship between researchers using both qualitative and quantitative methods.

Those in the field of youth development have made important strides in better assessing the benefits of intervention and how they can be measured and maximized (Dworkin & Bremer, 2004; MacDonald & Valdivieso, 1998; Roth, 2004; Sengstock & Hwalek, 1999). These pioneering efforts can easily be used to focus on youth-led research, not only furthering knowledge specific to the field but also bridging youth-led research with youth development.

The field of youth development, in turn, can benefit immensely from inclusion of youth in their research efforts. The knowledge derived from evaluating youth-led research projects can, and must, filter its way into university settings and educational programs specifically tailored to advance the field of youth development and youth-led initiatives. This process will understandably be slow-paced for most advocates of these types of interventions, but necessary, nevertheless.

A better grasp of the factors that maximize youth-led research initiatives can play an influential role in helping to craft youth-led research projects that have specific goals for maximizing these efforts with youth facing certain types of challenges in their lives, or have certain sociodemographic characteristics. Thus, the process of undertaking youth-led research is of equal importance as the product outcome of the research. A better balance between the two cannot be achieved. Further, knowledge gained from these efforts will undoubtedly help other forms of youth-led initiatives in crafting evaluation models of those efforts. In short, the entire field of youth development and youth-led research will advance as a result.

❖ TO WHAT EXTENT DOES DIVERSITY BRING
WITH IT POTENTIAL CONFLICTS WITHIN
YOUTH-LED RESEARCH TEAMS?

The field of youth development has been quite explicit in advocating inclusiveness to reflect the richness of a community. Community-centered interventions can hold real meaning only if they reflect the composition of the community being addressed. However, diversity in composition places team leaders in a challenging position: They must not only expect conflicts, due to the differing backgrounds of youth participants, but also constructively address them in ways that enhance the research process.

Diversity as a value and goal, however, is not restricted to the more conventional references to ethnicity, race, socioeconomic class, and gender. It must also embrace sexual orientation and those with physical and cognitive challenges (Owens & Jones, 2004). Broadening what is meant by this construct also broadens what we mean when we say "community." Communities always consist of a multitude of groups and youth, and any definition of community is no exception. Consequently, a value stressing inclusiveness will necessitate that those involved in youth-led research be cognizant not only of what is meant by community but also of how youth struggle with issues and experiences commonly found in any effort to achieve social and economic justice for all, and not just some, youth.

❖ WHO SHOULD BE RESPONSIBLE FOR BUILDING YOUTH-LED RESEARCH COMPETENCIES?

The development of competencies represents the logical next step in the field. The importance of this step is too great to rest in one sector. The field will make significant strides from practice and academic perspectives when these two worlds combine to help develop competencies in youth involved in all facets of youth-led research, with youth helping to identify and create measures evaluating these competencies. These competencies can influence recruitment, development of training and field support, and evaluation of all aspects of the research process. This list of competencies would also require creation of scales that also need to be based on field research.

Identification and assessment of these competencies will necessitate a close working relationship between practitioners and academics. Their collaboration is a labor-intensive process that requires considerable expenditure of funds. Nevertheless, the benefits of such an effort will effectively and efficiently move the field forward in a manner that can be easily evaluated, eventually resulting in the creation of theories and constructs based in the world of practice rather than academia. Hopefully, this book represents the initial stage of synthesizing material from a variety of sources and identifying areas of collective agreement and potential disagreement.

❖ CONCLUSION

The reader's willingness and ability to read through to the end of this chapter speaks well to his or her fortitude and embrace of practice that is not only dynamic and challenging in nature but also full of unexpected rewards and opportunities for innovation. The reader may argue with the selection of the seven challenges highlighted in this chapter and may advocate for a set of challenges not mentioned. Nevertheless, the presence of challenges in the field of youth-led research necessitates the establishment of partnerships between professional groups, and between these groups and communities. Although fraught with considerations and labor intensive, these partnerships are essential to the development of solutions to challenges.

The excitement of being part of a movement such as that represented by youth-led initiatives speaks well to those practitioners and academics. These types of partnerships bode well for future undertakings by enriching all parties in these endeavors and in the communities that are the ultimate beneficiaries of research. The benefits are not only immediate, but they also set the stage for future rewards that will enrich the lives of countless numbers of individuals, communities, and professions, making the bold move to embrace youth-led research as a viable and important part of knowledge creation.

12

Epilogue

I need to address nine key topics that warrant attention before I can "officially" complete this journey and put this book to rest, so to speak, which is always a challenging task for me. The reader, I am sure, could easily come up with other subjects. In fact, I would be disappointed if this were not the case. Differences of opinion, as I emphasize throughout this book, are to be expected and even encouraged, as a means of engaging in dialogue and moving the field forward. Nevertheless, I have selected these topics because of their importance to moving the field forward during this first decade of the twenty-first century.

❖ INNOVATIONS AND RESEARCH

Innovations and emerging fields are synonymous, causing excitement and frustration at the same time. I must be honest with the reader: I was not expecting to find so many innovative advances in the field of youth-led research. The field is still relatively young, and, as is customary in these situations, advances are difficult to keep up with. Many of these advances are so new that they have not found their way into conventional communication channels so that they can be studied and applied to local situations, particularly when the advances have transpired internationally.

Penuel, Gray, and Kim (2004) report on exciting developments integrating technology into community youth research and its potential for enhancing youth's experience. However, it has its set of challenges. Using new forms of data analysis software, such as Tinkerplots and Entryware Pro, represents a creative and colorful way of making data meaningful. Handheld software for use in survey data collection is another example of how technology can make research exciting, educational, and easy to use in service to a community. Penuel et al. caution, however, that introducing new technology requires careful development of a plan, extensive training support, and funds to purchase equipment.

The international scope of this field makes it particularly conducive to innovative advances. There were times when I read a report about a "totally new" way of research, and this proved exciting. At times, an innovative method I was familiar with, such as the use of photography or video, would be applied in an unexpected manner, such as with youth who are deaf or hearing-impaired. The possibilities of using visual or nonverbal approaches to breach the gap between youth of different backgrounds or, for example, between youth who are literate or illiterate represent the openness of the field to embrace new methods and designs.

I cannot predict how many of these new advances will remain in use five to ten years from now. Some, I believe, will systematically work their way from "unorthodox" to "emerging" and eventually enter the realm of "conventional." Others, however, will simply disappear. Nevertheless, the spirit guiding the emergence of these youth-led research methods remains the same, regardless of the staying power of the approach.

❖ ADULT-YOUTH RELATIONSHIPS
   AND THE POTENTIAL FOR ABUSE

Any systematic review of the literature and field interviewers with youth and adults who work with youth will reveal one prevailing theme regardless of the setting and geographical representation. The breaking down of barriers between youth and adults gets mentioned over and over again. Mind you, it does not mean that youth and adults cannot collaborate on equal terms or that adults cannot function in positions subservient to youth. Nevertheless, the power differential between youth and adults is a significant barrier in the successful launching of youth-led initiatives of any kind. Youth-led research, however, brings to the fore the power differential even more so because of the role of expertise in research with its emphasis on formal education rather than local knowledge.

As funding circles grow to accept the legitimacy of youth-led research, the potential for adults to take advantage of this opportunity and possibly subvert the principles this form of research is predicated on increases ever more dramatically because of the involvement of money. The saying "Money is at the root of all evil" may seem drastic, but its implications for youth-led research are clear. The availability of large sums of funds to foster youth-led research will quickly translate into a new group of organizations entering the field. This can be positive if their involvement is spurred by a desire to embrace the goals and principles of youth-led initiatives. Conversely, funding can also attract organizations with no intent in fostering the values and purposes of youth-led initiatives, research or otherwise. The primary intent of these organizations is generating a new stream of funding that can be reallocated to other organizational functions.

❖ VALIDITY AND RELIABILITY

I am sure there are more than a few readers who question how valid and reliable are the data generated from youth-led research. This is certainly a valid (pardon the pun) point, particularly as this form of research continues to receive funding and attention from scholars and practitioners alike.

Youth-led research will probably never fully escape the gravitational pull, or trap, of being under the scrutiny of researchers and consumers of research who will attempt to judge it by rather narrow interpretations of validity and reliability.

What do I mean by this? Simply, that this form of research, particularly with its high reliance on innovative methods, will probably always face an uphill battle to find acceptance across all sectors of the research field. I sincerely hope that the field of youth-led research does not compromise its values and principles in pursuit of this form of acceptance. I think that avoiding this trap will ultimately only enhance the appeal of this field.

Heaney (1993) issued a dire warning about efforts to professionalize participatory research to the point that it might ultimately limit and circumscribe what counts for knowledge, and the university plays an increasingly influential role in dictating the outcome of these efforts. This warning is particularly relevant to youth-led research. The field of youth-led research must, too, fight this tendency because if professionalism is allowed to enter and ultimately dictate what can be considered legitimate youth-led research, adults will dominate this discussion and subvert the very principles on which this field is based.

Youth-led research will no doubt challenge the field of social research. This should not be viewed in a negative light, however. It does not necessarily result in creating schisms, divisions, or tensions. Youth-led research can be expected to continue to evolve over the next several decades and bring with it greater efforts to synthesize this progress and outline areas that require greater attention. As youth-led research continues to cross national boundaries, the need to modify methods to take into account local cultural contexts will increase. The field of youth-led research is too important to limit its reach to one nation, no matter how important this nation is to the advancement of scientific inquiry.

❖ CULTURAL COMPETENCE

The field of research, in general, has struggled mightily with the need to make research methods better able to capture the influence of cultural values and beliefs. This is not to say that the practice arena has been successful in developing culturally competent services. Nevertheless, the practice arena has generally marched forward with minimal aid for culturally competent research. Research must ultimately play a more informative and critical role in highlighting best practices from a cultural competence perspective (Delgado et al., 2005).

The history of research within undervalued population groups is fraught with numerous examples of racial, ethnic, socioeconomic, gender, disability, and sexual orientation biases. In fact, research within undervalued communities, such as those found in U.S. inner cities, has resulted in social interventions that have dramatically represented the opposite outcomes of what they sought to change. This, in turn, has made communities suspicious of outside researchers coming in and further stigmatizing residents.

Youth-led research has the potential to establish a new way of conducting research within communities and the programs that serve them. Research will never again be considered "just research" because of the goals this form of activity has embraced as critical to its functioning. Consequently, it is natural to consider the use of innovative methods in research led by youth as normative and to be encouraged whenever possible. These methods bring a degree of excitement to what can be easily considered "routine" data gathering.

However, when this form of research is grounded within a cultural competence perspective, it facilitates the development of research methods that capture the importance of cultural beliefs, values, customs, and interactions. This aspect of youth-led research takes on added significance when applied to newcomer groups and communities that are so new or numerically small, scholarly publications documenting them do not exist, or if they do exist, much more knowledge is needed to influence policies and service delivery interventions. Youth from these respective communities bring with them a set of skills and functions that assist in the design and implementation of research and analysis of findings.

❖ THE BROAD REACH OF YOUTH DEVELOPMENT

I cannot help but marvel at the long reach of youth development and its potential to continue to grow and expand in influence. When the fields of "youth-led research," "youth participation," and "youth development" are examined, they all essentially are making reference to the same phenomenon, which many label "youth development." The expansiveness of the field goes beyond national boundaries and professional disciplines, as I hope to have illustrated with this book.

However, this does not take into account those circumstances where settings such as museums, libraries, zoos, and outdoor adventure, too, are using principles that can rightly be considered youth development inspired—the activities are simply being called by another label. It is necessary to pull back and fully appreciate the majestic nature of this field with all of its lofty goals and countless ways to reach them. It seems like no professional field has escaped its gravitational pull and the energy and drive associated with it.

Much work remains within the field of youth development to coalesce all of the "strains" of youth work that exist. Youth-led initiatives and youth participation or engagement, for example, are but two examples of work that can be classified as youth development but go under other names or labels, not to mention work that is classified as recreational, after-school, or social that, too, can be grouped within this paradigm (Dworkin & Bremer, 2004; Larson et al., 2004). These efforts will prove time-consuming but essential to move the field forward. Efforts to unify these movements under one heading, youth development or otherwise, will prove rewarding for youth and the organizations that serve their needs.

The continued articulation of principles allows youth development practitioners to reach out to other staff who may be practicing youth development but calling it by other labels. This process of consolidation will ultimately benefit all youth but must be viewed developmentally or evolutionary. A strategic and systematic effort to bridge these fields and the professionals practicing them will be required, along with an openness of integrating terms, strategies, and activities, used by non-youth development labeled practice. Language is important, particularly when it comes time to evaluate initiatives. Thus, the funding of initiatives necessitates a multidisciplinary approach that will go a significant way toward the creation of a nomenclature that will unify the field and make it politically more viable for lobbying stakeholders on behalf of youth.

❖ YOUTH CONFERENCES

The reader will probably ask why I include such a mundane topic as conferences in this chapter. Historically, I have not been a big fan of professional conferences. I found occasions when I needed to attend a conference for a period of time that could easily have been devoted to more constructive pursuits. Nevertheless, as time has passed, I have found these meetings to be more worthwhile because of their potential to fulfill multiple functions. Conferences that are youth-led provide youth with an opportunity to learn from other youth; these conferences also serve to engage and sustain youth once they have returned to their communities (Pancer, Rose-Krasnor, & Loiselle, 2002). There are relatively few instances where youth can be in control of these types of meetings. It is as if we, as adults, fear that turning over these meetings will result in youth rioting!

Conferences on youth led by adults do have a place in this society, but I have found them to encapsulate many of the problems associated with adults telling youth what they need. Occasionally an adult-led conference on youth will have one youth speaker or even a panel of youth. This is not my idea of youth participation or engagement, and it certainly does not represent the prevailing philosóphy of youth-led movements.

Youth-led conferences should incorporate all of the principles and goals articulated throughout this book. Youth-led conferences should be by youth, for youth, with adults invited only as guests. Opportunities for youth to share and hear their own voices will prove beneficial for all those advocating this field of youth development practice. Voakes's (2003) description and analysis of a conference planned by youth, but attended by both youth and adults, notes that the process of evaluation is as important as, if not more so than, the actual results.

❖ WHO CONTROLS THE PRODUCTION OF KNOWLEDGE?

The question of who ultimately controls the production of knowledge within a society is bound to be controversial, regardless of the forum within which it is raised. The answer to this question will no doubt vary according to the position of the person asking it. Bell (1974) made what can be considered a profound observation over thirty years ago, with direct implications for the central theme of this book:

> Industrial society is the coordination of machines and men for the production of goods. Post-industrial society is organized around knowledge, for the purposes of social control, and the direction of innovation and change, and this in turn will give rise to new social relationships and new structures which have to be managed polit-ically. (p. 20)

Bell's prediction of who has control over the production of knowledge has certainly not been disproven, and the arena of social research serves as an excellent case in point.

The question of who controls the production of knowledge is one that is being asked in a variety of scientific circles. The *British Medical Journal,* in an editorial ("Involving Patients in Clinical Research," 1999), calls for new standards for consumer input into all stages of clinical research submitted for publication review, instead of just informed consent. The editorial even goes so far as to suggest that consumers be involved in peer review of manuscripts. These recommendations serve to increase scientific rigor and relevance of future research. The position advocated by the *British Medical Journal* attempts to interject a role for consumers in the generation of knowledge and in safeguarding the rights of consumers during research undertakings.

Advocates would argue that youth are the ultimate stakeholders, so why not formally recognize them in this position? Formalizing a research role for youth represents a critical step in advancing this field of research, eventually leading to more efficient and productive advances that will benefit not only youth more directly but also society in the process (Schensul, Berg, et al., 2004).

Having youth play an active and increasingly major role in the production of knowledge directly impacting their lives typifies the need for research models that take into account the entrance of a new cadre of researchers, and one with the sole purpose of making the research authentic to their lives and their communities. Such a model must enjoy appeal across a variety of spectrums because of the democratic principles it is based on and its potential for increasing the capacities of youth, their communities, and their society. However, advocating for a youth-led model means that youth are to influence what is considered knowledge and how that knowledge should be used to benefit their lives.

❖ HUMANIZATION OF RESEARCH

There is little dispute that youth-led research humanizes a process that many critics have argued has essentially dehumanized people, particularly those in groups that are undervalued in U.S. society. Statistics are not just numbers. Numbers represent lives and stories that are oftentimes very tragic. It is not usual for youth to be able to put a face and a name to some statistic within their neighborhood or community. This personal connection serves to personalize, or contextualize, data and provides an opportunity for youth to analyze their daily experiences. Youth's being able to accomplish these three tasks will serve them both immediately and in later situations as they grow into adults.

Historically, one of the major, if not the foremost, criticisms of social research has been that it fails to humanize people's experiences. The emergence of qualitative research has been fueled largely as a response to this criticism. Combining quantitative and qualitative research methods is one proposal for making research more meaningful. This mixing of methods is a lot easier said than done, because it often requires bringing in a wide range of expertise to a project, adding significant costs, and opening up possibilities for major differences of opinions.

Youth are able to make connections between the findings from their research and their own lives. I could recount numerous stories of youth discussing research findings and pause to make side comments about their own lives, their friends, families, and neighbors. The search for solutions to problems takes on added prominence in these situations, and this makes youth-led research very important in the lives of youth. Making research relevant is a goal that we must never lose sight of. Involving the ultimate beneficiaries of the research helps us to not lose sight of why the research is being undertaken.

❖ WHO SHALL SPEAK FOR AND SHAPE THE YOUTH-LED MOVEMENT?

To say that it does not matter who is the spokesperson for a movement, and that a movement speaks for itself, would be a serious misstatement. The youth-led movement, of which research will become more and more a prominent part of, must find a way of maintaining youth participation after they have grown up and assumed an adult role. For youth who have played a prominent part in the origins of this movement, this continued involvement is important because of the perspective and legitimacy that they bring to these forms of youth initiatives. This involvement, however, can be as advisors, consultants, and even co-leaders, where applicable.

The leadership of the youth-led research movement must ultimately rest in the hands of youth and those adults able and willing to take a secondary role in this type of initiative. Leadership takes time to develop with the proper support. However, once established, it will have lasting influence on succeeding generations. Leadership, it should be noted, must not be defined in a conventional manner that stresses hierarchy and has one individual wielding tremendous influence and enjoying vast adulation. Leadership must be conceptualized as it is in the field of youth development; that is, individuals possessing various leadership competencies can step forward when needed and step back when others can better accomplish the tasks on hand. This fluidity strengthens the concept of team in research.

❖ CONCLUSION

I sincerely hope that the reader has developed a new, or renewed, appreciation for the field of youth-led research and the many different forms and goals it can embrace. Research, particularly when it is socially focused, cannot be considered boring or irrelevant if it is true to its social mission. Anything less than these lofty goals would truly be a major disappointment and would not do justice to this form of intervention. Further, an inability to embrace a social mission goal will effectively disengage youth and other marginalized groups from participating or leading such endeavors.

This epilogue brings this book to an end, although there are so many aspects of the topic that still deserve further attention and even an entire book devoted to them. It is my sincere hope that future scholarship on this subject will create the need for several other books on various aspects of youth-led research. Research plays an important role in any social intervention that seeks to achieve significant social change. This additional scholarship will result in "easier" access to material on this subject. However, it also signifies that the field has continued to evolve and mature and, in the process of doing so, has necessitated more and more information about these advances. This will certainly make me feel good about how youth have started to take their rightful place at the table where decisions are made about their immediate and future well-being!

References

Alawy, A. (2001, July 20). Peer evaluation of youth programs. *Public Welfare Foundation*, 1–13.

Alcoff, L. (1994). The problem of speaking for others. In S. U. Weisser & J. Fleischer (Eds.), *Feminist nightmares. Women at odds: Feminism and the problem of sisterhood* (pp. 285–309). New York: New York University Press.

Altpeter, M., Schopler, J. H., Galinsky, M. J., & Pennell, J. (1999). Participatory research as social work practice: When is it viable? *Journal of Progressive Human Services, 10,* 31–53.

Alvarez, A., & Gutierrez, L. (2001). Choosing to do participatory research: An example and issues fit to consider. *Journal of Community Practice, 9,* 1–20.

American Association for the Advancement of Science. (2003*). Community-based research for Africa.* Retrieved December 11, 2004, from http:///www .aaas.org/international/africa/cbr.shtml

American Statistical Association. (1997). *What are focus groups?* Alexandria, VA: Author, Section on Survey Research Methods.

Andersen, S. (1998, September). Service learning: A national strategy for youth development. *The Communitarian Network,* 1–8.

Anderson, D. S. (1999). *Kids, courts and communities: Lessons from the Red Hook Youth Court.* New York: Center for Court Innovation.

Anderson, M., Bernaldo, R., & David, J. (2003). *Youth speak out report.* Los Angeles: National Conference for Community and Justice.

Andrade, R. A. C. (1998). Life in elementary school: Children's ethnographic recollections. In A. Egan-Robertson & D. Bloome (Eds.), *Students as researchers of culture and language in their own communities* (pp. 93–114). Cresskill, NJ: Hampton Press.

Annie E. Casey Foundation. (2001). *Plain Talk implementation guide.* Baltimore: Author.

Anyon, Y., & Naughton, S. (2003, February). *Youth empowerment: The contributions and challenges of youth-led research in a high-poverty, urban community* (Issue Brief). Stanford, CA: John W. Gardner Center.

Armistead, P. J., & Wexler, M. B. (1998). Community development and youth development: The potential for convergence. *New Designs for Youth Development, 14,* 27–33.

Aspen Institute. (1997). *Voices from the field: Learning from the early work of comprehensive community initiatives.* Washington, DC: Author.

Asset-Based Community Development Institute. (2001). *Asset-mapping: A strengths-based approach.* Evanston, IL: Author.

Atweh, B., & Burton, L. (1995). Students as researchers: Rationale and critique. *British Educational Research Journal, 21,* 561–576.

Autz, R., Dillon, D., & Quay, R. (2001*). AuThenTiCITY—Engaging youth in community mapping.* Paper presented at the Annual American Planning Association Conference, New Orleans, LA.

Averch, H. A. (1994). The systematic use of expert judgment. In J. S. Wholey, H. P. Hatry, & K. E. Newcomer (Eds.), *Handbook of practical program evaluation* (pp. 293–309). San Francisco: Jossey-Bass.

Balcazar, F. E., Keys, C. B., Kaplan, D. L., & Suarez-Balcazar, Y. (1998). Participatory action research and people with disabilities: Principles and challenges. *Canadian Journal of Rehabilitation, 12,* 105–112.

Becker, A. L. (2003, August 16). Teens identify risk factors. *Hartford Courant,* p. 1.

Bell, D. (1974). *The coming of post-industrial society.* London: Heinemann.

Benson, P. L. (2003a). Developmental assets and asset-building communities: Conceptual and empirical foundations. In R. M. Lerner & P. L. Benson (Eds.), *Developmental assets and asset-building communities: Implications for research, policy, and practice* (pp. 19–43). New York: Kluwer Academic/Plenum.

Benson, P. L. (2003b). Toward asset-building communities: How does change occur? In R. M. Lerner & P. L. Benson (Eds.), *Developmental assets and asset-building communities: Implications for research, policy, and practice* (pp. 213–221). New York: Kluwer Academic/Plenum.

Benson, P. L., & Pittman, K. J. (Eds.). (2001). *Trends in youth development: Visions, realities and challenges.* New York: Kluwer Academic/Plenum.

Benson, P. L., & Saito, R. N. (1998). The scientific foundations of youth development. In *Youth development: Issues, challenges and directions* (pp. 125–147). Philadelphia: Public/Private Ventures.

Berg, M. J. (2004). Education and advocacy: Improving teaching and learning through student participatory action research. *Practicing Anthropology, 26,* 20–24.

Berg, M. J., Owens, D. C., & Schensul, J. J. (2002). Participatory action research, service-learning, and community youth development. *CYD Journal, 3,* 20–25.

Biklen, S. K., & Moseley, C. R. (1998). "Are you retarded? No I'm Catholic": Qualitative methods in the study of people with severe handicaps. *Journal of the Association for Persons with Severe Handicaps, 13,* 155–162.

Billig, S. H. (2000a). The effects of service learning. *The School Administrator, 57,* 14–18.

Billig, S. H. (2000b). Research on K-12 school-based service-learning: The evidence builds. *Phi Delta Kappan, 82*, 658–664.

Billig, S. H., & Conrad, J. (1997). *An evaluation of the New Hampshire service-learning and educational reform project.* Denver, CO: RMC Research.

Billig, S. H., & Furco, A. (2002). Service-learning through a multidisciplinary lens. In S. H. Billig & A. Furco (Eds.), *Advances in service-learning research: Vol. 1. The essence of the pedagogy* (pp. 201–222). Greenwich, CT: Information Age.

Bjorhovde, P. O. (2002). Teaching philanthropy to children: Why, how, and what. In P. O. Bjorhovde (Ed.), *Creating tomorrow's philanthropists: Curriculum development for youth* (pp. 7–19). San Francisco: Jossey-Bass.

Blanchard, K., Carlos, J., & Randolph, A. (1996). *Empowerment takes more than a minute.* San Francisco: Berrett-Koehler.

Bloom, D., & Padilla, A. M. (1979). A peer interviewer model in conducting surveys among Mexican-American youth. *Journal of Community Psychology, 7*, 129–136.

Bloome, D., & Egan-Robertson, A. (1998). Introduction. In A. Egan-Robertson & D. Bloome (Eds.), *Students as researchers of culture and language in their own communities* (pp. xi–xxii). Cresskill, NJ: Hampton Press.

Blyth, D. A., & Burden, L. M. (2003). *Stimulating research, promoting youth development: Final report of the national youth development research response initiative.* Minneapolis: University of Minnesota Extension Service.

Bogdan, R., & Biklen, S. K. (1992). *Qualitative research for education.* Boston: Allyn & Bacon.

Boston Plan for Excellence. (2004a). *School climate in Boston's high schools: What students say.* Boston: Author.

Boston Plan for Excellence. (2004b). *What students at Boston High School are saying about school climate.* Boston: Author.

Boston's student researchers looking at high school "climate." (2003, June 2). *Boston Herald,* p. 65.

Bowes, A. M. (1996). Evaluating an empowering research strategy: Reflections on action-research with South Asian women. *Sociological Research Online, 1*(1). Retrieved July 12, 2003, from http://www.socresonline.org.uk/socresonline/1/1/1.html

Boyden, J., & Ennew, J. (Eds.). (1997). *Children in focus—A manual for participatory research with children.* Stockholm, Sweden: Rädda Barnen.

Boyer, E. L. (1990). *Scholarship reconsidered: Priorities of the professorate.* Princeton, NJ: Carnegie Foundation for the Advancement of Teaching.

Brase, M., Pacheco, V., & Berg, M. J. (2004). Diffusing ICR's youth participatory action research model. *Practicing Anthropology, 26*, 15–19.

Bringle, R. G., & Hatcher, J. A. (2000). Meaning measurement of theory-based service-learning outcomes: Making the case for quantitative research. *Michigan Journal of Community Service Learning, 6*, 68–75.

Broad, B., & Saunders, L. (1998). Involving young people leaving care as peer researchers in a health research project: A learning experience. *Research, Policy and Planning, 16*, 1–9.

Brown, K. M., Bryant, C. A., Landis, D., Forthofer, M. S., McDermott, R. J., & Calkins, S. (2000). *Developing youth capacity for community-based research: Evaluation results from the Sarasota Youth Initiative.* Tampa, FL: University of South Florida, Florida Prevention Research Center.

Brown, K. M., McDermott, R. J., Bryant, C. A., & Forthofer, M. S. (2003). Youth as community researchers: The Sarasota County Demonstration Project. *CYD Journal, 4*, 40–45.

Brown, L. D., & Tandon, R. (1983). Ideology and political economy in inquiry: Action research and participatory research. *Journal of Applied Behavioral Science, 19*, 277–294.

Bryant, C., Brown, K. M., Landis, D. C., Alfonso, M., Abrenica, K., McDermott, R. J., et al. (2000, November). *Using youth administered research to address alcohol and tobacco use prevention in adolescents: Applications, results and lessons learned.* Paper presented at the 128th annual meeting of the American Public Health Association, Boston.

Brydon-Miller, M. (1993). Breaking down barriers: Accessibility self-advocacy in the disabled community. In P. Park, M. B. Miller, B. Hall, & T. Jackson (Eds.), *Voices of change: Participatory research in the United States and Canada* (pp. 125–143). Westport, CT: Bergin & Garvey.

Bumbarger, B., & Greenberg, M. T. (2002). Next steps in advancing research on positive youth development. *Prevention & Treatment, 5*, 1–7.

Burg, S. (1998). Keep the peace: Learn from the past. How neighborhood policing is making history in Boston. *New Designs for Youth Development, 14*, 12–17.

Burgess, J. (2000). Youth involvement can be the key to community development. *CYD Journal, 1*, 38–41.

Caldwell, L. L., & Baldwin, C. K. (2003). A serious look at leisure: The role of leisure time and recreation activities in positive youth development. In F. A. Villarruel, D. F. Perkins, L. M. Borden, & J. G. Keith (Eds.), *Community youth development programs, policies, and practices* (pp. 181–200). Thousand Oaks, CA: Sage.

Calvert, M., Zeldin, S., & Weisenbach, A. (2002). *Youth involvement for community, organizational and youth development: Directions for research, evaluation and practice.* Madison: University of Wisconsin, Human Development and Family Studies.

Camino, L. (1992). *What differences do racial, ethnic, and cultural differences make in youth development programs?* Washington, DC: Carnegie Council on Adolescent Development.

Campbell, P., Edgar, S., & Halstead, A. L. (1994). Students as evaluators: A model for program evaluation. *Phi Delta Kappan, 76*, 160–165.

Campbell, R. (2002). *In search of the holy grail of youth participation*. Retrieved from http://www.youthinclusion.org/Pdfstore/Holy_Grail_Report.pdf

Canadian Health Network. (2001). *How does meaningful youth participation work to improve the health of youth?* Retrieved from http://www.canadian-health-network.ca/html1/newnotable/apr1_2001e.html

Carnegie Council on Adolescent Development. (1992a). *A matter of time: Risk opportunity.* New York: Carnegie Corporation of New York.

Carnegie Council on Adolescent Development. (1992b). *Turning points: Preparing American youth for the 21st century.* New York: Carnegie Corporation of New York.

Carnegie Council on Adolescent Development. (1994). *Consultation on after-school programs.* New York: Carnegie Corporation of New York.

Carver, R. (1997). Theoretical underpinnings of service learning. *Theory and Practice, 36*, 143–149.

Castex, G. M. (1997). Immigrant children in the United States. In N. K. Phillips & S. L. A. Straussner (Eds.), *Children in the urban environment: Linking social policy and clinical practice* (pp. 43–60). Springfield, IL: Charles C Thomas.

Catalano, R. F., Berglund, M. L., Ryan, J. A. M., Lonczak, H. S., & Hawkins, D. J. (2002). Positive youth development in the United States: Research findings on evaluations of positive youth development programs. *Prevention & Treatment, 5*, 10–29.

Center for Popular Education and Participatory Research. (2003). *What is participatory research?* Berkeley: University of California.

Center for Youth Development. (2000). *Calculating the return on investment: What could be.* Washington, DC: Academy for Educational Development.

Center for Youth Development and Policy Research. (1995a). *Community youth mapping: A ten-step process.* Washington, DC: Academy for Educational Development.

Center for Youth Development and Policy Research. (1995b). *Community youth mapping.* Washington, DC: Academy for Educational Development.

Centre for Addiction and Mental Health. (2001). *More about VALIDITY.* Toronto, ON: Author.

Centre for Youth and Society. (2003). *Counting on research and making research count: Suggestions for community research projects.* Victoria, BC: University of Victoria.

Cervone, B., & Cushman, K. (2002). Moving youth participation into the classroom: Students as allies. In B. Kirshner, J. L. O'Donoghue, & M. McLaughlin (Eds.), *Youth participation: Improving institutions and communities* (pp. 83–99). San Francisco: Jossey-Bass.

Chan, B., Carlson, M., Trickett, B., & Earls, F. (2003). Youth participation: A critical element of research on child well-being. In R. M. Lerner & P. L. Benson (Eds.), *Developmental assets and asset-building communities: Implications for research, policy, and practice* (pp. 65–96). New York: Kluwer Academic/ Plenum.

Checkoway, B., Dobbie, D., & Richards-Schuster, K. (2003). Involving young people in community evaluation research. *CYD Journal, 4,* 7–11.

Checkoway, B., & Goodyear, L. (Eds.). (2003). Youth engagement in community evaluation research [Special Issue]. *CYD Journal, 4*(1).

Checkoway, B., & Richards-Schuster, K. (2002). *Youth participation in community evaluation research.* Ann Arbor: University of Michigan, Center for Community Change.

Cheshire, J., & Edwards, V. (1998). Knowledge about language in British class-rooms: Children as researchers. In A. Egan-Robertson & D. Bloome (Eds.), *Students as researchers of culture and language in their own communities* (pp. 191–214). Cresskill, NJ: Hampton Press.

Children's Society. (2001*). Children and young people as citizens now: Participation in local democracy.* London: Author.

Chin, E. (2004). Action research in the classroom: A case study from New Haven, Connecticut. *Practicing Anthropology, 26,* 40–44.

Chinman, M. J., & Linney, J. A. (1998). Toward a model of adolescent empow-erment: Theoretical and empirical evidence. *The Journal of Primary Prevention, 18,* 393–413.

Chow, J., & Crowe, K. (2004). Community-based research methods in commu-nity practice. In M. Weil (Ed.), *The handbook of community practice* (pp. 604–619). Thousand Oaks, CA: Sage.

Clacherty, G., & Kistner, J. (2001, October*). Child rape and abuse: Guns, power and identity.* Alrode, South Africa: Ekupholeni Mental Health Centre.

Claus, J., & Ogden, C. (1999*). Service learning for youth empowerment and social change.* New York: Lang.

Community Connections. (1997). First annual community youthmapping confer-ence. 4, 1, 4. Washington, DC: Academy for Educational Development.

Community Unity Matters. (2000*). Youth-led community meetings, forums, and summits.* Retrieved August 12, 2004, from http://www.commatters.org/ youth/summit.htm

Community Youth Development. (2000). *Community youthmapping.* Washington, DC: Academy for Educational Development.

Comstock, D. E., & Fox, R. (1993). Participatory research as critical theory: The North Bonneville, USA, experience. In P. Park, M. B. Miller, B. Hall, & T. Jackson (Eds.), *Voices of change: Participatory research in the United States and Canada* (pp. 103–124). Westport, CT: Bergin & Garvey.

Connell, J. P., Gambone, M. A., & Smith, T. J. (1998). Youth development in community settings: Challenges to our field and our approach. In *Youth development: Issues, challenges and directions* (pp. 281–299). Philadelphia: Public/Private Ventures.

Convention on the Rights of the Child. (1989). New York: United Nations.

Cook, P., Cook, M., Tran, L., & Tu, W. (1997). Children enabling change: A multicultural participatory, community-based rehabilitation research project involving Chinese children with disabilities and their families. *Child and Youth Care Forum, 26*, 205–219.

Council of Chief State School Officers. (1995). *Integrating service learning into teacher education: Why and how?* Washington, DC: Author.

Counts, G. S. (1932). *Dare the school build a new social order?* New York: John Day.

Cousins, J. B., Donohue, J. J., & Bloom, G. A. (1996). Collaborative evaluation in North America: Evaluators' self-reported opinions, practices and consequences. *Evaluation Practice, 17*, 207–226.

Cousins, J. B., & Earl, L. M. (1992). The case for participatory evaluation. *Educational Evaluation and Policy Analysis, 14*, 394–418.

Cullen, F. T., & Wright, J. P. (2002). Criminal justice in the lives of American adolescents. In J. T. Mortimer & R. W. Larson (Eds.), *The changing adolescent experience: Societal trends and the transition to adulthood* (pp. 88–128). New York: Cambridge University Press.

Curry, T., & Bloome, D. (1998). Learning to write by writing ethnography. In A. Egan-Robertson & D. Bloome (Eds.), *Students as researchers of culture and language in their own countries* (pp. 37–58). Cresskill, NJ: Hampton Press.

Dale, E. (1946). *Audio-visual methods in teaching.* New York: Dryden.

Davidoff, P. (1965). Advocacy and pluralism in planning. In R. LeGates & F. Stout (Eds.), *The city reader* (pp. 421–432). New York: Routledge.

Dean, D. L. (1994). How to use focus groups. In J. S. Wholey, H. P. Hatry, & K. E. Newcomer (Eds.), *Handbook of practical program evaluation* (pp. 338–349). San Francisco: Jossey-Bass.

Deans, T. (1999). Service-learning in two keys: Paulo Freire's critical pedagogy in relation to John Dewey's pragmatism. *Michigan Journal of Community Service Learning, 5*, 15–29.

Deatrick, J. A., & Faux, S. A. (1991). Conducting qualitative studies with children and adolescents. In J. M. Morse (Ed.), *Qualitative nursing research: A contemporary dialogue* (pp. 203–223). Newbury Park, CA: Sage.

Delgado, M. (1979). A grass-roots model for needs assessment in Hispanic communities. *Child Welfare, 58*, 571–576.

Delgado, M. (1981). Using Hispanic adolescents to assess community needs. *Social Casework: The Journal of Contemporary Social Work, 62*, 607–613.

Delgado, M. (1995). Community asset assessment and substance abuse prevention: A case study of a Puerto Rican community. *Journal of Child and Adolescent Substance Abuse, 4*, 57–77.

Delgado, M. (1996). Community asset assessments by Latin youths: Lessons from the field. *Social Work in Education, 18*, 169–178.

Delgado, M. (1998). Community asset assessment and substance abuse prevention: A case study involving the Puerto Rican community. In

M. Delgado (Ed.), *Social services in Latino communities: Research and strategies* (pp. 5–23). New York: Haworth Press.

Delgado, M. (1999). *Community social work practice within an urban context: The potential of a capacity enhancement perspective.* New York: Oxford University Press.

Delgado, M. (2001). *New arenas for community social work practice with urban youth: Use of the arts, humanities, and sports.* New York: Columbia University Press.

Delgado, M. (2002). *New frontiers for youth development in the twenty-first century: Revitalizing and broadening youth development.* New York: Columbia University Press.

Delgado, M. (2003). *Early death and the urban scene: The case for memorial murals and community healing.* Westport, CT: Praeger.

Delgado, M. (2004). *Social youth entrepreneurship: The potential for youth and community transformation.* Westport, CT: Praeger.

Delgado, M., Jones, K., & Rohani, M. (2005). *Social work practice with refugee and immigrant youth in the United States.* Boston: Allyn & Bacon.

Delgado, M., & Staples, L. (2005). *Youth-led community organizing.* Manuscript in preparation.

Denner, J., Kirby, D., & Coyle, K. (2000). How communities can promote positive youth development: Responses from 49 professionals. *CYD Journal, 1,* 31–35.

Designing questionnaires and conducting surveys for health data. (2002, May). *Great Lakes Epicenter Newsletter, 3*(2), 1–2.

Dewey, J. (1938). *Experience and education.* New York: Collier Books.

DiBenedetto, A. (1992). Youth groups: A model for empowerment. *Networking Bulletin, 2,* 19–24.

Diener, E., & Crandall, R. (1978). *Ethics in social and behavioral research.* Chicago: University of Chicago Press.

Dorfman, D., Douglas, R., Ellis, D., Fisher, A., Geiger, E., Hughes, K., et al. (2001). *Planning for youth success: Resources and training manual.* Portland, OR: NW Educational Laboratory.

Dworkin, J., & Bremer, K. (2004). Youth talk about their participation in extracurricular activities. *The Prevention Researcher, 11,* 14–16.

Dworkin, J., Larson, R., & Hansen, D. (2003). Adolescents' accounts of growth experiences in youth activities. *Journal of Youth and Adolescents, 32,* 17–26.

Earls, F., & Carlson, M. (2002). Adolescents as collaborators: In search of well-being. In M. Tienda & W. J. Wilson (Eds.), *Youth in cities: A cross-national perspective* (pp. 58–83). New York: Cambridge University Press.

Eccles, J., & Gootman, J. (Eds.). (2002). *Community programs to promote youth development.* Washington, DC: National Academy Research.

Edwards, J. (2000, November 27–28). *Students-as-researchers.* Paper presented at the annual meeting of the Australian Association of Research in Education, Melbourne, Adelaide, Australia.

Egan-Robertson, A. (1998). "We must ask our questions and tell our stories": Writing ethnography and constructing personhood. In A. Egan-Robertson & D. Bloome (Eds.), *Students as researchers of culture and language in their own communities* (pp. 261–284). Cresskill, NJ: Hampton Press.

Egan-Robertson, A., & Bloome, D. (Eds.). (1998). *Students as researchers of culture and language in their own communities.* Cresskill, NJ: Hampton Press.

Egan-Robertson, A., & Willett, J. (1998). Students as ethnographers, thinking and doing ethnography: A bibliographic essay. In A. Egan-Robertson & D. Bloome (Eds.), *Students as researchers of culture and language in their own communities* (pp. 1–32). Cresskill, NJ: Hampton Press.

Estes, R. J. (2004). Global change and indicators of social development. In M. Weil (Ed.), *Handbook of community practice* (pp. 508–528). Thousand Oaks, CA: Sage.

Eyler, J., & Giles, D. E. (1999). *Where's the learning in service-learning?* San Francisco: Jossey-Bass.

Fai-Borda, O., & Rahman, M. A. (1991). *Action and knowledge: Breaking the monopoly with participatory action research.* New York: Apex Books.

Falk, K. (2002). Teaching the next generation about philanthropy: A case study of the AFP New Jersey chapter's youth in philanthropy program. In P. O. Bjorhovde (Ed.), *Creating tomorrow's philanthropists: Curriculum development for youth* (pp. 55–71). San Francisco: Jossey-Bass.

Farrakhan praises gang members. (1993, July 18). *Star Tribune,* p. 1.

Farrell, W. C., & Johnson, J. H. (2004). Investing in socially and economically distressed communities: Comprehensive strategies for inner-city community and youth development. In M. Weil (Ed.), *Handbook for community practice* (pp. 494–507). Thousand Oaks, CA: Sage.

Faulkner, J. (1998). Participatory videomaking in Brazil. In V. Johnson, E. Ivan-Smith, G. Gordon, P. Pridmore, & P. Scott (Eds.), *Stepping forward: Children and young people's participation in the development process* (pp. 50–59). London: Intermediate Technology.

Fernandez, M. A. (2002, October). *Creating community change: Challenges and tensions in community youth research* (Issue Brief). Stanford, CA: John W. Gardner Center.

Ferrari, T. M. (2003). Working hand-in-hand: Community youth development and career development. In F. A. Villarruel, D. F. Perkins, L. M. Borden, & J. G. Keith (Eds.), *Community youth development programs, policies, and practices* (pp. 201–223). Thousand Oaks, CA: Sage.

Fetterman, D. M. (2001). *Foundations of empowerment evaluation.* Thousand Oaks, CA: Sage.

Fetterman, D. M. (2002). *Collaborative, participatory, and empowerment evaluation.* Palo Alto, CA: Stanford University School of Education.

Fetterman, D. M. (2003). Youth and evaluation: Empowered social change agents. In K. Sabo (Ed.), *Youth participatory evaluation: A field in the making* (pp. 89–92). San Francisco: Jossey-Bass.

Fisher, R. (2004). History, context, and emerging issues for community practice. In M. Weil (Ed.), *Handbook for community practice* (pp. 34–58). Thousand Oaks, CA: Sage.

Flanagan, C., & Van Horn, B. (2003). Youth civic development: A logical next step in community youth development. In F. A. Villarruel, D. F. Perkins, L. M. Borden, & J. G. Keith (Eds.), *Community youth development programs, policies, and practices* (pp. 273–297). Thousand Oaks, CA: Sage.

Fletcher, A. (2002). Meaningful involvement benefits all students. *Service Line: Revitalizing Schools and Communities Through Service-Learning, 12,* 1–12.

Fletcher, A. (2003). *Unleashing student voice: Research supporting meaningful student involvement.* Retrieved April 8, 2004, from http://www.studentinvolvement.net/article.103.htm

Forum for Youth Investment. (2001). *Youth engagement: The state of cities.* Takoma Park, MD: Author.

Forum on Child and Family Statistics. (2002). *America's children 2002.* Retrieved July 7, 2004, from http://childstats.gov/ac2002/highlight.asp

France, A. (2000). *The Triumph and Success Peer Research Project.* Canberra, Australia: National Youth Agency Foundation.

France, A. (2002). *Youth researching youth: The Triumph and Success Peer Research Project.* Leicester, UK: National Youth Agency Foundation.

Fraser, M. W., & Galinsky, M. J. (1997). Toward a resilience-based model of practice. In M. W. Draser (Ed.), *Risk and resilience in childhood: An ecological perspective* (pp. 265–275). Washington, DC: National Association of Social Works Press.

Fussell, E. (2002). Youth in aging societies. In J. T. Mortimer & R. W. Larson (Eds.), *The changing adolescent experience: Societal trends and the transition to adulthood* (pp. 18–51). New York: Cambridge University Press.

Gamble, D. N., & Hoff, M. D. (2004). Sustainable community development. In M. Weil (Ed.), *Handbook of community practice* (pp. 169–188). Thousand Oaks, CA: Sage.

Gambone, M. A., & Connell, J. P. (2004). The community action framework for youth development. *The Prevention Researcher, 11,* 17–20.

Garbarino, J. (1985). Human ecology and competence in adolescence. In J. Garbarino (Ed.), *Adolescent development: An ecological perspective* (pp. 40–86). Columbus, OH: Merrill.

Gardner, H. (1993). *Multiple intelligences: The theory in practice.* New York: Basic Books.

Gaventa, J. (1993). The powerful, the powerless, and the experts: Knowledge struggles in an information age. In P. Park, M. B. Miller, B. Hall, & T. Jackson (Eds.), *Voices of change: Participatory research in the United States and Canada* (pp. 21–40). Westport, CT: Bergin & Garvey.

Gertler, B. (2003, Spring). Self-knowledge. In E. N. Zalta (Ed.), *Stanford encyclopedia of philosophy.* Retrieved June 15, 2004, from http://plato.stanford.edu/archives/spr2003/entries/selfknowledge/

Gildin, B. L. (2003). All stars talent show network: Grassroots funding, community building, and participatory evaluation. In K. Sabo (Ed.), *Youth participatory evaluation: A field in the making* (pp. 77–85). San Francisco: Jossey-Bass.

Giles, D. E., & Eyler, J. (1993). *The theoretical roots of service-learning in John Dewey: Toward a theory of service-learning.* Nashville, TN: Vanderbilt University.

Ginsburg, K. R. (1996). Searching for solutions: The importance of including teenagers in the research process. *Journal of Developmental and Behavioral Pediatrics, 17,* 255–257.

Giri, G. (1995). *Focus group discussion—Special needs.* London: Save the Children UK.

GirlSource. (2000). *It's about time! A book by and for young women about our relationships, rights, futures, bodies, minds, and souls.* Berkeley, CA: Ten Speed Press.

Gloucester County Youth Council. (2002). *Hearing the youth voice.* Gloucester County, NJ: Author.

Goggin, S., Powers, J., & Spano, S. (2002). *Profiles of youth engagement and voice in New York State: Current strategies.* Ithaca, NY: Cornell University.

Golombek, S. (Ed.). (2002). *What works in youth participation: Case studies from around the world.* Baltimore: International Youth Foundation.

Goodyear, L. (2003). Engaging young people in evaluation as a strategy for evaluation field-building and innovation. *CYD Journal, 4,* 54–55.

Goodyear, L., & Checkoway, B. (2003). Establishing the importance of youth participation in community evaluation and research. *CYD Journal, 4,* 5.

Grave, M., & Walsh, D. (1998). *Studying children in context: Theories, methods and ethics.* Thousand Oaks, CA: Sage.

Greig, A., & Taylor, J. (1999). *Doing research with children.* Thousand Oaks, CA: Sage.

Greiner, J. M. (1994). Use of ratings by training observers. In J. S. Wholey, H. P. Hatry, & K. E. Newcomer (Eds.), *Handbook of practical program evaluation* (pp. 239–270). San Francisco: Jossey-Bass.

Guishard, M., Fine, M., Doyle, C., Jackson, J., Roberts, R., Singleton, S., et al. (2003). *"As long as I got breath, I'll fight": Participatory action research for educational justice.* Cambridge, MA: Harvard Family Research Project.

Guyll, M., Spoth, R., & Redmond, C. (2003). The effects of incentives and research requirements on participation rates for a community-based preventive intervention research study. *The Journal of Primary Prevention, 23,* 25–41.

Hackman, D. (1997). *Student-led conferences at the middle level.* Champaign, IL: ERIC Clearinghouse on Elementary and Early Childhood Education. (ERIC Document Reproduction No. ED407171)

Hall, B. (1992). From margins to center? The development and purpose of participatory research. *The American Sociologist, 23,* 15–28.

Hamilton, S. F. (1981). Adolescents in community settings: What is to be learned? *Theory and Research in Social Education, 9,* 23–38.

Hamilton, S. F., & Hamilton, M. A. (1994). *Opening career paths for youth: What can be done? Who can do it?* Washington, DC: American Youth Policy Forum.

Hanley, B., Truesdale, A., King, A., Elbourne, D., & Chalmers, I. (2001). Involving consumers in designing, conducting, and interpreting randomised controlled trials: Questionnaire survey. *British Medical Journal, 322*, 519–523.

Hanna, P. R. (1937). *Youth serves the community.* New York: Appleton Century.

Harkavy, I., & Benson, L. (1997). *De-platonization and democratization of education as the basis of service learning.* Philadelphia: University of Pennsylvania.

Harley, D. A., Stebnicki, M., & Rollins, C. W. (2000). Applying empowerment evaluation as a tool for self-improvement and community development with culturally diverse populations. *Journal of Community Development Society, 31*, 348–364.

Harper, G. W., & Carver, L. J. (1999). Out of the mainstream youth as partners in collaborative research: Exploring benefits and challenges. *Health Education and Behavior, 26*, 250–256.

Hart Leadership Program. (2003*). Mapping refugee communities: An introduction to research service learning.* Durham, NC: Duke University, Terry Sanford Institute of Public Policy.

Hart, R. (1992). *Ladder of participation, children's participation: From tokenism to citizenship.* New York: UNICEF.

Hart, R. (1997). *Children's participation: The theory and practice of involving young citizens in community development and environmental care.* London: Earthscan & UNICEF.

Hart, R., & Rajbhandary, J. (2003). Using participatory methods to further the democratic goals of children's organizations. In K. Sabo (Ed.), *Youth participatory evaluation: A field in the making* (pp. 61–75). San Francisco: Jossey-Bass.

Harter, S. (1993). Causes and consequences of low self-esteem in children and adolescents. In R. Baumeister (Ed.), *The puzzle of low self-regard* (pp. 87–116). New York: Plenum Press.

Hartman, A., DePoy, E., Francis, C., & Gilmer, D. (2000). Adolescents with special health care needs in transitions: Three life histories. *Social Work & Health Care, 31*, 3–58.

Hatch, J., Moss, N., Saran, A., Presley-Cantrell, L., & Mallory, C. (1993). Community research: Partnership in Black communities. *American Journal of Preventive Medicine, 9*(Suppl.), 27–31.

Hatry, H. P. (1994). Collecting data from agency records. In J. S. Wholey, H. P. Hatry, & K. E. Newcomer (Eds.), *Handbook of practical program evaluation* (pp. 374–385). San Francisco: Jossey-Bass.

Hatry, H. P., Newcomer, K. E., & Wholey, J. F. (1994). Conclusion: Improving evaluation activities and results. In J. S. Wholey, H. P. Hatry, & K. E. Newcomer (Eds.), *Handbook of practical program evaluation* (pp. 590–602). San Francisco: Jossey-Bass.

Heaney, T. W. (1993). If you can't beat 'em, join 'em: The professionalization of participatory research. In P. Park, M. B. Miller, B. Hall, & T. Jackson (Eds.), *Voices of change: Participatory research in the United States and Canada* (pp. 40–46). Westport, CT: Bergin & Garvey.

Hein, K. (2000). Joining creative forces with adolescents. *CYD Journal, 1*, 44–47.

Hein, K. (2003). Enhancing the assets for positive youth development: The vision, values, and action agenda of the W. T. Grant Foundation. In R. M. Lerner & P. L. Benson (Eds.), *Developmental assets and asset-building communities: Implications for research, policy, and practice* (pp. 97–117). New York: Kluwer Academic/Plenum.

Hendricks, M. (1994). Making a splash: Reporting evaluation results effectively. In J. S. Wholey, H. P. Hatry, & K. E. Newcomer (Eds.), *Handbook of practical program evaluation* (pp. 549–575). San Francisco: Jossey-Bass.

Heritage Community Foundation. (2002a). *Fish bowls and bloopers: Oral history in the classroom.* Edmonton, AB: Author.

Heritage Community Foundation. (2002b). *Why have students conduct an oral history project?* Edmonton, AB: Author.

Hester, R. T., Jr. (1984). *Planning neighborhood space with people.* New York: Van Nostrand Reinhold.

Hetzel, S., Watson, S., & Sampson, L. (1992). Participation and partnership. *Youth Studies Australia, 11*, 33–39.

Hicke, C. (2002). *One-minute guide to oral histories.* Edmonton, AB: Heritage Community Foundation.

Hill, M. (1997). Participatory research with children. *Child and Family Social Work, 2*, 171–183.

Hine, T. (2000). *The rise and fall of the American teenager: A new history of the American adolescent experience.* New York: Perennial.

Hodgson, D. (1995). *Participation of children and young people in social work.* New York: UNICEF.

Holden, D. J., Pendergast, K., & Austin, D. (2000). *Literature review for American Legacy Foundation's statewide youth movement against tobacco use.* Research Triangle Park, NC: Research Triangle Institute, Center for Economics Research.

Homan, M. S. (2004). *Promoting community change: Making it happen in the real world* (3rd ed.). Belmont, CA: Brooks/Cole.

Honnet, E. P., & Poulsen, S. (1989). *Principles of good practice in combining service and learning.* Racine, WI: Johnson Foundation.

Horsch, K., Little, P. M. D., Smith, J. C., Goodyear, L., & Harris, E. (2002). Issues and opportunities in out-of-school time evaluation briefs. *Youth Involvement in Evaluation & Research, 1*, 1–15.

Horton, R. L., Hutchinson, S., Barkman, S. J., Machtmes, K., & Myers, H. (1999). *Developing experientially based 4-H curriculum materials* (Report No. 4-H 897). Columbus, OH: Ohio State University.

Howard, J., & Scott, J. (Eds.). (1998, Fall). [Special Issue on Service Learning]. *Michigan Journal of Community Service Learning, 3.*

Howard, S., Hoyer, L. A., MacGregor, L., Maltmann, S., Specer, A., Skelly, C., et al. (2002). *Moving from research "on" or "about" to research "with" or "by" . . . : Exploring the roles of young people in educational research.* Paper presented at the Australian Association for Research in Education Conference, Adelaide University, South Australia.

Huber, M. S. Q., Frommeyer, J., Weisenbach, A., & Sazama, J. (2003). Giving youth a voice in their own community and personal development. In F. A. Villarruel, D. F. Perkins, L. M. Borden, & J. G. Keith (Eds.), *Community youth development programs, policies, and practices* (pp. 297–323). Thousand Oaks, CA: Sage.

Huebner, A. J. (1998). Examining "empowerment": A how-to guide for the youth development professional. *Journal of Extension, 36,* 6–12.

Huebner, A. J. (2003). Positive youth development: The role of competence. In F. A. Villarruel, D. F. Perkins, L. M. Borden, & J. G. Keith (Eds.), *Community youth development programs, policies, and practices* (pp. 341–357). Thousand Oaks, CA: Sage.

Huebner, A. J., & Betts, S. C. (2002). Exploring the utility of social control theory for youth development: Issues of attachment, involvement, and gender. *Youth & Society, 34,* 123–145.

Hughes, D. M., & Curran, S. P. (2000). Community youth development: A framework for action. *CYD Journal, 1,* 7–13.

Innovation Center for Community and Youth Development. (2001). *At the table: Making the case for youth in decision-making.* Madison: University of Wisconsin.

Innovation Center for Community and Youth Development. (2003). *Extending the reach of youth development through civic activism.* Takoma Park, MD: Author.

Innovation Center for Community and Youth Development. (2004). *Creating change: How organizations connect youth, build communities, and strengthen themselves.* Takoma Park, MD: Author.

Institute for Community Research. (2004a). *About ICR.* Hartford, CT: Author.

Institute for Community Research. (2004b). *Participatory action research training and evaluation.* Hartford, CT: Author.

Institute for Community Research. (2004c). *Resident engagement through action research for community and family strengthening.* Hartford, CT: Author.

Institute for Community Research. (2004d). *Youth Action Research Institute.* Hartford, CT: Author.

International Youth Foundation. (2000). Us. *CYD Journal, 1,* 54–56.

Involving patients in clinical research [Editorial]. (1999). *British Medical Journal, 319,* 724–725.

Irby, M., Pittman, K., & Tolman, J. (2003). Blurring the lines: Expanding learning opportunities for children and youth. In K. J. Pittman, N. Yohatem, & J. Tolman (Eds.), *When, where, what, and how youth learn: Blurring school and community boundaries* (pp. 13–27). San Francisco: Jossey-Bass.

Israel, B. A. (2000). Community-based participatory research: Principles, rationale and policy recommendations. In L. R. O'Fallen, F. L. Tyson, & A. Dearry (Eds.), *Successful models of community-based participatory research* (pp. 16–29). Washington, DC: National Institute of Environmental Health Services.

Ivan-Smith, E. (1999). *Child focus development manual.* London: Save the Children UK.

Jablon, R. (2003, February 6). Hispanic babies majority of newborns in California. *Associated Press State & Local Wire,* p. 1.

Jacoby, B. (Ed.). (2003). *Building partnerships for service-learning.* San Francisco: Jossey-Bass.

James, T., & McGillicuddy, K. (2001). Building youth movements for community change. *Nonprofit Quarterly, 8,* 1–3.

Jobes, K. (1997). *Participatory monitoring and evaluation guidelines: Experiences in the field.* London: Social Development Division, DFID.

John W. Gardner Center. (2001). *A handbook for supporting community youth researchers.* Palo Alto, CA: Stanford University.

Johnson, E. B. (2002). *Contextual teaching and learning: What it is and why it's here to stay.* Thousand Oaks, CA: Sage.

Johnston, P. H., & Nichols, J. (1995). Voices we want to hear and voices we don't. *Theory into Practice, 34,* 94–100.

Jones, K. R., & Perkins, D. F. (2002). *Youth-adult partnerships.* University Park: Pennsylvania State University.

Jovenes Unidos & Padres Unidos. (2004). *North High School report: The voice of over 700 students.* Denver, CO: Author.

Kaba, M. (2000). They listen to me . . . But they don't act on it: Contradictory consciousness in decision-making. *School Journal, 84,* 21–35.

Kahne, J., Nagaoka, J., Brown, A., O'Brien, J., Quinn, T., & Thiede, K. (2001). Assessing after-school programs as contexts for youth development. *Youth & Society, 32,* 421–446.

Kato, M., Zwahlen, D., & Hubbard, B. D. (2002, November 12). *Using participatory research with local youth to assess health risk posed by heavy use of pesticide in a rural community in El Salvador.* Paper presented at the American Public Health Association Annual Meeting, Philadelphia.

Kelly, D. M. (1993). Secondary power source: High school students as participatory researchers. *The American Sociologist, 1,* 8–26.

Kendall, J. (1990). Principles of good practice in combining service and learning. In J. Kendall et al. (Eds.), *Combining service and learning: A resource book for community and public service* (Vol. 2, 37–55). Raleigh, NC: National Society for Internships and Experiential Education.

Kendrick, J. R. (1996). Outcomes of service-learning in an introduction to sociology course. *Michigan Journal of Community Service Learning, 2,* 72–81.

Kerckhoff, A. C. (2002). The transition from school to work. In J. T. Mortimer & R. W. Larson (Eds.), *The changing adolescent experience: Societal trends and the transition to adulthood* (pp. 52–87). New York: Cambridge University Press.

KIDS Consortium. (2001). *Kids as planners: A guide to strengthening students, schools, and communities through service-learning.* Lewiston, ME: Author.

Kids First. (2003). *Student voices count: A student-led evaluation of high schools in Oakland.* Oakland, CA: Author.

Kielsmier, J. C. (2000). *Service-learning.* Washington, DC: National Youth Leadership Council.

Kim, S., Crutchfield, C., Williams, C., & Hepler, N. (1998). Toward a new paradigm in substance abuse and other problem behavior prevention for youth: Youth development and empowerment approach. *Journal of Drug Education, 28,* 1–17.

Kincheloe, J. L., & McLaren, P. (2000). Rethinking critical theory and qualitative research. In N. K. Denzin & Y. Lincoln (Eds.), *Handbook of qualitative research* (2nd ed., pp. 138–157). Thousand Oaks, CA: Sage.

Kingsland, S. F., Richards, M., & Coleman, L. (1995). *A status report for KIDS-NET, year one, 1994–1995.* Portland: University of Southern Maine.

Kinkade, S., & Macy, C. (2003). *What works in youth media: Case studies from around the world.* Seattle, WA: The Freechild Project.

Kinsley, C. (1997, October). Service-learning: A process of connecting learning and living. In Service-learning: Leaving footprints on the planet. *National Association of Secondary School Principals Bulletin,* 1–7.

Kirby, D. (2001). *Emerging answers: Research findings on programs to reduce teen pregnancy.* Washington, DC: National Campaign to Prevent Teen Pregnancy.

Kirby, P. (1999). *Involving young researchers: How to enable young people to design and conduct research.* London: Joseph Rowntree Foundation.

Kirshner, B., O'Donoghue, J. L., & McLaughlin, M. (2002). Issue editor's notes. In B. Kirshner, J. L. O'Donoghue, & M. McLaughlin (Eds.), *Youth participation: Improving institutions and communities* (pp. 5–7). San Francisco: Jossey-Bass.

Klindera, K., & Menderwald, J. (2001). *Youth involvement in prevention programming.* Washington, DC: Advocates for Youth.

Knopf, T. A. (1970). Youth patrols: An experiment in community participation. *Civil Rights Digest, 3,* 1–4.

Kolb, D. (1984). *Experiential learning: Experience as the source of learning and development.* Englewood Cliffs, NJ: Prentice Hall.

Kraft, R. (1996). Service learning. *Education & Urban Society, 28,* 131–159.

Krasny, M., & Doyle, R. (2002). Participatory approaches to program development and engaging youth in research: The case of an intergenerational urban community gardening program. *Journal of Extension, 40,* 3–10.

Krogh, K. (2001, June 20–23). *Video action research: Possibilities as an emancipatory research methodology and reflections on a health policy study for people with disabilities.* Paper presented at the Democracy, Diversity, and Disability Conference of the Society for Disability Studies, Winnipeg, MB.

Krueger, R. A. (1988). *Focus groups: A practical guide for applied research*. Newbury Park, CA: Sage.

Lakes, R. D. (1996). *Youth development and critical education: The promise of democratic action*. New York: State University of New York Press.

Landis, D. C., Alfonso, M., Ziegler, S. E., Christy, J., Abrenica, K., & McCormack Brown, K. (1999). Training youth to conduct focus groups and interviews. *Social Marketing Quarterly, 5*, 23–29.

Lansdown, G. (2001). *Promoting children's participation in democratic decision-making*. Florence, Italy: UNICEF Innocenti Research Center.

Larson, R., Eccles, J., & Gootman, J. A. (2004). Features of positive developmental settings. *The Prevention Researcher, 11*, 8–13.

Lau, G., Netherland, N. H., & Haywood, M. L. (2003). Collaborating on evaluation for youth development. In K. Sabo (Ed.), *Youth participatory evaluation: A field in the making* (pp. 47–59). San Francisco: Jossey-Bass.

Leffert, N., Saito, R. N., Blyth, D. A., & Kroenke, C. H. (1996). *Making the case: Measuring the impact of youth development programs*. Minneapolis, MN: Search Institute.

Lerner, R. M. (1995). *America's youth in crisis: Challenges and options for programs and policies*. Thousand Oaks, CA: Sage.

Lerner, R. M., Brentano, C., Dowling, E. M., & Anderson, P. M. (2002). Positive youth development: Thriving as the basis of personhood and civil society. In R. M. Lerner, C. S. Taylor, & D. von Eye (Eds.), *Pathways to positive youth development among diverse youth* (pp. 11–33). San Francisco: Jossey-Bass.

Lerner, R. M., Taylor, C. S., & von Eye, D. (Eds.). (2002). *Pathways to positive youth development among diverse youth*. San Francisco: Jossey-Bass.

Lewis-Charp, H., Yu, H. C., Soukamneuth, S., & Lacoe, J. (2003). *Extending the reach of youth development through civic activism: Outcomes of the youth leadership for development initiative*. Takoma Park, MD: Innovation Center for Community and Youth Development.

Loesch-Griffin, D., Petrides, L., & Pratt, C. (1995). *A comprehensive study of Project Yes—Rethinking classroom comments: Service-learning as educational reform*. San Francisco: East Bay Conservation Corps.

London, J. (2000). Youth development through youth-led research evaluation and training: The experience of Youth in Focus. *Focal Point: A National Bulletin on Family Support and Children's Mental Health, 14*, 35–36.

London, J. (2002, June 7–9). *Youth involvement in community research and evaluation: Mapping the field* [Draft Discussion Paper]. Paper presented at the Wingspread Symposium on Youth Involvement in Community Research and Evaluation, Racine, WI.

London, J., Zimmerman, K., & Erbstein, N. (2003). Youth-led research and evaluation: Tools for youth, organizational, and community development. In K. Sabo (Ed.), *Youth participatory evaluation: A field in the making* (pp. 33–45). San Francisco: Jossey-Bass.

Lopez, M. H. (2002). *Youth demographics.* College Park, MD: Center for Information and Research on Civic Learning and Engagement.

Lorion, R. P. (2000). Theoretical and evaluation issues in the promotion of wellness and the protection of "well-enough." In D. Cichetti, J. Rappaport, I. Sandler, & R. Weisberg (Eds.), *The promotion of wellness in children and adolescents* (pp. 1–28). Washington, DC: Child Welfare League of America.

Lorion, R. P., & Sokoloff, H. (2003). Building assets in real-world communities. In R. M. Lerner & P. L. Benson (Eds.), *Developmental assets and asset-building communities: Implications for research, policy, and practice* (pp. 121–156). New York: Kluwer Academic/Plenum.

Macaulay, A. C., Commanda, L. E., Freeman, W. L., Gibson, N., McCabe, M. L., Robbins, C. M., et al. (1999). Participatory research maximizes community and lay involvement. *British Medical Journal, 319,* 774–778.

MacDonald, G. B., & Valdivieso, R. (1998). Measuring deficits and assets. In *Youth development: Issues, challenges and directions* (pp. 149–184). Philadelphia: Public/Private Ventures.

MacNair, R. H. (1996). A research methodology for community practice. *Journal of Community Practice, 3,* 1–19.

Maguire, P. (1993). Challenges, contradictions and celebrations: Attempting participatory research as a doctoral student. In P. Park, M. Brydon-Miller, B. Hall, & T. Jackson (Eds.), *Voices of change: Participatory research in the United States and Canada* (pp. 157–176). Westport, CT: Bergin & Garvey.

Males, M. A. (1996). *The scapegoat generation: America's war on adolescents.* Monroe, ME: Common Courage Press.

Males, M. A. (1998). *Framing youth: Ten myths about the next generation.* Monroe, ME: Common Courage Press.

Marcantonio, R. J., & Cook, T. D. (1994). Convincing quasi-experiments: The interrupted time series and regression-discontinuity designs. In J. S. Wholey, H. P. Hatry, & K. E. Newcomer (Eds.), *Handbook of practical program evaluation* (pp. 133–154). San Francisco: Jossey-Bass.

Marin, G., & Marin, B. V. (1991). *Research with Hispanic populations.* Newbury Park, CA: Sage.

Markus, G. B., Howard, J., & King, D. (1993). Integrating community service and classroom instruction enhances learning: Results from an experiment. *Educational Evaluation and Policy Analysis, 15,* 410–419.

Marques, E. (1999). *Youth involvement in policy-making: Lessons from Ontario school boards* (Institute on Global Policy Brief No. 5). Toronto, ON: Canadian Institute on Governance.

Marsh, D. (2002). Youth speak out, a participatory research model: Assignment, asset development, and knowledge building to good health. *The Great Lakes Epicenter News, 3,* 4–5.

Matysik, G. J. (2000). Involving adolescents in participatory research. *CYD Journal, 1,* 15–19.

McAleavey, S. J. (1997). *Service-learning: Theory and rationale.* Mesa, AZ: Mesa Community College, Center for Public Policy and Service.

McCall, D. (2000). *Selected case studies of youth involvement in public decision making.* Ottawa, ON: Canadian Association for School Health for the Division of Childhood and Adolescence Health, Centre on Community and School Health.

McCall, D. S., & Shannon, M. M. (1999). *Youth led health promotion, youth engagement and youth participation.* Ottawa, ON: Health Canada.

McCreary Centre Society. (2002). *Youth participation—What is it about?* Retrieved September 21, 2004, from http://www.mes.bc.ca/ya_base.htm

McGillicuddy, K. (2003, June). Youth leaders and heroes. A veteran activist talks about the power of youth organizing. *What Kids Can Do,* 16–20.

McKnight, J. L., & Kretzmann, J. P. (1990). *Mapping community capacity.* Evanston, IL: Northwestern University, Center for Urban Affairs and Policy Research.

Mead, J. P. (2003). Map it! And turn up the volume of youth voices. *CYD Journal, 4,* 12–18.

Melchior, A. (1997). *National evaluation of Learn and Serve America and community-based programs: Interim report.* Waltham, MA: Brandeis University, Center for Human Resources.

Melchior, A. (1999). *Summary report: National evaluation of Learn and Serve America.* Waltham, MA: Brandeis University, Center for Human Resources.

Melchior, A., & Bailis, L. N. (2002). Impact of service-learning on civic attitudes and behaviors of middle and high school youth: Findings from three national evaluations. In A. Furco & S. Billig (Eds.), *Advances in service-learning research: Vol. 1. The essence of the pedagogy* (pp. 201–222). Greenwich, CT: Information Age.

Mercado, C. I. (1998). When young people from marginalized communities enter the world of ethnographic research: Scribing, planning, reflecting and sharing. In A. Egan-Robertson & D. Bloome (Eds.), *Students as researchers of culture and language in their own communities* (pp. 69–92). Cresskill, NJ: Hampton Press.

Merrifield, J. (1993). Putting scientists in their place: Participatory research in environmental and occupational health. In P. Park, M. B. Miller, B. Hall, & T. Jackson (Eds.), *Voices of change: Participatory research in the United States and Canada* (pp. 65–84). Westport, CT: Bergin & Garvey.

Midgley, J., & Livermore, M. (2004). Development theory and community practice. In M. Weil (Ed.), *Handbook of community practice* (pp. 153–168). Thousand Oaks, CA: Sage.

Miller, D. L., College, D., McVea, K. L. S. P., Creswell, J. W., Harter, L., Mickelson, W., McEntarffer, B. A., Ollerenshaw, J., & Plano-Clark, V. (2001). *Engaging high school students as co-researchers in qualitative research: Logistical, methodological, and ethical issues.* Paper presented at the American

Educational Association Annual Conference, April 14, Seattle, Washington.

Miller, T. I. (1994). Designing and conducting surveys. In J. S. Wholey, H. P. Hatry, & K. E. Newcomer (Eds.), *Handbook of practical program evaluation* (pp. 271–292). San Francisco: Jossey-Bass.

Milner, P., & Carolin, B. (1999*). Time to listen to children: Personal and professed communication*. London: Routledge.

Molnar, D., & Kammerud, M. (1977). Developing priorities for improving the urban social environment: A use of Delphi. In N. Gilbert & H. Specht (Eds.), *Planning for social welfare: Issues, models, and tasks* (pp. 324–348). Englewood Cliffs, NJ: Prentice Hall.

Montero-Sieburth, M. (1998). Reclaiming indigenous cultures: Student-developed oral histories of Talamanca, Costa Rica. In A. Egan-Robertson & D. Bloome (Eds.), *Students as researchers of culture and language in their own communities* (pp. 217–241). Cresskill, NJ: Hampton Press.

Moore, K. A., & Lippman, L. (Eds.). (2005). *What do children need to flourish? Conceptualizing and measuring indicators of positive youth development.* New York: Springer.

Morgan, D. L. (Ed.). (1993). *Successful focus groups: Advancing the state of the art.* Newbury Park, CA: Sage.

Morgan, W., & Streb, M. (2001). Building citizenship: How student voice in service-learning develops civic values. *Social Science Quarterly, 82,* 155–169.

Morris, J. (2000). *Don't leave us out: Involving disabled children and young people with communication impairments.* London: Joseph Rowntree Foundation.

Morrow, V., & Richards, M. (1996). The ethics of social research with children: An overview. *Children and Society, 10,* 90–105.

Mortimer, J. T., Harley, C., & Staff, J. (2002). The quality of work and youth mental health. *Work and Occupations, 29,* 166–197.

Mortimer, J. T., & Larson, R. W. (2002). Macrostructural trends and the reshaping of adolescence. In J. T. Mortimer & R. W. Larson (Eds.), *The changing adolescent experience: Societal trends and the transition to adulthood* (pp. 1–17). New York: Cambridge University Press.

Morton, K., & Troppe, M. (1996). From the margin to the mainstream: Campus compact's project on integrating service with academic study. *Journal of Business Ethics, 15,* 21–33.

Mothers on the Move. (2004). *Oral history project agenda.* New York: Author.

Mullahey, R., Susskind, Y., & Checkoway, B. (1999). *Youth participation in community planning.* Washington, DC: American Planning Association.

Munoz-Laboy, M., Almeida, V., Nascimento, L. F. R., & Parker, R. (2004). Promoting sexual health through action research among young male sex workers in Rio de Janeiro, Brazil. *Practicing Anthropology, 26,* 30–34.

Murphy, D. E. (2003, February 17). New Californian identity predicted by researchers: Most newborns in state are now Hispanic. *New York Times,* p. A13.

Murphy, P. W., & Cunningham, J. V. (2003). *Organizing for community controlled development: Renewing civil society.* Thousand Oaks, CA: Sage.

Muscott, H., & O'Brien, S. T. (1999). Teaching character education to students with behavioral and learning disabilities through mentoring relationships. *Education and Treatment of Children, 22,* 373–390.

Nation of Islam offers to patrol housing. (1991, December 22). *Los Angeles Times,* p. 2.

National Latino Research Center. (2002). *Youth research.* San Diego, CA: San Diego State University.

National Service-Learning Cooperative. (1999). *Essential elements of service-learning for effective organizational support.* St. Paul, MN: Author.

National Youth Leadership Council. (1994). *Service-learning.* Washington, DC: Author.

Naughton, S. (2000). *Understanding service-learning.* Wellesley, MA: Wellesley College Center for Research on Women, National Institute on Out-of-School Time.

Newman, S., Smith, S. M., & Murphy, R. (2001, January). Youth development. *Reading for Child and Youth Care Workers, 24,* 1–5.

Nicholls, J. G., & Hazzard, S. P. (1995). Students as collaborators in curriculum construction. In J. G. Nicholls & T. A. Thorkildsen (Eds.), *Reasons for learning* (pp. 114–136). New York: Teachers College Press.

Nightingale, D. S., & Rossman, S. B. (1994). Managing field data collection from start to finish. In J. S. Wholey, H. P. Hatry, & K. E. Newcomer (Eds.), *Handbook of practical program evaluation* (pp. 350–373). San Francisco: Jossey-Bass.

Noam, G. G., & Miller, B. M. (Eds.). (2003). *Youth development and after-school time: A tale of many cities.* San Francisco: Jossey-Bass.

Norman, J. (2001). Building effective youth-adult partnerships. *Transitions, 14,* 1–5.

O'Donoghue, J. L., Kirshner, B., & McLaughlin, M. (2002). Introduction: Moving youth forward. In B. Kirshner, J. L. O'Donoghue, & M. McLaughlin (Eds.), *Youth participation: Improving institutions and communities* (pp. 15–26). San Francisco: Jossey-Bass.

Oliver, M. (1995). *The sociology of liberation and the liberation of sociology.* Paper presented at Hull Seminar, University of Greenwich, London, UK.

Oliver, S., Milne, R., Bradbum, J., Buchanan, P., Kerridge, L., Walley, T., et al. (2001). Involving consumers in a needs-led research programme: A pilot project. *Health Expectations, 4,* 18.

O'Looney, J. (1998). Mapping communities: Place-based stories and participatory planning. *Journal of the Community Development Society, 29,* 201–236.

Owens, D. C., & Jones, K. T. (2004). Adapting the youth participatory model to serve LBGTO youth of color. *Practicing Anthropology, 26,* 25–29.

Ozer, E. M., Macdonald, T., & Irwin, C. E. (2002). Adolescent health care in the United States: Implications and projections for the new millennium. In J. T. Mortimer & R. W. Larson (Eds.), *The changing adolescent experience:*

Societal trends and the transition to adulthood (pp. 129–174). New York: Cambridge University Press.

Pace, K. L. (2003). The character of moral communities: A community youth development approach to enhancing character development. In F. A. Villarruel, D. F. Perkins, L. M. Borden, & J. G. Keith (Eds.), *Community youth development programs, policies, and practices* (pp. 248–272). Thousand Oaks, CA: Sage.

Padilla, E. R., Padilla, A. M., Morales, A., Olmedo, E. L., & Ramirez, R. (1979). Inhalant, marijuana, and alcohol abuse among barrio children and adolescents. *International Journal of the Addictions, 14,* 945–964.

Pancer, S. M., Rose-Krasnor, L., & Loiselle, L. D. (2002). Youth conferences as a context for engagement. In B. Kirshner, J. L. O'Donoghue, & M. McLaughlin (Eds.), *Youth participation: Improving institutions and communities* (pp. 47–84). San Francisco: Jossey-Bass.

Park, P. (1993). What is participatory research? A theoretical and methodological perspective. In P. Park, M. B. Miller, B. Hall, & T. Jackson (Eds.), *Voices of change: Participatory research in the United States and Canada* (pp. 1–19). Westport, CT: Bergin & Garvey.

Pass, S., & Vasquez, E. (2004). Contributions and challenges of observation in evaluating PAR. *Practicing Anthropology, 26,* 56–60.

Patmor, G. L. (1998). *Student and school council members views of student involvement in decision-making in Kentucky high schools.* Unpublished doctoral dissertation, Southern Illinois University at Carbondale.

Patton, M. Q. (1990). *Qualitative evaluation and research methods* (2nd ed.). Newbury Park, CA: Sage.

Pennell, J., Noponen, H., & Weil, H. (2004). Empowerment research. In M. Weil (Ed.), *The handbook of community practice* (pp. 620–635). Thousand Oaks, CA: Sage.

Penuel, R., Gray, J. H., & Kim, D. (2004, January*). Integrating technology into community youth research* (Issue Brief). Stanford, CA: John W. Gardner Center.

Perez, R., Padilla, A. M., Ramirez, A., Ramirez, R., & Rodriguez, M. (1980). Correlates and changes over time in drug and alcohol abuse within a barrio community. *American Journal of Community Psychology, 8,* 621–636.

Perkins, D. F., & Borden, L. M. (2003). Key elements of community youth development programs. In F. A. Villarruel, D. F. Perkins, L. M. Borden, & J. G. Keith (Eds.), *Community youth development programs, policies, and practices* (pp. 327–340). Thousand Oaks, CA: Sage.

Perkins, D. F., & Jones, K. (2002). *Comprehensive community assessment of youth development opportunities.* College Park: Pennsylvania State University.

Perry-Williams, J. (1998). *An evaluation, primarily by children evaluators, on the SC UK female headed households project in Tajikistan.* London: Save the Children UK.

Phillips, T., Stacey, K., & Milner, J. (2001) You're a peer what?! *Youth Studies Australia, 20,* 4–8.

Pittman, K. (2000). Balancing the equation: Communities supporting youth, youth supporting communities. *CYD Journal, 1*, 32–36.

Pittman, K., Irby, M., & Ferber, T. (1998). Unfinished business: Further reflections on a decade of promoting youth development. In *Youth development: Issues, challenges and directions* (pp. 17–64). Philadelphia: Public/Private Ventures.

Pittman, K., Yohalem, N., & Tolman, J. (Eds.). (2003). *When, where, what, and how youth learn: Blurring school and community boundaries*. San Francisco: Jossey-Bass.

Poole, D. L. (1997). Building community capacity to promote social and public health: Challenges for universities. *Heath & Social Work, 22*, 163–170.

Pritchard, I. (2002). Travelers and trolls: Practitioner research and institutional review boards. *Educational Researcher, 31*, 3–13.

Prop-agandists or saviors? (1994, September 12). *U.S. News & World Report*, p. 14.

Prout, A. (2000). Children's participation: Control and self-realisation in British late modernity. *Children and Society, 14*, 304–315.

Putnam, R. (2000). *Bowling alone*. New York: Simon & Schuster.

Puuronen, V. (1993). Research design in applied youth research. *Young, 1*, 1–13.

Rappaport, J., Swift, C., & Hess, R. (Eds.). (1994). *Studies in empowerment: Steps toward understanding and action*. New York: Haworth Press.

Rappoport, A. L. (2002). Building social and civic capital through service-learning: In practice and in systematic study. *CYD Journal, 3*, 26–32.

Rauner, D. M. (2000). *The role of caring in youth development and community life*. New York: Columbia University Press.

Rein, M. (1977). Planning by what authority? Social planning: The search for legitimacy. In N. Gilbert & H. Specht (Eds.), *Planning for social welfare: Issues, models, and tasks* (pp. 50–77). Englewood Cliffs, NJ: Prentice-Hall.

Reisch, M. (2004). Community practice in the global economy. In M. Weil (Ed.), *Handbook of community practice* (pp. 529–547). Thousand Oaks, CA: Sage.

Rennekamp, R. A. (2001, October). Youth as partners in program evaluation. *Hear It From the Board*, pp. 1–4.

Rhodes, J. E. (Ed.). (2002). *A critical view of youth mentoring*. San Francisco: Jossey-Bass.

Rhodes, J. E., & Roffman, J. G. (2003). Nonparental adults as asset builders in the lives of youth. In R. M. Lerner & P. L. Benson (Eds.), *Developmental assets and asset-building communities: Implications for research, policy, and practice* (pp. 195–209). New York: Kluwer Academic/Plenum.

Ribisl, K. M., Steekler, A., Linnan, L., Patterson, C. C., Pevzner, E. S., Markatos, E., et al. (2004). The North Carolina Youth Empowerment Study (NCYES): A participatory research study examining the impact of youth empowerment for tobacco use prevention. *Health Education Behavior, 31*, 597–614.

Richards, H. M., & Schwartz, L. J. (2002). Ethics of qualitative research: Are there special issues of health services research? *Family Practice, 199*, 135–139.

Richmond, J. (2000). New partnerships and new systems: Supporting young people's growth and job readiness. *CYD Journal, 1*, 20–25.

Riorden, R., & Fulwiler, T. (1992, December 1). *Writing it down, writing it up.* Ithaca, NY: Cornell Youth Apprenticeship Demonstration Project.

Rissel, C., Perry, C., & Finnegan, J. D. (1996). Toward the assessment of psychological empowerment in health promotion: Initial tests of validity and reliability. *Journal of the Royal Society of Health, 116,* 211–218.

Root, S. C. (1997). School-based service: A review of research for teacher educators. In J. Erickson & J. Anderson (Eds.), *Learning with the community: Concepts and models for service-learning in teacher education* (pp. 42–72). Washington, DC: American Association for Higher Education.

Rosenberg, S. L., McKeon, L. M., & Dinero, T. E. (1999). Positive peer solutions: One answer for the rejected student. *Phi Delta Kappan, 81,* 114–118.

Roth, J. L. (2004). Youth development programs. *The Prevention Researcher, 11,* 3–7.

Royle, J., & Oliver, S. (2001). Letters: Consumers are helping to prioritise research. *British Medical Journal, 322,* 519–523.

Rubin, H., & Rubin, I. (1995). *Qualitative interviewing: The art of hearing data.* Thousand Oaks, CA: Sage.

Ruth, J., Brooks-Gunn, J., Murrey, L., & Foster, W. (1998). Promoting healthy adolescents: Synthesis of youth development program evaluations. *Journal of Research on Adolescence, 8,* 423–459.

Sabo, K. (2003a). Editor's notes. In K. Sabo (Ed.), *Youth participatory evaluation: A field in the making* (pp. 1–11). San Francisco: Jossey-Bass.

Sabo, K. (2003b). A Vygotskian perspective on youth participatory evaluation. In K. Sabo (Ed.), *Youth participatory evaluation: A field in the making* (pp. 13–24). San Francisco: Jossey-Bass.

Sagawa, S. (1998). *Ten years of youth in service to America.* Washington, DC: American Youth Policy.

San Francisco Department of Children, Youth and Families. (2002). *Youth IMPACT: Youth-led evaluation of city-funded youth service agencies.* San Francisco: Author.

Save the Children. (2000). *Children and participation: Research, monitoring and evaluation with children and young people.* London: Author.

Scales, P. C., Blyth, D. A., Berkas, T. H., & Kielsmeier, J. C. (2000). The effects of service-learning on middle school students' social responsibility and academic success. *Journal of Early Adolescence, 20,* 332–358.

Scales, P. C., & Leffert, N. (1999). *Developmental assets: A synthesis of the scientific research on adolescent development.* Minneapolis, MN: Search Institute.

Schaafsma, D. (1998). Telling stories with Ms. Rose Bell: Students as authors of critical narrative and fiction. In A. Egan-Robertson & D. Bloome (Eds.), *Students as researchers of culture and language in their own communities* (pp. 243–259). Cresskill, NJ: Hampton Press.

Schensul, D. (2004). Mapping the PAR path: Outcome evaluations of participatory action research interventions with youth. *Practicing Anthropology, 26,* 51–55.

Schensul, J. J. (1994*). The development and maintenance of community research partnerships.* Hartford, CT: Institute for Community Research.

Schensul, J. J., & Berg, M. J. (2004). Introduction: Research with youth. *Practicing Anthropology, 26*, 1–4.

Schensul, J. J., Berg, M. J., Schensul, D., & Sydio, S. (2004). Core elements of participatory action research for educational empowerment and risk prevention with urban youth. *Practicing Anthropology, 26*, 5–9.

Schensul, J. J., LoBianco, L., & Lombardo, C. (2004). Youth participatory action research (Youth-Par) in public schools: Opportunities and challenges in an inner-city high school. *Practicing Anthropology, 26*, 10–14.

Schensul, J. J., Wiley, K., Sydlo, S., & Brase, M. (1999). *Youth as action researchers for HIV prevention: Translating youth research to prevention with peers.* Paper presented at the 1999 National HIV Prevention Conference, Atlanta, GA.

Schilling, T., & Martinek, T. (2000). Learning through leading in the Project Effort Youth Leader Corps. *CYD Journal, 1*, 24–30.

Schulz, A. J., Parker, E. A., Israel, B. A., Becker, A. B., & Maciak, B. (1998). Conducting a participatory community-based survey: Collecting and interpreting data for a community health intervention on Detroit's east side. *Journal of Public Health Management and Practice, 4*, 10–24.

Schwandt, T. A. (1996). New songs of innocence and experience (with apologies to William Blake). In L. Heshusius & K. Ballard (Eds.), *From postivisim to interpretivism and beyond: Takes of transformation in educational and social research* (pp. 155–160). New York: Teachers College Press.

Schwartz, R. G. (1998). Juvenile justice and positive youth development. In *Youth development: Issues, challenges and directions* (pp. 233–280). Philadelphia: Public/Private Ventures.

Scottish Parliament. (2002, April 29). Youth participation. *SPICe Briefing 02/44,* 8pp.

Seattle Youth Involvement Network. (2000). *Initial research: Youth forums.* Seattle, WA: Author.

Sengstock, M. C., & Hwalek, M. (1999). Issues to be considered in evaluating programs for children and youth. *New Designs for Youth Development, 15*, 8–12.

Shaw, J. A. (1996). The ethnographer as youth's apprentice. *Journal of Child and Youth Care Work, 1*, 61–71.

Sherman, R. F. (2002). Building young people's public lives: One foundation's strategy. In B. Kirshner, J. L. O'Donoghue, & M. McLaughlin (Eds.), *Youth participation: Improving institutions and communities* (pp. 65–82). San Francisco: Jossey-Bass.

Shrestha, I. (2000). *Participatory research involving people as principal actors.* Paper presented at the Conference of Public Health Association, Savar, Dhaka.

Sigmon, R. (1996). The problem of definition in service-learning. In R. Sigmon et al. (Eds.), *The journey to service-learning* (pp. 112–119). Washington, DC: Council of Independent Colleges.

Smilowitz, B. (2000). The youth movement: Claiming our piece of the pie. *CYD Journal, 1*, 42–45.

Smith, J. C. (2001). Pizza, transportation, and transformation: Youth involvement in evaluation and research. *The Evaluation Exchange, 7*, 10–11.

Smith, J. E. (1983). *The spirit of American philosophy.* Albany: State University of New York Press.

Smith, L. T. (1999). *Decolonizing methodologies: Research and indigenous people.* New York: Zed Books.

Smith, M. K. (1996). *Action research: The encyclopedia of informal education.* Retrieved October 23, 2004, from http://www.infed.org/research/b-actres.htm

Smyth, J. (1999). *Voiced research: Bridging in the epistemology marginalised?* Paper presented to the annual meeting of the Australian Association for Research in Education, Melbourne, Australia.

Sohng, S. S. L. (1995, November 1–3). *Participatory research and community organizing.* Paper presented at the New Social Movement in Community Organizing Conference, Seattle, WA.

Sonnichsen, R. C. (1994). Evaluators as change agents. In J. S. Wholey, H. P. Hatry, & K. E. Newcomer (Eds.), *Handbook of practical program evaluation* (pp. 534–584). San Francisco: Jossey-Bass.

Spangler, K., & Teter, W. (2002). Service-learning for community change: A national level initiative. *Generator: Journal of Service-Learning and Youth Leadership, 21*, 5.

Spano, S. (2003, April). Best practices for youth development programs. *Research Facts & Findings*, 1–5.

Spradley, J. P. (1980). *Participant observation.* New York: Holt, Rinehart & Winston.

Steinberg, S. R., & Kincheloe, J. L. (Eds.). (1998). *Students as researchers: Creating classrooms that matter.* Bristol, PA: Falmer Press.

Steinke, P., & Buresh, S. (2002). Cognitive outcomes of service-learning: Reviewing the past and glimpsing the future. *Michigan Journal of Community Service Learning, 8*, 5–14.

Stoecker, R. (1997). *Are academics irrelevant? Roles for scholars in participatory research.* Paper presented at the American Sociological Society Annual Meeting, Toronto, ON.

Strand, K., Marullo, S., Cutforth, N., Stoecker, R., & Donohue, P. (2003). *Community-based research and higher education: Principles and practices.* San Francisco: Jossey-Bass.

Stringer, E. T. (1999). *Action research: A handbook for practitioners.* Thousand Oaks, CA: Sage.

Stubbs, S. (1996). *Engaging with differences: Methodology in evaluation.* London: Save the Children UK.

Student Researchers for High School Renewal. (2003). *School climate in Boston's high schools: A presentation.* Boston: Author.

Stukas, A. A., Clary, G. E., & Synder, M. (1999). Service learning: Who benefits and why. *Social Policy Report, 8*, 1–22.

Sugar, J., & Livosky, M. (1988). Enriching child psychology courses with a preschool journal option. *Teaching of Psychology, 15*, 93–95.

Susskind, Y. (2003). A framework for youth empowerment. *Children, Youth and Environments, 13*, 1–3.

Sustain. (2000). *Reaching the parts. Community mapping: Working together to tackle social exclusion and food poverty.* London: Author & Oxfam's UK Poverty Programme.

Swanson, N. (2002). The power of youth in philanthropy fundraising. In P. O. Bjorhovde (Ed.), *Creating tomorrow's philanthropists: Curriculum development for youth* (pp. 91–99). San Francisco: Jossey-Bass.

Tandon, R. (1988). Social transformation and participatory research. *Convergence, 21*, 5–15.

Tena, J. (2001). *Youth IMPACT.* San Francisco: Youth IMPACT.

Terry, J., & Woonteiler, D. (2000). An interview with Craig Kielburger, founder of Free the Children. *CYD Journal, 1*, 14–19.

Theis, J., Pickup, K., Hoa, T., & Lan, M. (1999). *Visions of children who can't hear.* London: Save the Children UK.

Tienda, M., & Wilson, W. J. (2000a). Comparative perspectives of urban youth: Challenges for normative development. In M. Tienda & W. J. Wilson (Eds.), *Youth in cities: A cross-national perspective* (pp. 3–18). New York: Cambridge University Press.

Tienda, M., & Wilson, W. J. (2000b). Prospect and retrospect: Options for healthy youth development in changing urban worlds. In M. Tienda & W. J. Wilson (Eds.), *Youth in cities: A cross-national perspective* (pp. 269–277). New York: Cambridge University Press.

Toole, J. (2000). Implementing service-learning in K-8 schools: Challenging the learning grammar and the organizational grammar of "Real School." Paper presented at the American Educational Research Association Annual Meeting, New Orleans, LA.

Torre, M. E., & Fine, M. (2003). Youth reframe questions of educational justice through participatory action research. *The Evaluation Exchange, 9*, 1–3.

Torres, M. (1998). Celebrations and letters home: Research as an ongoing conversation among students, parents, and teachers. In A. Egan-Robertson & D. Bloome (Eds.), *Students as researchers of culture and language in their own communities* (pp. 59–68). Cresskill, NJ: Hampton Press.

Triumph and Success Peer Research Project. (2002). *Involving young people in research projects.* Sheffield, UK: Author.

Trivedi, P., & Wykes, T. (2002). From passive subjects to equal partners: Qualitative review of user involvement in research. *The British Journal of Psychiatry, 181*, 468–472.

Ungar, M. (2002). *Playing at being bad: The hidden resilience of troubled teens.* Washington, DC: National Association of Social Workers Press.

Ungar, M. (2003). *Nurturing hidden resilience in troubled youth.* Washington, DC: National Association of Social Workers Press.

UNICEF. (2002). *Working for and with adolescents—some UNICEF examples.* Geneva, Switzerland: Author.

Upshur, C. C., & Barreto-Cortez, E. (1995). Participatory evaluation. *The Evaluation Exchange, 1,* 1–3.

Van Til, J., & Paarz, K. (with Brennan, S., Cisse, T., Conner-Morris, A., et al.). (2001). *Youth as resources in Northern Ireland.* Camden, NJ: Rutgers State University of New Jersey, Department of Urban Studies and Community Planning.

Villarruel, F. A., Perkins, D. F., & Keith, J. G. (Eds.). (2003). *Community youth development: Practice, policy and research.* Thousand Oaks, CA: Sage.

Voakes, L. (2003). Listening to the experts. In K. Sabo (Ed.), *Youth participatory evaluation: A field in the making* (pp. 25–32). San Francisco: Jossey-Bass.

W2 Forum. (2002). *U.S. is hottest mobile youth growth market in the world.* London: Author. Retrieved October 11, 2004, from http://www.mobileyouth.org/news/mobileyouth382.html

Walker, G. (1998). The policy climate for early adolescent initiatives. In *Youth development: Issues, challenges and directions* (pp. 65–80). Philadelphia: Public/Private Ventures.

Wallerstein, N. (1998). *Empowerment education: Freire's theories applied to health: A case study of alcohol prevention for Indian and Hispanic youth.* Unpublished doctoral dissertation, University of California, Berkeley.

Ward, L. (1997). *Seen and heard: Involving disabled children and young people in research and development projects.* London: Joseph Rowntree Foundation.

Watkins, M., & Iverson, E. (1998). Youth development principles and field practicum opportunities. In R. R. Greene & M. Watkins (Eds.), *Serving diverse constituencies: Applying the ecological perspective* (pp. 167–197). New York: Aldine de Gruyter.

Weah, W., Simmons, V. C., & Hall, M. (2000). Service-learning and multicultural/multiethnic perspectives from diversity to equity. *Phi Delta Kappan, 81,* 673–683.

Weil, M. (2004). Introduction: Contexts and challenges for 21st century communities. In M. Weil (Ed.), *Handbook of community practice* (pp. 3–33). Thousand Oaks, CA: Sage.

Weiler, D., LaGoy, A., Crane, E., & Rovner, A. (1998). *An evaluation of K-12 service-learning in California: Phase II Final Report.* Emeryville, CA: RPP International & Search Institute.

Weiss, H. B., & Lopez, M. E. (2000). New strategies in foundation grantmaking for children and youth. *CYD Journal, 1,* 52–59.

Weiss, M. (2003). *Youth rising.* Oakland, CA: Applied Research Center.

Westheimer, J., & Kahne, J. (2000). *Report to the Surdna Board—D.V.I.* New York: Surdna Foundation.

Whitlock, J. (2003, April). Social capital and the well-being of youth. *Research Facts & Findings*, 1–3.

Whitlock, J., & Hamilton, S. F. (2002). *Youth surveys and youth development strategies: Lessons from the field.* Ithaca, NY: Cornell University Cooperative Extension.

Wilkins, V., & Bryans, K. (1993). Youth participation in youth-focused research. *Youth Studies, 12,* 3–9.

Williams, B. (1996). Skinfolk, not kinfolk: Comparative reflections on the identity of participant-observations in two field situations. In D. Wolf (Ed.), *Feminist dilemmas in fieldwork* (pp. 72–95). Boulder, CO: Westview Press.

Williams, G., Ng'ang'a, L., & Ngugi, J. (1998). Youth-led responses to HIV and AIDS in Kenya. *Wajibu: A Journal of Social & Religious Concerns, 13,* 1–6.

Williams, M., & Roche, A. M. (1999). Young people's initiation into injecting drug use: The role of peer interviewers in risk reduction research. *Health Promotion Journal of Australia, 9,* 219–229.

Wilson, C. C., & Gutierrez, F. (1985). *Minorities and media: Diversity and the end of mass communication.* Beverly Hills, CA: Sage.

Wingspread Symposium on Youth Participation in Community Research. (2002). [Summary of Proceedings]. Racine, WI. Author. Retrieved October 22, 2004, from http://www.ssw.umich.edu/youthandcommunity/pubs/SymposiumII.pdf 10/22/04

Woods, G. (1990). Teaching for democracy. *Educational Leadership, 48,* 32–37.

Wyn, J. G., & White, R. (1997). *Rethinking youth.* Thousand Oaks, CA: Sage.

Yeager, B., Floriani, A., & Green, J. (1998). Learning to see learning in the classroom: Developing an ethnographic perspective. In A. Egan-Robertson & D. Bloome (Eds.), *Students as researchers of culture and language in their own communities* (pp. 115–139). Cresskill, NJ: Hampton Press.

YELL. (2002). *Hear us YELL: A new beginning* [Report]. Oakland, CA: Author. Retrieved September 3, 2004, from http://www.whatkidscando.org/studentresearch/images/GardnerCtrWestOaklandYELL.pdf

Youniss, J., & Ruth, A. J. (2002). Approaching policy for adolescent development in the 21st century. In J. T. Mortimer & R. W. Larson (Eds.), *The changing adolescent experience: Societal trends and the transition to adulthood* (pp. 250–271). New York: Cambridge University Press.

YouthAction. (1998). *Why youth organizing?* Albuquerque, NM: Author.

Youth and STD/HIV Prevention Project. (2002). [Summary and Community Report]. Winnipeg, MB: Health Canada & Winnipeg Foundation.

Youth IMPACT. (2001). *Youth voices inspiriting creative change: Youth-led evaluation.* San Francisco: Author.

Youth IMPACT. (2002). Youth evaluating programs for youth: Stories of Youth IMPACT. In B. Kirshner, J. L. O'Donoghue, & M. McLaughlin (Eds.), *Youth participation: Improving institutions and communities* (pp. 101–117). San Francisco: Jossey-Bass.

Youth in Focus. (2002). *Youth rep step by step: An introduction to youth-led research and evaluation.* Oakland, CA: Author.

Youth Media Council. (2002). *Is KMEL the people's station? A community assessment of 106.1 KMEL.* Oakland, CA: Author.

Youth Research Institute. (2002). *Youth research institute/California wellness.* San Marcos, CA: National Latino Research Center.

Zeldin, S. (1995a). *Making research relevant to community mobilization efforts for youth development: A project and conference summary.* Washington, DC: Academy for Educational Development, Center for Youth Development and Policy Research.

Zeldin, S. (1995b). *Preparing youth for adulthood: Common ground between the school-to-work and youth development fields.* Washington, DC: Academy for Educational Development, Center for Youth Development and Policy Research.

Zeldin, S., & Camino, L. (1998). Nothing as theoretical as good practice: Improving partnerships with researchers. *New Designs for Youth Development, 14,* 34–36.

Zeldin, S., Kimball, M., & Price, L. (1995). *Day-to-day experiences that promote youth development: An annotated bibliography.* Washington, DC: Academy for Educational Development.

Zeldin, S., McDaniel, A., Topitzes, D., & Calvert, M. (2000a). *A study on the impacts of youth on adults and organizations.* Madison: University of Wisconsin.

Zeldin, S., McDaniel, A., Topitzes, D., & Calvert, M. (2000b). *Youth in decision-making: A study on the impacts of youth on adults and organizations.* Chevy Chase, MD: Innovation Center for Youth and Community Development & University of Wisconsin Extension.

Zimmerman, M. A. (1990). Taking aim on empowerment research: On the distinction between individual and psychological conceptions. *American Journal of Community Psychology, 18,* 169–177.

Index

This item is to be returned on or before the last due date stamped below .
Items can be renewed 3 times unseen.If a fourth renewal is required the item must be brought to the library.

Me   ice
at]   :ial
wo   ɔm
Bra   nd
nuɪ   nd
sch   lar
foc   ity
enr   ;.

Liverpool Hope University
The Sheppard-Worlock Library
Tel: 0151 291 2000
http://www.hope.ac.uk/library